Adolph Rupp

Kentucky's Basketball Baron

Russell Rice

Sagamore Publishing
Champaign, IL

Production supervision and interior design: Brian J. Moore
Dustjacket and photo insert design: Michelle R. Dressen
Editors: Chris Mackey, Dan Heaton
Proofreader: Phyllis L. Bannon

Library of Congress Catalog Card Number: 94-68641
ISBN: 0-915611-98-8

To My Six Granddaughters

Lori, Cindy, Tracy, Kristen, Lindsay and Kaitlyn

And Matthew

Contents

Acknowledgments vi

Foreword viii

Introduction xi

1   From Kansas Soil 1

2   Jayhawker 7

3   Bluegrass Bound 13

4   Young Wildcat 19

5   Motivation Through Fear 27

6   Friends and Family 33

7   The Pursuit of Perfection 43

8   Earning a Reputation 51

9   Victory Garden 69

10   Postwar 87

11   Fabulous Five 101

12   Shaving Glory 109

13   Wall of Shame 117

14   Unbearable Pair 129

15   Fiddlers Five 143

16   Shades of Gray 151

17   Mountain to Mohammads 157

18   Picking Cotton 165

19   Rupp's Runts 175

20   Issel—Pratt—Casey 183

21   Milestones 193

Epilogue 201

Appendices 207

Acknowledgments

First, I thank my wife Doris. I also thank our daughter, Judy Covington, and her boss, Ken Wright, for their early assistance. Ken is instructional supervisor of the Scott County (KY) Schools. Sagamore wanted the book on Macintosh disks. IBM-PC is my bag. Judy and Ken solved that problem. They provided a Mac LC; then a LaserWriter Select printer. It is important to have such people in your corner.

Thanks to Ira and Judy Gewirtzman. Ira is a UK sports guru. He keeps us informed on the home front while we winter in Florida. John (Pistol) and Jean Woodard are our Florida neighbors. "Pistol" is from Harrodsburg, KY. We go back a long way. Start with the Marine Corps on Guadalcanal (W.W. II) and then at UK, where he was one of Bear Bryant's sweat hogs. He has been a supportive friend.

We owe much to Cliff and Meredith Barker. The fact that Cliff was a member of the "Fabulous Five" has little to do with our friendship. Their Florida home is on Dunnes Creek near Palatka. It is a retreat. While fishing, we do not discuss basketball or Rupp. At dinner, we do not talk UK. Breakfast is a time to share Meredith's crossword puzzles.

I appreciate the Rupp family's trust and willingness to let me do things my way. Their concern is the racist image placed on the patriarch by persons who did not know him or live in his time. Perhaps I know the answers, but questions linger: Why doesn't someone blame those members of the black community who did not step forward to help him recruit their "boys?" Why didn't they encourage those boys to challenge the system? Better yet, why doesn't someone criticize Paul "Bear" Bryant for not being the first to break the color barrier? I interviewed Bryant a few years before his death, but I did not ask that question. What was the use? We talked about UK and Rupp.

Thanks to S. T. Roach—as a sports editor, I worked his Dunbar High School games—for sharing his views on the racial situation. I was not aware of an embarrassment he suffered at a UK basketball game. Neither was Rupp. Coach Roach did not contest the situation because his job was at stake. Perhaps Rupp faced a similar fate in the racist Southeastern Conference. Hopefully, I have provided some insight into those changing times. There is blame to share, both black and white, not placed on one person. For those who wanted to talk off the record, thanks, but no thanks.

Foreword

I'm glad I had the opportunity to play basketball for Adolph Rupp. He was one of the great coaches. Many of the offensive philosophies we had in the '60s in college basketball would not apply in the NBA today, but the discipline, structure, and organization are very important. Adolph had a lot to do with that.

He was one of the main reasons I went to Kentucky. I knew he brought out the talent in his players. Adolph and Harry Lancaster were two of the best people I ever knew in basketball. Theirs was a relationship born out of loyalty because Harry could have left Adolph a number of times. He could have gone to great institutions in this country and become a head coach. Who knows what kind of career he could have had as one of the great coaches. He was simply a coach who loved Kentucky, the guy that made much of it work. Adolph was the patriarchal figure. He was the father who yielded the discipline sword. Adolph rarely gave you any sugar. Any time you needed a little bit of sugar, Harry was there. He took care of the damage control. There was a great balance between them.

I was as close to Adolph as a player could be under his system. I always felt comfortable with him. So did other members of our 1966 "Rupp's Runts" team. We knew he held a special place in his heart for us. It went beyond winning 23 games in a row before losing to Tennessee at Knoxville. He took a group of "runts," molded them into a smooth-operating basketball machine, and took them all the way to the NCAA championship game. His biggest disappointment came when we lost to Texas Western, 72-65, at College Park, MD. The fact that the Miners started an all-black team was not a major factor to us at the time.

We did not realize the game was going to be so (socially) significant, that we were going to be part of history. Nobody really talked about it. Back in 1966, we were really going through a tremendous cultural change. Basketball and sports at the time were still the choice department in human affairs. You left all the conflicts and hatreds out of it. People knew about five black guys from the inner city and five white guys from the South playing each other for the most important prize in college basketball, but there wasn't much written about it.

I coached a player in the '80s with the Lakers, Bob MacAdoo, who simply was one of the great players in the NBA. He used to kid me about that game. Bob came to me one day and said, "You don't realize it, but because you got beat by Texas Western, it allowed me to go to North Carolina."

The game really helped open the door for great, black players in the South to go to southern institutions. They can thank Martin Luther King, Jr. and those people in Selma, AL, during that time for opening the door, not just that game, but it was a watershed for many blacks.

Coach Rupp and I were going to Schenectady that year for "Pat Riley Day," in which he came for nothing. He would always do something for his boys if they ever needed it. I believe he really felt deeply for us all but had to keep this hard shell around himself to maintain discipline.

When we were on the plane, he asked if I needed any-thing and I said, "No." He asked if there was anything special he should say at the banquet or to my parents and I said, "No!" So knowing Coach Rupp and how he was about any of his boys getting something extra other than what their scholarships called for, I was greatly surprised when he pulled out a $50 bill and said, "Here, in case you have to buy your cronies some Cokes at home."

To show how concerned he was about his players, when they started passing out All-America honors that "Rupp's Runts year," I made the second and third teams on the first two lists and Louie (Dampier) made first team. I guess Adolph thought that might bother me because we were just going to the playoffs and maybe I might get down or something like that. After practice one day, he got me aside and said, "You know you are going to make the *Look Magazine* All-America first team?" I said "No, I was not aware." Then he said, "You know you are going to be named SEC Player of the Year?" and I said "No." "Well anyway, I think you're the best goddam player in the nation this year," he said, "so get your dobber up."

I cannot think of a more logical person to write the Rupp story than Russell Rice. When I arrived at UK, Russell was sports editor of *The Lexington Leader.* He attended practically every practice session and traveled with us on the road. He wrote a daily column that covered all sports, not just basketball and football. Sometimes he would write about catching nightcrawlers while others wrote about Keeneland racing that afternoon and Kentucky playing Georgia in football that night. For the combined Sunday paper, Russell preferred to write the "sidebar" story about human elements of a game and let the *Herald* sports editor do the game story. Russell was resourceful. After we lost to Texas Western, he beat us to the dressing room and hid in the shower while Harry Lancaster kept out other members of the press. When I took off my shoe, Russell stepped out of the shower and watched the team doctor inspect my swollen toe. The fact that Harry didn't show him the door speaks for itself.

Russell often traveled with Adolph on the coach's various speaking engagements. After he joined the UK sports information staff, he and Adolph became even closer, with Russell taping Coach Rupp's life story over a period of three or four years. Russell tells the Rupp story from an investigative reporter's point of view, but also with a personal touch that comes from knowing the "other side" of a great basketball coach.

—Pat Riley

Introduction

Each time I start a new project, I say it will be the last. That was true with the Rupp Tape, which consists of audio excerpts from a series of interviews with Rupp, that Paul Willman and I produced in 1992. It was also true of several other projects since I "retired" from the University of Kentucky Athletic Department in 1989. My wife and I bought a small winter home in Florida, where we planned to live happily ever after. I would plant a garden, catch a few fish, and read some books; Doris would watch soaps in the daytime and game shows at night. These would be our Golden Years.

A call from Sagamore Publishing changed all that. Joe Bannon, the president, was looking for someone to write the life story of Adolph Rupp, and he said my name kept coming up as the guy to write it. Having written a few books, I was well aware that writing a book is hard work.

Still, I agreed to think about the Rupp story. When Joe called again, I said, "Send me some of your publications." Four books arrived the following afternoon. Whew, this guy was serious.

My one concern was that I might be too close to the forest to see the trees. I knew Rupp intimately, worked with him, traveled with him, learned a lot from him. My office was across the hall from his. Much of my philosophy of life comes from him. Then, too, I know the Rupp family. Some writers who never knew the man have so distorted the image of a husband and father that the family who truly knew Rupp scarcely recognized the portrait. My charge was simple: don't sugarcoat, don't sensationalize, just present the truth to the best of my ability. I hoped my newspaper training would help keep me on that simple path—*if* I tackled the project.

I began to sift through the "Rupp Stories," the stuff of legend in Kentucky. I interviewed former players and talked to people who knew him but never played for him, from bankers to farmers to Shriners. All the while I guarded against getting bogged down with thrice-told tales, game scores, statistics. One statistic, though, was unavoidable: Adolph Rupp won 896 basketball games, more than any college coach living or dead.

Rupp was brash, arrogant, and antagonistic in his drive to make basketball matter as much as football in the South. Rupp would take the best basketball team in the nation into Atlanta and seethe when the local sports editor played the story below a dog show. When basketball season was reaching a climax, Rupp's teams had to compete for attention with spring football practice, and again Rupp would get his dander up. He lived to see basketball become a major sport in Dixie.

Sometimes, of course, he built his own roadblocks. His reluctance to recruit black players—probably his major flaw—is well documented. I am not an apologist for Rupp; he needs no apology.

If I were to take on this project, my prime objective would be to explore the person behind the headlines—while always remembering that the headlines were a big part of his life. And forget about easy answers: the Adolph Rupp of my book would neither be branded a racist nor canonized as a saint. I'd just present things as they occurred and let opinions fall as they may. When I thought about it that way, all of a sudden I had no choice; I had to write the book. That's OK, though: when I thought about it that way, all the work seemed worthwhile. The Golden Years could wait.

—Russell Rice

Chapter
One

From Kansas Soil

Astrologers say that a person born between August 23 and September 22 has a practical mentality. A Virgo, they say, is painstakingly thorough, methodical, and exact. Feeling seldom takes precedence over thinking. Virgos are detail oriented and demand perfection; they are often insensitive about the feelings of others. Virgos choose their friends carefully, but they want people around them because they find it difficult to be alone. Above all, they thrive on recognition.

Adolph Rupp, born on September 2, 1901, fit the Virgo profile. To the Reverend Ed Beck, who played for Rupp, he was a human computer, "not in the mechanical sense, but in the ability to look into the future and decide what to do. He made a decision, started at the beginning, and worked toward his goals." Harry Lancaster said Rupp's image—arrogant, egocentric, sometimes just plain rude—came from a relentless dedication to success. "Nobody is really a good loser, but that is an easy way out," Lancaster said. Rupp wouldn't pretend to take losses easily. He was, Lancaster said, "a perfectly honest man." Rupp spared no effort to succeed. Time meant nothing to him. He concentrated only on what was important. He had no hobbies; he couldn't sit and watch television; he couldn't even take a vacation. Rupp's objectives were always clear. He became so submerged in molding his basketball teams that he often seemed aloof. But he was a perfectionist in everything he did, whether coaching a team, making a speech, or operating a farm.

At the turn of the century, Halstead was a small frontier town along the Santa Fe Railroad in central Kansas, a few miles north of the urban sprawl of Wichita and a dozen miles east of Newton, the Harvey County seat. Before 1868, it was a feeding place for countless buffalo, deer, and antelope, and it was home to sodbusters, outlaws, cowboys, and Indians. Pioneers settled under the Homestead Act of 1862, which offered 120 acres of public land to eligible families. It was a life of hard work on the rough, raw, unplowed, unfenced parcels. The newcomers plowed the soil, dug wells, graded roads, planted crops, and built sod shanties.

A majority of all immigrants to the United States in the late 1800s located in Kansas. The frontier line extended through the central part of the state, in Harvey, McPherson, and Reno counties. Most of Kansas's European settlers were members of the Mennonite Church, a Protestant sect founded in Freisland more than four hundred years ago. In new Mennonite settlements, the church was always built first and the school second. Because it was important to the church to preserve the German language, Mennonite children attended two months of German school each year. German was the only foreign language taught in high school, and parents subscribed to two German-language papers that gave news from the ports back east. A group of Mennonites built Halstead's first church in 1892.

The Mennonites had moved to Kansas for two reasons: to escape compulsory military service and to farm the land. They were a hard-working lot, erecting houses and sowing the hard-seed wheat that would later become famous throughout the West. At the turn of the century, Halstead's main street was four or five blocks long, with a hardware store, a post office, a grocery store, and a drug store. The feed store, the implement store, and the flour mills lay beyond the main street.

It was in this setting that Adolph Frederick Rupp spent the first eighteen years of his life. His parents were Heinrich and Anna Lichti Rupp, Mennonites who immigrated to America in the late 1800s. Rupp's father settled in Halstead after coming from Austria in 1883 with his mother, two brothers, and two sisters. He worked as a mill hand before taking up farming and became a citizen in 1892. Rupp's mother emigrated from Germany in 1891, accompanied by her father and her youngest brother. Heinrich and Anna married in 1893 and lived on two small farms before claiming a 120-acre homestead seven miles north of Halstead. Six children were born to the union: Otto, Henry, Theodore, Adolph, Elizabeth, and Alfred.

Adolph knew little English when he enrolled in District 33 School, which had one room and one teacher. At the beginning of the year, Anna outfitted each boy with a pair of overalls, two or three gingham shirts, plow shoes, and a heavy jacket. The Rupp children walked a mile to and from school, avoiding fence rows during heavy snowfalls. Apart from school, the church dominated all social activities. By the age of six, the children were reciting in church. On Christmas Eve, they performed a play that took weeks to prepare. The younger ones had only a few lines, but the parts became more complicated with each birthday.

Heinrich Rupp was a strict disciplinarian. After dinner he would adjourn to the living room, and silence would prevail. His children would creep to bed in order not to disturb him. "His word was law, and if you forgot it, he'd be there with a lash," Elizabeth Rupp Lawson remembered. "We inherited much of our self-reliance and independence from him." After Heinrich, just 48 years old, died of pneumonia in 1910, Rupp's older brother Otto quit school and took over running the farm. Anna became head of the household, a short, stout woman whose iron hand ruled the roost. A driver and pusher, Anna was always on the move. She tended her garden, sewed, ironed, cooked, and did all the other duties of her station. She believed that the future of each child rested with the individual. Her duty was to prepare them for high school; after that, they were on their own.

The Rupp home consisted of a living room, three bedrooms, a bath, a large kitchen, a dining room that also served as a family room, and two porches. An oak tree shaded the front of the house; fruit trees and a cottonwood dotted the rest of the property. The older boys worked in the field, while the younger ones milked the cows, fed the hogs, and performed other light chores. At the age of ten, Adolph took his turn on the mowing machine, staying in the field all day long. By the time he was thirteen, he operated a Kansas threshing machine. The boys ate breakfast by the light of a kerosene lamp and were in the fields ready to thresh or cut grain when the sun peeped over the horizon. Adolph helped farm wheat, oats, corn, and alfalfa every summer until he graduated from college. What he dreaded most was the most monotonous job of the year: plowing the half-mile-long Kansas corn rows. On the other hand, he enjoyed haymaking season, when all of the neighbors got together and put up prairie grass to feed the livestock in winter. It was a time for hard work, clean fun, and plenty of gossip.

To earn extra money, the Rupp boys broke wild horses for their neighbors, who let them work the animals for one summer. Adolph also filled silos and pitched wheat. "None of us were skilled at the time, so we did that kind of work," Otto said. Each fall, the Rupps slaughtered a steer and three or four hogs. Anna cured hams, ground sausage, and fried or baked meat, later preserving it in lard. She and Elizabeth canned vegetables from the garden and preserved plums and cherries from trees that grew wild in the area. Butter, cream, and milk were stored in a pump house. The Rupps traded surplus food for salt, sugar, and other staples. The boys took wheat to the mill, where it was ground into flour for the winter. They caught catfish in the Little Arkansas River and hunted rabbits, ducks, geese, quail, and prairie chickens, which were abundant in the area.

Adolph was in the second grade when District 33 erected a basketball goal at the school. On the farm, the Rupp boys nailed a barrel ring to a tool shed and played with a ball their mother made by stitching a feed sack filled with rags and straw. "The thing about that ball was that you couldn't dribble it," Adolph would recall. "There was no such thing as individual play." Henry described his brother as a leader who insisted that things be done the right way, and Otto said, "Adolph took to the game right away. He was a person who always seemed to get things done."

The Rupp house became a meeting place for Eugene Thornhill and other boys from town who went there to play basketball with Adolph and his buddies. The district schools formed teams and played against each other. Adolph practically ran the District 33 team. He was also the school janitor. He banked the fires in the afternoon and was the first to arrive at the school in the morning to start them up again. He swept the floor, wiped blackboards, dusted erasers, and filled coal buckets, all for fifty cents a month.

Halstead High School played its basketball games on a regulation basketball court in the city hall. Because the ceiling was only three feet above the backboards, protective wire baskets covered the lights. A few miles away, Sedgwick High School played in a general store with a stove in one corner. Moundridge High School played in an old church, and before Burrton could play, students had to remove cars from an old garage, sweep the floor, and hang baskets.

When Halstead won the first of its two consecutive state championships, Adolph was six years old. "We had no telephones, and sometimes it took days to find out what was going on," he said. "When we heard that Halstead High School had won, everybody went crazy about the game." By the time Adolph enrolled at Halstead in 1915, the basketball program had become weak. W. A. Lee coached the team because he was the school's only male teacher. Jeptha Carl Stone succeeded Lee and coached until he joined the military in 1917. Neither knew much about basketball. "I got hold of a whistle and practiced blowing until I knew how to blow a whistle, but I wasn't too sure when to blow it," Stone said in a 1979 interview. He admitted that any of the school's four female teachers would have been a better coach. Henry and Theodore Rupp were among the twenty-five boys who reported for basketball practice in 1915. The team lost its opener to Moundridge by fifty points and ended a disastrous season with a 110-13 loss to Newton. In addition to winning only one of sixteen games, the local boys scored almost five hundred fewer points than their opponents.

While a freshmen, Adolph joined Der Deutsche Verein, a literary society whose motto was "Ubung Macht den Meister"— Practice makes the master. That would prove to be a prophetic choice. Stone, who remembered young Adolph as "just another farm boy," played him sparingly as a sophomore, but he said Rupp seemed interested in what few plays they ran. Halstead defeated Bonner Springs and lost to El Dorado in the state tournament that year.

During the fall, the Rupp boys traveled to school by horse and buggy. When the winter snows set in, they rented a house in town with some other boys. Adolph worked odd jobs— mainly at Williams' Grocery—to pay expenses. He waited on customers, stocked shelves, and cleaned. In the summer, he worked on a threshing crew, pitching stacked wheat and oats into the machines. After the work day, crew members bathed in a nearby creek or a stock tank and slept outdoors on beds of straw. "It was hard work from sunup until sundown," Adolph said. "I enjoyed that."

During Adolph's junior year, the weekly newspaper started publishing high school box scores. He had ten field goals in an opening 67-17 victory over Sedgwick and thirty-seven points in a 79-19 win over Burrton. He averaged nine-teen points a game, and Halstead won the Mid-Kansas League championship.

Adolph was one of sixteen seniors in the 1919 class at Halstead High School. The basketball players elected the team captain, and Rupp let it be known that he wanted the job. He told Claude Thornhill that a vote for him meant Thornhill would start the opening game. Once Rupp became captain, he unofficially ran the team because the coach knew so little about the game; Thornhill started the first five games. "He's been a politician all his life," Thornhill said in a 1974 letter to the author. "He likes to be in the middle of the action." Adolph scored his career-high 33 points in a 50-30 drubbing of Florence and later led Halstead to its sixth straight win with twenty-three points against Burrton. Halstead closed the season with victories over Florence, Sedgwick, and Nickerson but lost to Nickerson in the district tournament. Rupp averaged 19.1 points a game.

Adolph was much more than a basketball star at Halstead High School. He was the school's best debater and a leader in class projects. His was the starring role— a football hero—in the senior class play. After graduation, Adolph used the money he had saved from summer work to travel by rail to Emporia, where he planned to attend the state college. He spent two hours in Emporia before deciding that wasn't the place for him. He put his trunk back on the train and headed for the University of Kansas. It was a decision he would never regret.

Chapter Two

Jayhawker

At the University of Kansas, Rupp encountered two men whose names are synonymous with basketball: Dr. James A. Naismith, inventor of the game, and Dr. Forrest "Phog" Allen, who some would say invented basketball coaching. "I had heard of Dr. Naismith while I was playing high school basketball, and he may have refereed a game at Halstead," Rupp said. "I didn't meet him until we freshmen reported for medical examinations." They formed a bond at Kansas that would last until Naismith's death in 1939. Naismith told Rupp that he came to Kansas to run the physical education program and pray in chapel, not because he invented basketball.

When Rupp was chairman of the Junior Olympics Committee during his senior year, Dr. Naismith introduced a new game he called war-ring, predicting that it would become more popular than basketball. The setting was a football field, with tires and rims placed at the fifty-yard line. Opposing teams lined up at the goal lines. At a signal, they rushed together and tried to carry the rings over the other team's goal. Every ring they got across a goal earned them five points. At the end of each ten-minute period, the referee awarded points according to the position of each ring. The game was so strenuous that the players quit after the first half. That was the first and last of war-ring.

Naismith told Rupp that he had played basketball only twice, once at Springfield, Massachusetts, where he invented the game, and once at Kansas. He formed the first teams at KU and introduced the game to both the college and the town. He thought coaching was unnecessary in a game intended for amusement. As coach at Kansas from 1899 to 1907, he had a record of fifty-four wins and sixty losses. Naismith's star pupil, Allen, was a logical choice to become the new coach of the Jayhawkers, as they were then called. After posting an impressive 43-9 record at Kansas, Allen became a teacher and coach at the Haskell Institute. He also coached at Central Missouri in Warrensburg before returning to Kansas in 1919 as the athletic director. He was also the freshman basketball coach. When the varsity coach, Carl Schlademan, resigned that post before the season began, Allen took over his duties.

In mid-October, students intending to try out for the freshman basketball squad reported to Allen's office, where he drilled them in the fundamentals of the game. That was Rupp's first meeting with a person who would have a profound influence on his life. Allen was a trim, alert six-footer who obviously took pride in his appearance. He wore loud clothes, leaning to gray or brown imported tweeds with big spots. He had closely cropped brown hair, a pink face, and tiny lines under his eyes. His players were clean-shaven and neatly dressed. A man who felt his personal habits were constantly being watched and copied by his players, Allen denounced the use of tobacco or liquor, and he warned of the dangers of gambling on sporting events. He was "Dr. Allen" or "Doc" to his players, never "Phog." Discipline was so demanding under Allen that the players spoke only when they had a question. They conversed freely, however, when invited to Allen's home. "We would talk basketball," Rupp said. "He would give us pep talks."

Allen talked nonstop to visitors, all the while eating horehound candy, which he claimed was good for the larynx. "Dr. Allen needed it at times in practice because he yelled himself hoarse," Rupp said. Allen was very health conscience and thought everyone should exercise. "He would make us do push-ups on our fingertips, not letting the heel of the hand touch the floor," Rupp recalled. "I had a sprained finger all the time I was there." Most of Allen's athletes were in awe of him —all had a tremendous respect for their coach. "We respected him because he stood for everything," Rupp said. "He just took care of himself."

The first days of basketball practice under Allen were "just plain brutal," Rupp said, and they didn't get easier. Sometimes the team practiced twice a day; if Allen had worked them three times a day, Rupp said, "some of us might not have survived." Rupp thought some of Allen's drills were unnecessary. "We would pivot and pivot and do all those things until the blisters on our feet would be the size of a silver dollar," he said. "We would spend ten or twelve minutes on hook passing, and we would throw that pass probably once a year, and that usually sailed out the window." On defense, Allen, who thought there was too much use of arms and too little use of feet in basketball, would have his players imagine they had no forearms. He introduced them to his "ape man" theory, which put every player in a crouch on both offense and defense. "We would raise our arms and hands like claws in the face of the man we were guarding," Rupp said. "Then we would yell at him," sometimes startling the player into dropping the ball.

Allen retained all the first-year players who reported to him. He felt a large squad touched more lives, created keener interest, and spawned unselfishness. The players spent most of their time learning the basics of the game. Allen's insistence on mastering the fundamentals was one reason his teams often looked ordinary at the start of a season and brilliant at the end, and Rupp would later adopt a similar regimen. When Allen's team played at home, he would take the players to a dormitory and put them to bed. After they awoke, he would lead them on a one-mile walk. Dinner usually consisted of two slices of whole wheat bread, a portion of honey, half a grapefruit, and celery. Later the players would sit before a big fireplace and place their feet close to the flames for fifteen minutes. "I never saw a man with cold feet who wasn't nervous and jumpy," Allen said. "Keep your feet warm, and you keep your nerves warm." (Years later, when Rupp was coaching at Freeport High School in Illinois, his team traveled to games in private automobiles; the coach heated bricks, wrapped them in towels, and placed them on the floorboard to keep his players' feet and nerves warm.) In the locker room, the players never knew what to expect from Allen. One of his favorite tricks was to turn out the lights before his pregame talk. His first freshman team won only ten of eighteen games, but they filled Robinson Gym.

The 1921-22 KU varsity took a 12-2 record into Columbia for the biggest game of the season, a rematch with a favored Missouri team that had already won at Lawrence. After holding a two-point lead at the half, the Jayhawkers stopped the Tiger offense and won 26-16, then won their remaining four games. "The Missouri game forced us to go into a zone defense," Rupp said. "It was a 3-2 zone." Rupp, a guard, played in the back line near the basket, with the other guard on the opposite side. Their job was to get the ball off the board and throw it to the front men for a fast break. "It was a good zone," Rupp said. "We hustled, which is the secret of any defense." You didn't stand around when you played for Allen.

The 1922-23 opening game was at Creighton, so Allen let the players go home for the holidays. They reported to him on December 26 in Omaha. He woke them up every day at 5 a.m. After a long hike in the country, they would practice, eat lunch, take a nap, and practice again. "It was exhausting, but we didn't mind," Rupp said. "We knew we were a good team." Kansas had a fine shooting and ballhandling team that was big enough to control the boards. Allen used a fast break, but he had no screening plays. Since most of the players had been together for three years, they ran their plays with precision. "We were always on the move," Rupp said. "You had to move with every pass." Playing before a capacity crowd, the Jayhawkers held Creighton to one late field goal in a 29-7 victory. They also beat Nebraska 30-20 on that trip.

Tusten Ackerman, Waldo Bowman, Charlie Wulf, Charlie Black, and Paul Endacott were the Kansas starters; and Rupp was a member of what Allen called his Meat Packers, a group that got in a game when the outcome was secure. (At Kentucky, Rupp would call his group the Lost Battalion or the Turds.) KU lost only to the Kansas City Athletic Club 34-32 and was 16-1 when Missouri came to town for the season finale. Long before the game, an unprecedented crowd gathered outside the gym, and cars lined the road that ran through the campus.

Endacott was only six feet tall, but he was a good jumper. In those days, a player could jump and tip the ball to himself. In the last minute and a half of the Missouri game, Endacott tipped the ball and let Missouri tie him up. The clock kept running, and he had possession of the ball when the game ended, Kansas winning 23-20. The Jayhawkers, undefeated in collegiate play, claimed the nation's championship. Endacott and Charlie Black were named All-America, and Endacott was named Player of the Year by the Helms Foundation.

Allen described Rupp as an intelligent player who excelled in the classroom and was one of the most popular students on campus. He said Rupp might have been a star had the two guards that played ahead of him not been so perfect. "Throw me that ball," Rupp told Endacott during a team reunion. "I never got it when we were playing." John Bunn, an assistant coach at Kansas, said Rupp was not a great player, but he was an excellent student of the game. "He was always somewhat of a character," Bunn said. "Customers would flock to the Jayhawk Cafe just to be around him."

Rupp drew much of his philosophy from Naismith, but it was Allen's quirks and habits he copied. He differed from both of his mentors, however, in the way he treated his players. "His door was always open to basketball players," Rupp said of Naismith. "I spent many hours talking to him." Allen, too, got close to his players. Rupp, though, kept his "boys" at a distance. Allen appealed to men's loves; his goal was to get into their hearts, know their families, discover their interests, study their temperaments, and feel their sorrows. He never cursed at his players. Rupp also wrote that a coach should control his temper, refraining from striking or cursing a player. "Don't call a boy yellow or a quitter," he advised. "He may be fighting his soul out for you at the time and be giving you all that he can." But in truth he cursed at some players and cajoled others. He praised sparingly and used satire effectively. He said that if he wanted to hear about personal problems, he would take his players to the farm and raise white-faced cattle. "I don't care if your girlfriend leaves you or if your pet rabbit dies," he said. "I just care if you produce for me on the basketball court." There was no getting close to Rupp; he felt he couldn't be a coach and a pal at the same time. Someone had to be in charge, and he made it quite clear that he was the boss.

After spending four years at the University of Kansas, Rupp had picked up more than Allen's mannerisms; he had studied the techniques of some of the finest coaches of that era. The wealth of basketball knowledge that he absorbed would serve him well in the future.

Chapter
Three

Bluegrass Bound

R upp graduated from the University of Kansas in 1923, just as the end of the big-spending boom of World War I was putting a damper on the nation's economy. Unable to find a job, he returned to the university and began work on an advanced degree. The Jayhawk Cafe gave him his old job back, and he also worked as an assistant in the Department of Home Economics, where one of his duties was grading test papers. It was a thankless task, he said, but there were benefits: the girls began to notice him. Sometimes he would find blank pages where they had failed to answer any questions.

"They would come to me crying and wanting to know if I could help them," he said. "I did get a little lenient with the essay papers, but there wasn't much I could do with the true and false ones." As an undergraduate, he was chairman of the varsity dance committee, which indicated his growing interest in girls, but basketball, studies, and the cafe had taken up all of Rupp's spare time. Rupp never did have a steady girlfriend at Kansas. He was happy to socialize with girls in a group, but he was not a one-on-one person.

At the end of the 1923-24 school year, he accepted a teaching and coaching position at Burr Oak High School in Kansas, but the primitive conditions his teams labored under must have reminded him of his high school days. "I discovered on the first day of football practice that the team had no uniforms," he said. "We finally received approval from the school board to buy some equipment, but were told to order as little as possible."

The basketball team played its games in a skating rink, and the baseball and track facilities were also below the standards of other schools in the area. When Rupp went home for Thanksgiving that year, he got a lucky break when he met the principal of the high school at Marshalltown, Iowa, B. R. Miller, who hired Rupp as a teacher and a coach.

"I thought I would coach the basketball team," Rupp said. "Imagine my surprise when they told me I was to coach the wrestling team." He had never even seen a wrestling match, but he persuaded Allie Morrison, a former AAU champion, to help coach the team. With Morrison's expert assistance, Rupp's team went undefeated and qualified for the state tournament at Ames.

During the season, Rupp gave a preview of his uncompromising attitude toward competition. One of his wrestlers injured a shoulder in a fall from a bunk, but Rupp insisted that he compete in the next match. Although the boy did not have a chance of winning, his refusal to default gave the team a point that proved to be the winning margin in the match.

Rupp moved to Freeport High School in northern Illinois in the fall of 1926. In addition to a full teaching load, he coached the line in football and the track and heavyweight basketball teams. The 1915 Freeport team, led by captain Pat Holmes, had won the state tournament, and Holmes himself coached the school to another state championship in 1926. When Holmes left Freeport to become freshman football coach at the University of Wisconsin, Rupp succeeded him. Rupp knew he would lose his job unless he maintained Freeport's winning tradition. Freeport had a new high school, a new gym, and was near Chicago. The metropolitan newspapers listed area high school scores, and they even wrote about the coaches. Rupp couldn't have dreamed of a better setup.

Rupp's players quickly learned of the intensity that would become famous. "Rupp wouldn't let you waste time," George Schmelzle remembered. "You automatically played to win basketball games." Lightweight coach George Kloos said his main job was sitting on the bench and holding Rupp down. Like his old coach, Allen, Rupp began by teaching the fundamentals of the game, drilling his players for hours before allowing them to scrimmage. He installed a new system to replace the slow-down offense used by Holmes. His offense relied on a fast break and two or three set plays built around the screens that he picked up from Dr. Walter E. Meanwell, a highly successful coach at the University of Wisconsin. The pivot man mainly fed the ball to the other players. Rupp chose Meanwell's man-to-man defense rather than Allen's zone because it was easier to teach. He taught his players to be sensitive on defense to openings where they could slide through and stay with their men. And sometimes, as Rupp put it, "we just made our boys put their heads down and go through the screens." Kloos said he never saw Rupp use any defense other than a man-to-man.

Rupp was home for the holidays when Freeport played an exhibition game against the Illinois School for the Deaf, losing 16-14 in two overtimes. Two days later, players from the 1926 state championship team defeated the varsity. Rupp returned from vacation and whipped the squad into shape, and the Pretzels defeated Dubuque 21-16 in the regular-season opener, but later that week, a concerned Rupp planted a story in the local newspaper:

> If the heavies do not come through in proper shape this season, the blame is due to the fact that there are too many blind girls in Freeport High School.
>
> Every time there is a call for classes at the school each day, most major basketball players lead fair co-eds through the   halls of the building and up to their classrooms. The broad-shouldered athletes invariably have one or two of the co-eds hanging on well-muscled arms.
>
> Coach Rupp has come to the conclusion that the fair damsels must be blind or they could find their way to the classroom without the aid of the gallant cage warriors. He added that the interference of the maids upset his well-laid plans to make his athletes think basketball as well as play it.

Of course, he also wants them to think of their studies, but he feels that the athletes cannot devote a certain portion of their minds to the co-eds, another portion to their studies and still have another portion left for basketball.

Rupp lived at the YMCA in adjoining rooms with Elmer Hoffman, his scorekeeper and best friend. Each evening, they would buy a newspaper at Tinsley's Cigar store and check on the stock market, then track down certain players who sometimes could be found at a girl's house. He enforced a 10 p.m. curfew, even discouraging social organizations from inviting players to functions that might keep them out late, but he was particularly nervous about the effect of females on his boys' rest and on their powers of concentration. Once Rupp banned two players from practice for a week for parking with girls in a cemetery.

"Love affairs have wrecked many a good ballclub," he told a civic group. "I consider them along with the player's physical development and proper basketball instruction."

Rupp admitted years later that he was shy and secretly afraid of women. He had been a timid youngster who put on a bold front to scare people off, giving them the impression that he was brash, and as a coach, he became suspicious, jealous, and resentful of women who associated with his basketball players. When Kentucky player Wallace Jones married Edna Ball, "Coach Rupp objected because he didn't feel like he had complete charge of his program," Jones said. "He thought maybe somebody at home was in charge."

In spite of Rupp's social vigilance, Freeport continued to struggle. Belvidere held the Pretzels without a field goal in the first half and won 16-12, and Aurora shut out Rupp's team in the first half en route to a 41-10 romp, forcing him to make defensive changes and insert new plays. Freeport closed on a strong note and qualified for the district tournament, winning three games before falling to Rockford in the finals. The Pretzels finished 10-6 in Rupp's first year and improved in 1928 to 11-5 and second in the district. In 1929, they went 20-4 and were sectional champs, finishing third in the state tournament. They won the district tourney again in 1930.

Hoffman and a group of boosters and parents of players formed a car pool to transport the boys to their games. "We were a tight little unit of followers and players traveling as a group," George Kloos said. Though he still shied from most social contacts, Rupp was a member of the Elks Club, the City Club, and the exclusive Germania Society, whose members often conversed in German. He played handball and golf with Hoffman but never developed a serious interest in the games. Always the coach, he suggested during a round of golf that Hoffman switch to his left hand; he became one of the best left-handed golfers in the state.

Even when he worked up the courage to ask a girl on a date, he couldn't step out of character. When Rupp dined at a restaurant with Esther Schmidt, one of the most popular young ladies in town, he drew basketball plays on the table-cloth.

University of Illinois coach Craig Ruby was the speaker at Freeport's 1930 basketball banquet. He told Rupp that John Mauer had resigned as head coach at the University of Kentucky. Rupp was a hot coaching prospect, with a four-year record of 59-21. He had developed seven all-conference players and three scoring champions. Still, Rupp was thinking about giving up the sport. He was a trained school administrator, and they made more money than coaches. But when Ruby agreed to recommend him for the college job, Rupp decided to see what Kentucky had to offer.

The Illinois influence was already strong on the UK campus. The Wildcat football coach was Harry Gamage, who had played center for Bob Zuppke at the University of Illinois. Line coach Bernie Shively had been an All-America guard who blocked for Red Grange. Fred Major, another assistant coach with Illini connections, coached the UK freshmen in basket-ball and football. Basketball coach John Mauer had played in the Illini backfield with Grange. Mauer also played basketball at Illinois.

From 1920 to 1924 Illinois graduate George Buchheit had coached the UK basketball team to a 44-27 record. In 1921, they were recognized as the first basketball champions of the South after winning the first SIAA Tournament in Atlanta. When Buchheit left Kentucky in 1924, assistant football coaches C.O. Applegran and Ray Eklund—two more former Illini stars—coached the team for two years. In 1927, the job was offered to Basil Hayden, Kentucky's first All-

American. "I was selling insurance and out of touch when the university called me to coach the team," Hayden said. "I agreed to take the job on a temporary basis." Devastated by football injuries to two-sport players, the Wildcats finished 3-13, still the school's worst record. Hayden was glad to turn the job over to Mauer, who compiled a 40-16 record in three seasons, including a 16-3 mark in 1930. He quit because the university would not give him a pay raise. The school newspaper called Mauer a "Moses" who had led the Wildcats out of the basketball wilderness. His influence spread throughout the South, as other coaches adopted his style.

Two university officials who came to the station to greet a candidate for the basketball job saw a strong young man standing about 6-foot-2, a little on the portly side, get off the train. The candidate dressed conservatively, combed his hair neatly, spit-shined his shoes, and carried himself well. Bernie Shively said he looked like a preacher.

The route through Lexington went past a slum. Arriving late for lunch, the trio settled for cold fish, cornbread, and coffee. "I thought the people of Kentucky had poor houses," Rupp said, "and they also didn't eat so good." The interview went well, but Rupp wasn't interested in a short contract, a long contract, or any contract at all. He simply wanted an opportunity to show the people at Kentucky what he could do. If they liked him and he liked them, they would talk about a contract. If he didn't like them, he would quit; if they didn't like him, they could fired him.

Pat Harmon, a Freeport native and the sports editor of the *Cincinnati Post* and *Times-Star*, asked a council member why they hired Rupp. "Because he told us he was the best damned basketball coach in the United States," the administrator replied, "and he convinced us he was."

Chapter Four

Young Wildcat

When Adolph Rupp arrived at the University of Kentucky, he wanted to be more than just another assistant football coach coaching basketball. He went through the motions of helping coach the football reserves and track, which was part of his contract, but he was a man with a mission: to convert the natives to a new and exciting brand of basketball. His salary was about the same he made at Freeport: $2,800 for the 1930-31 academic year and $3,000 for 1931-32. His football assignment, assisting Birkett Pribble with the freshmen, was about as low as you could get in the coaching ranks.

The 1929 Kentucky football team had compiled a 6-1-1 record, and fan interest was high. Some even dared to dream of an invitation to the Rose Bowl. But after winning their first four games, the Wildcats lost three of the last four, and thoughts turned to basketball. Rupp was already drilling some members of the squad.

One of the first things he had done when he got to Lexington was set up a meeting with Carey Spicer, the lone returning basketball starter. Rupp congratulated Spicer on winning All-America honors and asked him to continue as team captain. Then they sat down and talked basketball. Rupp had conducted a similar session with Ralph Ruhe at Freeport five years earlier. Rupp had told Ruhe, the only returning starter from Freeport's state championship team, that the slow-down offense used by coach Pat Holmes was going out the window. From that time on, the Pretzels would run. Spicer got the same message: a new sheriff was in town and the boys were going to have fun. "Carey got the word around to the others," Rupp said. "They got a little confident that maybe the new coach was going to give them a better opportunity to shoot and score."

Spicer remembers, though, that Rupp asked him about Mauer's offense. Spicer lent him Mauer's playbook and never saw it again. He said Rupp used the same plays, even the same numbers, throughout his career. That may be an exaggeration, but Rupp did reject Phog Allen's style in favor of the Illinois system of play. Craig Ruby taught a guard-around offense at Illinois that featured short passes and shots close to the basket. The plays began with a guard passing the ball to the post man and moving to the outside while a forward set a pick; then the guard cut to the basket and took a pass from the pivot. Rupp let his players create variations and use their own natural ability. He also told them to run, throwing all caution to the wind.

In the mid 1930s, Rupp—or rather his team—developed an inside screen. The players were scrimmaging during spring practice one day when he stopped the action and asked them to repeat what they had just done. By the time the season started, the inside screen was part of the offense. The two screens allowed the guard to go either inside or outside the screening forward after the guard passed to the post man. Another innovation was the second guard-around play, in which the first guard set a pick for the second.

Cotton Nash was an All-American for Kentucky in the early 1960s, but his assessment of the coach's style could have been made by one of Rupp's first Wildcats: "We knew what we had to do and we did it. It was very efficient, with no wasted motion. He gave his players a lot of freedom, and I think he was successful because of that wide-open style. You had to be an all-around player to play for Rupp. You couldn't be a specialist." Kentucky and 12 other schools left the Southern Conference and formed the Southeastern Conference in December 1932. Using screening plays, the Wildcats won forty-eight games before losing to an SEC team. Rupp claimed the inside screen was UK's big contribution to the game of basketball.

Rupp continued John Mauer's winning tradition on the court, and unlike his predecessor, he presented a winning image off the court as well. Rupp was outgoing and cheerful; when he entered a room, he drew a crowd. Mauer was a brilliant teacher, but a dour person who alienated people. The media, which had never warmed to Mauer, loved Rupp, who carried a lucky buckeye in one pocket and a pack of superstitions in the other. Rupp's most intriguing superstition was about the color brown. Once when he was at Freeport, he had bought a blue suit to replace his old brown one. He wore the new suit to a game, and his team got clobbered. Rupp never again wore anything but brown to games; he became known as "The Man in the Brown Suit." His favorite sign of good luck was finding a pin, especially a bobby pin, and particularly on the afternoon of a game. His players began dropping pins where he would be sure to find them. He would pick up a pin and say, "My gawd, boys, there's no way we can lose this game!" Asked once if he was superstitious, Rupp said he had learned long ago that it was bad luck to be superstitious.

Neville Dunn, sports editor of the Lexington *Herald,* offered his opinion of the new coach: "Rupp is a person with a gloriously developed sense of humor, a droll, witty man who knows basketball, makes a friend out of every new acquaintance, and is, in all the popular meaning of the phrase, 'a good sport.'" Lexington's social life revolved around the big horse farms in the area, but Rupp wasn't interested in hobnobbing with that group. He didn't even read the society pages. The only date he had was the time Esther Schmidt and some friends came to see his team play. Instead Rupp spent his spare time with reporters, fishing, trying polo, and going to the races. He made friends early in his tenure because he knew there would be plenty of time to make enemies. He cared little what they might say about him in Chicago or New York, but he did not want a bad local press.

Kentucky had lost some key players, and the writers predicted that the rookie coach would be lucky to win half his games. But Rupp knew that the cupboard was far from bare. Besides Spicer, the returnees included lettermen Jake Bronston, Louis McGinnis, and George Yates, and sophomores Forest "Aggie" Sale and Ellis Johnson were future All-Americans.

Rupp often speculated that Sale might have been the best player he coached. Sale, 6-foot-5 and a tremendous rebounder, specialized in following shots on the offensive board. Sale also liked to outjump the opposing center, get the tap himself—a legal maneuver in those days—and dribble the length of the floor for a layup. Johnson was the best athlete on the team, a four-sports star who had won All-America honors in both basketball and football at Ashland High School. He was the Most Valuable Player of the 1928 national high school basketball tournament, which his Tom Cats won, and he was also an outstanding student.

Sale and McGinnis were the only non-football players in the group. The other players would report to Rupp after the annual Thanksgiving football game with Tennessee. Though he was charged with working with the freshmen, Rupp knew very little about football and had less to say about it. On the Saturday of a game, he would sit in the press box and chart yards made through the line, turning the stats in to Gamage at halftime and after the game. Rupp turned basketball workouts over to Pisgah Combs, who had played for Mauer the previous year, though the head coach would hurry to the gym after football practice.

A record forty-six candidates showed up for the first varsity practice. Rupp arranged them in a semicircle at midcourt and made a simple speech: "I want it understood that there will be no loafers on this team. Every man has to play ball or be gone; that's final." Two weeks before Christmas, the varsity defeated the freshmen 75-21 in their first scrimmage. Afterward Rupp worked the varsity overtime on defense for letting the freshmen attempt thirty-one shots. Two days later the varsity won 75-9, and the freshman shot only six times in forty-five minutes.

A few days after the football players reported for basketball, Rupp made Johnson a starting guard, joining Spicer,

McGinnis, Yates, and Bill Trott in the first five. "Coach Rupp didn't believe in someone resting on his laurels," Johnson said in 1975. "He apparently had seen enough to feel that I should be one of the guards on his team." Although he was only six feet tall, Johnson played under the basket and was a leading rebounder on the team. He would grab the ball off the backboard and start the fast break with a long pass. "We got an awful lot of birdies because the opposition didn't know what we were doing," he said.

From previews in the press, basketball fans knew that they should expect a new style of play, and they would soon be able to judge for themselves: the Wildcats played their first five games at home. Rupp would always remember how he felt before they opened with nearby Georgetown College: like having lye on your stomach. He would feel that way before every game his teams played.

Rupp was no inspirational coach in the Knute Rockne mold. During pregame warm-ups, he watched the other team, observing how the players moved and took their shots. In the dressing room, he gave his starters the numbers of the men they were to guard and told them what plays to run. There were no pep talks; he wanted his players to go onto the floor poised, cool of nerve, and keen of judgment, not nervous or excited. The team took the floor in a pecking order that never varied: team captain and players, support personnel, assistant coaches, and Rupp. He entered after the last bar of the national anthem; it was more dramatic that way. His quick eye noted whether the managers had folded the towels correctly and distributed the right quantity of chewing gum. There was a place for everything, and everything had to be in its place. At intermission, he would hang his coat in the first locker, use the urinal, wash his hands, and then talk to the boys. When the occasion warranted it, he delivered scorching criticism; then he would hand the chalk to his assistant.

On its first possession, Rupp's team always ran No. 6, a guard-around play to flush out the defense. Wildcat fans came to expect "Star Spangled Banner and then No. 6," as Rupp put it. As the action quickened, Rupp would squirm on the bench. "Play defense, dammit," he yelled after Georgetown captain Harry Lancaster scored the first field goal in that first game. "Get on him; he's going wild." Then Ellis Johnson scored two points for Kentucky, and the Wildcats were off to the races. Their fast breaks resulted in layups, and their screens left the defenders in their tracks. Led by Aggie Sale's nineteen points, Kentucky won 67-19; Rupp complained that they had let Lancaster score eleven. He used his entire squad of seventeen players. The next day's newspaper acknowledged that the game demonstrated the scoring potential of the new coach's fast-break system.

The first meeting between the young coach and Georgetown's best player hardly suggested the closeness the two would develop. During the three years that Lancaster played against Rupp's teams, the Baron never spoke to him. "He didn't change through the years," Lancaster said, "almost never speaking to a player on the opposing team."

After graduating from Georgetown, Lancaster was an assistant at Paris High School under his old coach, Blanton Collier. He became head coach at Bagdad High School and then principal at Gleneyrie. When the school fired its basketball coach before the end of the year, Lancaster took over the basketball team. Meanwhile, he worked on his master's degree at UK, and, now that he was no longer an enemy player, he found Rupp eager to talk to him when their paths crossed on campus—though Lancaster suspected that Adolph simply knew he was a high school coach and someday might have a good boy for the Baron.

Kentucky was 5-0 when Rupp took the team on the road for the first time. Some of the players showed up at the train station wearing sweat shirts and knickers. Rupp did not mind the stylish knickers, but he objected to the sweats. Each offending player had to go home and change into a dress shirt, a tie, and a coat. Rupp demanded class; sloppy business was unacceptable as long as he was their coach.

After a poor first half at Vanderbilt, Rupp asked Bronston what he was thinking. "I was wondering if you had on brown socks," Bronston said. Rupp pulled up his trousers to reveal brown socks. The Wildcats won 42-37. They defeated Tennessee by four points and returned home to play Washington & Lee. The day Kentucky played the Generals, Rupp was at a local horse farm with Elmer Hoffman, referee Dick Bray, and Lexington *Herald* sports editor Frank Hoover. They spied a black cat. Rupp crossed over, followed in the cat's footsteps, and said, "Boys, it's in the bag." That night the Wildcats won 23-18.

Rupp's first loss as a college coach was to Georgia, 25-16 at Athens. The game was played in Woodruff Hall, which Rupp called a museum piece. Ellis Johnson did not make the trip, and Georgia's Bill Strickland hit three straight shots late in the game. To make matters worse, Georgia football coach Harry Mehre sat in for Horace Stegeman, the Bulldog basketball coach. "Harry tells the story about as well as anyone," Rupp said. "He had two sporting goods salesmen referee the game." Actually, the UK scorebook lists only one official—O'Sullivan—for that game; next to O'Sullivan's name, in Rupp's handwriting, is the word *terrible*, underlined twice. Rupp later began having someone record every foul called during a game, with the name of the official making the call and the team penalized. An official whose stats weighed heavily against the Wildcats had to face the wrath of Rupp. After the victory, Mehre wired Stegeman in New York and asked whether he had any more tough games that he could coach. When Mehre's football team got stomped in California that fall, Rupp asked whether Mehre had any tough games he needed help with.

Neville Dunn speculated that the Wildcats lost to Georgia because Rupp's brown socks were in the laundry, or perhaps he had left his brown suit and brown tie at home. Dunn also noted that the Cats and Dogs played on Friday the thirteenth. Kentucky lost to Clemson and beat Georgia Tech on the same trip, and Rupp was still bemoaning the losses when he received a bill for $400 from the hotel where the team had stayed in Atlanta, payment for towels, lamps, blankets, and other missing items. Rupp, who always kept housing lists on road trips and filed them with the athletic director's office so he knew who stayed in which room, gave his players a deadline for returning the goods. The hotel got every item back, and Rupp never had any more trouble of that kind.

For the second year in a row, the Wildcats entered the conference tournament with only two losses. They beat North Carolina State, Duke, and Florida for the right to meet Maryland in what turned out to be a classic championship game. Kentucky had the lead only one time, with one minute left on the clock. Lewis "Buzzy" Berger hit a layup to tie the score for the Terrapins. Berger caught the ball on the ensuing center jump and shot from the middle of the floor, making the basket that beat the Wildcats.

After the final game, Rupp wired the Herald a brief description of the battle: "The boys from old Kentucky staged the greatest comeback of the tournament, and their loss to Maryland is no disgrace. I only wish that the people at home could have seen the battle; for the fight they put up in the last half will live in my memory forever." Kentucky placed three players on the All-Southern team: George Yates, unanimous choice at center; Louis McGinnis, the leading scorer; and Carey Spicer, the third-leading scorer. Spicer set a tournament record with twenty-two points against Florida.

Although John Mauer had won one more game than Rupp the year before, Kentucky fans had forgotten the former coach. Mauer's Miami University team went 5-10 that season and 46-79 in his eight years there. He then moved to Tennessee and haunted Kentucky for a few years, but Rupp did not worry about Mauer or anybody else. He had laid the groundwork for his program. It was just a matter of time before basketball would overshadow football at Kentucky. Rupp had one other program to get established. In August, he returned to Freeport for Esther Schmidt. They married in Chicago and had a twelve-day honeymoon. It was a good first year in Lexington.

Chapter
Five

Motivation through Fear

Every year on the first day of practice, Rupp would call the players to center court. "This basketball I have in my hand is not a toy," he would say. "It is a tool. Our purpose is to teach you to work with this tool so we can win basketball games." Rupp ran his practice sessions with the precision of a Marine Corps boot camp. Coaches wore starched khaki, and players dressed in white undershirts, shoes, socks, and shorts. The setting was solemn. "Adolph wore that khaki uniform every day, and I often wondered if he washed it," Alex Groza said. "Then I found out he had a whole supply." Dan Chandler and Vern Hatton wrote, in *From Both Ends of the Bench*, "You could almost see the sergeant's stripes. Uncle Sam was a breeze compared to [Rupp's drills]."

Rupp's philosophy was simple and straightforward: "It's the work we give them in the fundamentals that counts," he said. "There is no other way. The first thing you have to do is curtail the individual desire of the boy in the interest of team play. Then you have to correct two deficiencies every boy has—in playing defense and recognizing the value of ball possession."

Rupp surrounded himself with a good staff, which was one of the secrets of his success. Teaching fundamentals to freshmen was a job for the top assistant coach; Rupp had two of the best in Paul McBrayer (1934-43) and Harry Lancaster (1946-69). After a varsity practice, the ranking assistant would drill the freshmen for as long as three hours. Part of the freshman coach's responsibility was to weed out the players who couldn't play up to Rupp's standards. A player who couldn't put the ball in the basket did not have a prayer with Rupp, who expected recruits to have learned to shoot in high school. To Rupp, the outside shot was fundamental, because it made the defense come out and cover the perimeter, which in turn left areas close to the basket open for high-percentage shots. A long shot in those days was an 18-footer: most players had learned to shoot in facilities with low ceilings that made high-arched shots impossible. Rupp disapproved of jump shooting, and he was the last coach to abandon the two-handed set shot. But he believed in preserving a player's style of shooting, and when players who had learned the jump shot in high school started to arrive on campus, he gave in to the new style.

Rupp could adapt to new styles of play, but he was inflexible when it came to training players in his system. "From the first day I went to practice in 1930, he expected us to be simple with what we were doing," Ellis Johnson recalled. "He wanted us to run out on the fast break and get a good percentage shot." He also demanded that his players run their patterns and play defense.

And Rupp believed that games were won and lost in practice, Johnson said. Practice started at 3:30 p.m. and ended at 5; you could set your clock by it. James Dickerson of the *National Observer* came to Lexington in 1966 when the Wildcats were undefeated after twelve games. The drills reminded him of a taut, silent version of a forced march. Superbly conditioned athletes were gasping and grunting as though they were weightlifters or shot putters, he said. "On and on it goes, silent, efficient, implacable; basketball at Kentucky is like rolling a boulder uphill."

Practice began with thirty minutes of "spot" shooting and ended with fifteen-minute free throw sessions. Every drill in between followed the same rigid schedule. "Our boys have more fun playing at Kentucky than they will anywhere," Rupp contended. "They know every minute what they are going to do." There was no talk, no laughter, no clowning. Rupp called the basketball floor his classroom, and demanded complete silence. "You have to have complete concentration, the same as in law school," he said. "From the time you walked into the gym until you left, you were there to play basketball," Alex Groza said.

Rupp's philosophy was to establish rhythm through repetition. Players practiced the same maneuver until it became an automatic part of their game. Louie Dampier said that spot shooting—each player taking shots designed for his position—was the hardest drill of all. "You concentrated on *every* shot," Dampier said. "I got tired of it." During passing drills, the ball would pop-pop-pop with monotonous precision. A break in the rhythm would bring a roar from Rupp, who would chew the player out on the spot. Once Rupp stopped a scrimmage against Georgetown College to remind Willie Rouse that dribbling was to be used only for ball control and to get from one spot to another. "Men of Georgetown," he said, "let me introduce you to Willie Rouse, the God-damnedest dribbler in the world." He once told Tom Kron he was going to write a book about how not to play defense and devote a whole chapter to him.

Anyone who ever played for Rupp eventually learned the depth of the coach's repertoire of sarcasm:

> "I want you to make that crip shot. If you get killed doing it, we'll give you the finest funeral ever seen in Central Kentucky."
> "Get up Evans, there goes your man."
> "You have such great hands that we're going to immortalize you by casting them in bronze."
> "Why don't you go over in that corner and take a crap, so you can at least say you did something while you were here."
> "I want you to remain very nonchalant and aloof. Act like you don't know what's going on, and then break behind the screen to get the ball. Ah, hell, just act natural, and it's bound to work."

"Since you like that damn ball so much, you take it home tonight and sleep with it."

"You look like a Shetland pony in a stud horse parade."

"Stop practice and everyone take a shower. Rose got a rebound."

When Jack Tucker missed four free throws against Cincinnati, Rupp sat him in a chair on the foul line and made him stare at the goal throughout practice. "I was embarrassed enough without the other players coming by and making remarks to me," Tucker said. "My foul shooting improved the rest of the season." Another time the Wildcats were training for a visit to Madison Square, and Bill Spivey could not buy a basket. "Spivey, those New Yorkers up there won't think the Barnum & Bailey Circus has been in town," Rupp said, "but they'll think the biggest damn clown has." Spivey later observed, "I thought he had a writer who wrote all those quips, but I found out they just came off the top of his head."

And if he didn't focus all his ire on one player, he could insult the whole team at once. Stopping one ragged scrimmage session, Rupp raised his face and hands upward and pleaded, "Dear God, please send me someone who is worth a damn." At that moment, the governor of Kentucky, Albert B. "Happy" Chandler, walked into the arena. "Thank you, God," Rupp said. But when Chandler laughed, Rupp told him to shut up. "I don't care if you are the governor," he said. "Either be quiet or get out."

Chandler had broken a cardinal Rupp rule: speak only if you can improve on the silence. Harold Ross was whistling in practice once when Rupp yelled, "I didn't bring you here all the way from Hickman to listen to you sing. If you want to do that, you should talk to Warren Lutz [the UK band director], and maybe he will give you a scholarship." Alex Groza pranced into the dressing room one day singing, "I'm in the army now." When Rupp entered the room, he asked who in the hell was making all that noise. Groza sneaked through the row of lockers, went outside, and came back in with a serious look on his face. "I thought, 'If this is the atmosphere, and this is the way it's going to be, then it's also the way I'm going to be,'" he said. "It was the first time I realized basketball was a serious business there."

If players performed poorly, Rupp got after them. When they did well, he complimented sparingly; he figured that was what they were there for. "Those practices were rough, and there was always a man on the second string waiting to bump you off the starting five," Bobby Watson recalled. "I used to look forward to some games simply because there would be less pressure."

Spivey thought Rupp wanted everybody to hate him, and he often succeeded. Teammates told Scotty Baesler if the coaches didn't get after him, it meant they didn't like him; the time to start worrying, they said, was when Rupp and his staff ignored you. Baesler eventually learned that if you could not take the criticism, you were not going to play. "Joe B. Hall considered it an honor when Rupp chewed him out in practice. "To me, it was a sign of concern," he told Billy Reed of the *Courier-Journal*. "I knew that it mattered to him." C. M. Newton said it took a tough hide to play for Rupp, because he motivated through fear. Newton knew that if he had a bad practice, he might be "scalded" or invited back that night. There was also the possibility of a trip to the "nickel seats," a round trip to the top of the lower arena.

Rupp's intensity level peaked during defensive drills. Each season, defense was the last thing the team worked on, drilling for two weeks before the opening game. Rupp believed that emphasizing defense first would undermine the players' confidence in their offensive patterns. "Defense is like spreading fertilizer on the farm," he said. "It's dirty work that nobody wants to do, but it has to be done." And heaven help the player who failed to spread the fertilizer to Rupp's liking. "Oh, my Gawd!," the coach would bawl. "You just made the worst mistake since this building has been built. Burn the damn thing down if you're going to play defense like that. Don't burn down libraries or student centers. Burn this place down, because we're not going to have defense like that."

As Cliff Barker put it, Rupp would "blow you right off the floor." Cotton Nash, who played for Barker at Jeffersonville, Indiana, said that Rupp and Lancaster ran off many players who simply could not stand the heat. One practice was so intense that Roger Newman lost his cool and tried to escape by climbing the iron gate that barred visitors from the arena. Nash survived by listening to about half of what the coaches said.

"If you choked in practice," Barker said, "Adolph did not want you on the floor during a double-overtime game." Those who survived Rupp's wrath were so well-versed in fundamentals that Red Auerbach once said he would rather watch Kentucky practice than see most teams play. Many of Rupp's players felt the same way—once they'd graduated and left the practices to another generation of Wildcats.

Chapter Six

Friends and Family

Maybe Adolph Rupp didn't make a big first impression on Esther Schmidt, the young business college student he fell for in Freeport. Sixty-two years after the marriage, she couldn't remember how or where they first met. "Perhaps it was at a party," she said. "He was always so busy." She made an impression on Adolph, though, and marrying Esther turned out to be one of the smartest things he ever did. She was the centerpiece in the puzzle, the glue that held him together. If there is such a thing as a perfect marriage, Esther and Adolph—living proof that opposites attract—had one.

Everyone who knew Esther remembers her as a lovely person; some wonder what she saw in Adolph. When Esther visited Lexington in 1931, Adolph introduced her to the wives of the Kentucky coaches. After she returned to Freeport, he asked Ruth Shively and Stella Gilb if they thought Esther was good enough for him. "Anybody would be good enough for you," replied Ruth, who considered him the most self-centered person she had ever met. At age 90, she still couldn't find a good word to say about him.

"There are many people who let a little power go to their head. He got a reputation, and he thought he was the most important person in the world," said Ruth. "Esther was one of the most beautiful women I have ever seen, but she was completely submissive to Adolph. She was a charming and delightful person to be with. Her personality changed when she was around Adolph."

But Ruth's was a minority opinion among those who were close to Adolph. To Harry Lancaster, a longtime assistant, Rupp seemed rough and gruff, but he knew when to show a softer side. On the night Lancaster's mother died, he was in New Orleans scouting the Sugar Bowl. Rupp called him and gently broke the news; he had already called Lancaster's hotel, had his baggage sent to the airport, and bought him a ticket to Cincinnati. After meeting Lancaster at the airport at 4:30 a.m., Rupp drove him the seventy- five miles back to Lexington, then gave him his car to drive to Richmond, where his mother had lived.

Wayne Walker is another Rupp defender. In 1957 Walker was athletic director and coach of three sports at Kentucky Village, a juvenile facility run by the state. To compete on the high school level, the team needed uniforms and all types of equipment. Walker was a student in Lancaster's basketball class, for which Rupp was a frequent guest lecturer. Having met Rupp in the class, Walker called him to discuss his needs as a new coach.

"I'll never forget walking into his office with all the sports pictures on the wall and his delightful handshake," Walker said. "I went over my needs with him, and he sat there with his hand over his mouth for a moment. Then he got up and put his arm around me. He said, 'By Gawd, anybody that has the nerve, patience, and guts to work with these kids, I'm going to help. Let's go see the equipment manager.'" George Hukle gave Walker shoes, athletic supporters, practice shorts, shirts, uniforms, warm-up pants, and jackets. On the back of each jacket was a wildcat logo and the word *Kentucky* across the top; Walker had the word *Village* stitched underneath, and his team became the Kentucky Village Wildcats. "When my season started, all the opponents were complimentary of our uniforms," He recalled. "It gave us great pride in our accomplishments."

Lyman Ginger, an educator who held many positions at the university and in state government, and his wife Betty were longtime friends of the Rupps. The relationship began, not surprisingly, in the athletic arena. When Rupp arrived at Kentucky, Ginger was teaching and coaching at Winchester High School. They met when one of the officials failed to appear for a football game against Paris. In those days there were no trained officials, and the local coach grabbed anyone he could find who knew something about the game. The Paris coach, Blanton Collier, asked Rupp to help work the game, and both coaches agreed that he did a good job.

When Adolph and Esther set up housekeeping in Lexington, they lived in an apartment. Bill and Ethel Fish were their neighbors. Ethel invited Rosie Rash, Betty Ginger, Claire Bell and Esther in for bridge, and the group played once a week for the next forty years. Rosie later married Bob Sparks, a lumber dealer who became another of Adolph's close friends. Esther also struck up a friendship with Jeanette Sparks, who lived in the sorority house next door. Jeanette married Paul Nickell, a salesman for the Graves-Cox Company, owner of the best men's clothing store in town, a connection that benefited Adolph. "I patched his brown suit at least a half-dozen times," Nickell recalled in a 1994 interview. "He was only making $2,800 a year and didn't have the money to buy a new one."

Graves-Cox started Lexington's first sports radio program, a half-hour show on WLAP featuring interviews with the Kentucky football coach and coaches of the Wildcats' upcoming opponents. Nickell lined up the guests, but he needed an interviewer; Rupp agreed to do it for nothing. "The program was so popular that people would stop dinner to listen to Adolph," Nickell said. "He became known as the Will Rogers of Kentucky radio." In lieu of pay, the Graves-Cox owners told Nickell to take care of Rupp. Nickell did just that, outfitting the coach in the company's most expensive brown suit and matching accessories: brown hat, brown shirt, brown shoes, brown socks, and a brown tie. Nickell was Rupp's aide when Rupp was potentate of Oleika Temple Shrine. When Adolph died, Paul was at his bedside.

Rupp's circle of friends held cookouts in the summer and postgame parties in the winter. Adolph "would take over a party and be the center of attention, no matter who else was there," Lyman Ginger recalled. "He knew many things and had opinions about most of them." When Rupp ate dinner at the home of Cecil Bell, he always sat at a certain place at the table—they called it "Adolph's Chair." At the Nickells' cookouts, Rupp would prop his feet on the porch, accept a big glass of bourbon, and say, "By Gawd, Paul, let's get that incinerator going." The group talked about everything but basketball. Ginger and Rupp kept up a running debate on school consolidation. Rupp, who hated the idea, would reminisce about walking to school in Kansas. Ginger had also walked to a one-room school that contained the first eight grades, but he argued that consolidation gave students a much better opportunity.

Every year some members of the group—particularly the Bells and the Nickells, as well as Dr. Escumb Moore and his wife—took fishing vacations in Florida with the Rupps. Bell and Moore would operate the boat and do all the other chores, but when they caught a big fish, Rupp was first in line to have his picture taken with it. During one of those vacations in the early 1950s, Adolph became ill and stayed in his cabin most of the time. Nickell believes that was the first indication that Rupp had a blood sugar problem.

When Sparks' lumber business burned, the local newspaper reported that he had a $100,000 loss and only $80,000 in insurance. Two days later, when Adolph and Esther visited the Sparks home, Rupp asked to see a new room that Sparks had shown him before. "Hell, I don't want to see the room," Rupp said when they were alone. "I wanted to tell you that I have $20,000 that you're welcome to."

Rupp made some longtime friends as a teacher, too. While attending a psychology class at Kentucky, Ben Averitt had heard his professor talk about an instructor named Rupp who taught a class in basketball coaching strategies and who gave all of his students A's. That was news to Averitt, who was taking Rupp's class as well as keeping statistics and doing other minor chores. He asked Rupp whether what the professor had said was true. "Ben," Rupp replied, "what kind of teacher would I be if I couldn't teach you well enough to make an A?"

While Averitt was in central Africa for three years, he kept in touch with Rupp, who sent him letters and team statistics. When Averitt returned home during basketball season, team members wanted to know about the wildlife; Rupp asked whether Rhodesia had succeeding in crossing zebu cattle with the Brahma bulls that had been imported from India.

Once Averitt asked Rupp to sign a copy of *Championship Basketball* for two young nephews in Arizona. When Rupp asked what the boys were doing out West, Averitt told him they suffered from asthma. Rupp asked several more questions about the boys and discovered that their plight was serious. "Right now I am busy," he said. "Just put the book on my desk, give me the boys' names, and then pick it up in a few days." When Averitt returned for the book, he saw that Rupp had written a long, personal letter on the blank pages at the front, offering the boys encouragement and wishing them well. "Coach Rupp was a sincere and appreciative person," Averitt said. "He did fine and meaningful things for people in a quiet way."

Naturally, the people who meant most to Adolph were Esther and their only child, Adolph F. Rupp Jr. "Herky" was born on Sunday, June 30, 1940, with a triple hernia that kept him in Good Samaritan Hospital for ninety-one days. Rupp always had a close relationship with his son, and they shared many interests outside of basketball. In fact, baseball seems to have been their closest bond. "I guess we played baseball together more than basketball when I was growing up," Herky said. "Daddy always tried to attend my Little League games." Father and son shared a passion for major league baseball, as well; their goal was to visit all the big league parks, and they made it to most of them.

Fishing was another shared love. Adolph and Herky fished the salt waters of Florida and the fresh waters of Canada. According to Bob Sparks, though, Adolph's impatience made him a poor fisherman. Some of the Kentucky coaches built a camp on Herrington Lake, and Rupp would go there regularly. But he had a rusty little steel rod, a knobby reel, and a silk line that was rotten because he never dried it, recalled Sparks, who did triple duty as guide, rower, and hook baiter. Rupp would fish for about fifteen minutes and say, "Well, they're not biting, let's go." The Rupps traveled to every state in the union and to Canada, Mexico, and Puerto Rico when Herky was growing up, but Rupp's impatience took a toll on that pastime as well. He often cut vacations short to get back on the job.

One place Adolphs Senior and Junior could spend long stretches together was the family farm. Rupp bought his first farm—a two hundred-acre spread at Pinckard in Woodford County—in 1941, later incorporating the farm in the name of Adolph Rupp & Son. Herky loved to tour their farm. He worked the gates until he was big enough to drive a car. Then he would drive his father around to check up on the spread.

Rupp's practice sessions always ended in time for dinner, and his eagerness to be with his family was only part of the reason. Bob Sparks noticed that Adolph always ate dinner before or after sundown, but never while the sun was setting. When Sparks asked about the curious habit, Rupp explained: "The main crops we had on the plains of Kansas were corn and wheat. If we didn't have a rain, we went hungry. My mother went out on the porch every night and watched the sun go down. If the sun set in a pillow of clouds, we might have some rain, and she was happy. We had a drought every four or five years, and we wouldn't have any crops. My mother watched the sun go down all my childhood. I do the same thing." Sparks remembered, "No matter where you were with him, he'd watch the sun."

At the Rupp dinner table, Herky would ask his father how practice had gone that day, and after dinner, he would do homework while Adolph read one of the many publications he subscribed to. Besides papers and magazines devoted to business, farming, and insurance, he read anything published by the Masons, with whom he held advanced degrees. "He was under so much pressure all the time," Esther said. "Spending a few quiet evenings at home was his way of reducing that pressure."

Marvin Whitton, the recorder at Oleika Temple Shrine in Lexington for more than thirty-five years, praised Rupp's activities as a Shriner. "The world at large thought that, other than family, Adolph's two loves were basketball and Hereford cattle," Whitton said. "The Shriners Hospital for Crippled Children was his third love." Rupp cajoled wealthy people into contributing to the hospital. Herky's ordeal at birth may have given Rupp a particular interest in the children at the hospital. They, in turn, looked forward to visits from "Uncle Adolph," especially the older ones, who knew of Rupp's celebrity. Rupp kept his work with the hospital from the public, Whitton said.

He was a member of the hospital board for many years, and when Fred Bryant stepped down as chairman of the board in January 1971, Rupp was the logical choice as his successor. He served in that capacity until his death in December 1977.

Rupp was concerned with the welfare of his fellow Shriners, as well. In 1952, shortly after becoming the local imperial potentate, he led a group to the organization's international convention in Miami. His group chartered a train with eighteen cars and two diners. When Rupp discovered on the return trip that dining room prices had increased, he called a meeting with railway officials, demanding that prices be rolled back. "If we can't come to an agreement by the time we get to Jacksonville," he said, "I'm going to stop this damn train, take everybody off, and buy them breakfast." The railroad backed down, cringing as diners asked for the "Rupp Special" on the way back to Lexington.

Days after Rupp retired as potentate of Oleika Temple, he traveled with a local delegation to Imperial Council headquarters in St. Louis to secure approval of a bid of more than a million dollars for a new hospital in Lexington. Rupp's delegation returned with an extra $200,000 for operating equipment. Impressed with his unmatched ability to get things done, friends urged Rupp to run for imperial potentate, highest office in the Shrine. A majority of the voters were not UK basketball fans. Rupp lost the race.

Rupp was at his best when he could combine his love of family and friends with his passion for basketball. Lyman Ginger was director of the University School when Herky was in kindergarten. Rupp's team was taking a trip to Madison Square Garden, and Rupp sent a note to the teacher, proposing to take Herky along. No basketball fan, she said no. Rupp appealed to Ginger: "He'll learn more up there in one hour than he will in kindergarten in one week." Herky made the trip. After they returned, Rupp called Ginger to his office and pulled open a desk drawer containing a dozen watches, gifts from tournaments. He told Ginger to take his choice. "We really had a very warm, friendly situation," Ginger said. "He was very ambitious; his personality as far as his coaching was concerned was *win*."

When huge student crowds forced Kentucky to close most of its games to the public, Rupp's friends asked if he could sneak them in. Alumni Gym contained two old scoreboards with two control buttons each. "There are four buttons," Rupp said. "That will take care of four of you." Sparks got the job of firing a blank pistol at halftime and at the end of a game. Elmer Rix handled the keys to the locker room, and Louis Ades lasted a short while as the public address announcer. Ginger kept score. When the games moved to Memorial Coliseum in 1951, the group was again able to buy tickets, but Rupp—who said he didn't want students controlling factors that his job depended on—wouldn't let his "support staff" retire. Sparks operated the new game clock. Ginger, by this time the dean of the College of Education, could no longer keep score, so that job went to Jim Robinson, an official at the bank where Rupp kept his money. J. D. Reeves, also a bank official, kept track of rebounds.

With the new scoreboard, Sparks traded in his pistol for a buzzer. Once, with Kentucky leading by fourteen points, a Mississippi player sank a shot as the halftime buzzer sounded. The referee deferred to Sparks' judgment: "Just tell me where the ball was when the horn blew." Sparks told him it was in the air, and on the way back to the playing floor, Rupp scolded him: "Bob, I knew everybody else in this gym was against me, but I didn't think you were." Sparks replied, "If you want me to steal for you, turn out the lights. I won't steal before 11,500 people." Rupp said, "Oh, you know I didn't mean it." Sparks knew Rupp well enough not to believe him. "What difference does it make?" Sparks asked. "You were so far ahead they didn't have a chance." "Every time they score," Rupp answered, "my heart bleeds. I don't care what the score is."

Among Rupp's close circle of friends in his final years at UK were Lexington attorney Harry B. and Pat Miller, who often had movie actor George C. Scott as a house guest. Pat's father was Gerald Griffin, a UK graduate ('22) who was a writer for the Louisville *Courier-Journal*. Griffin interviewed the young coach Rupp from Freeport in 1930 and subsequently recommended him to the UK Athletic Council. When Joe B. Hall left UK for St. Louis in 1969, Harry Miller, UK board chairman Albert G. Clay and communications mogul Jim Host brought him back to Lexington.

Rupp dubbed as "Deadheads" non-UK persons who traveled with the Wildcats. Printers Herbie and Mary Lou Feedback, motel owners Bob and Lula Mae Lutes, druggists Gene and Gertrude Sageser, builders Bob and Pat Myers, news vendor Steve Rardin and Dr. and Mrs. V.A. Jackson.

Dr. Jackson moved his practice from Clinton in Western Kentucky, a distance of 300 miles to Lexington, in the mid-1960's so he could be closer to UK basketball. He became a fixture on the UK bench.

The late Steve Rardin, co-owner of Central Kentucky News Company, holds the record for attending the most consecutive UK basketball games. His string of 647 games began after the Wildcats lost to Wisconsin in Chicago on New Year's Eve 1968. Rardin was attending a wedding in Lexington. The streak ended when he became ill during a UK-Indiana game at Indianapolis in 1989. Prior to the Wisconsin game, Rupp looked around the Chicago hotel lobby and asked, "Where's Steve?"

On the road, Bob and Lula Mae Lutes would invite members of the traveling party to their room for snacks and drinks. Rupp would have two or three shots of bourbon, relax, go to his room, put on a pair of red pajamas, and worry about the upcoming game.

During the NCAA Mideast Regional at Columbus, Ohio, in 1970, Rupp presented a "Most Valuable Deadheads" plaque to Bob and Lula Mae Lutes.

"We always felt that Adolph appreciated us," Bob Lutes said in 1994, "but the plaque was a pleasant surprise." It is one of his most prized possessions.

Chapter
Seven

The Pursuit
of Perfection

W hen Rupp arrived in Lexington, most of the boys he recruited were Kentucky boys, many of them spotted at the state high school tournament. The university managed the tourney from 1918 until 1938, and the tournament remained on the UK campus for a few years after that.

Players sought to play for Kentucky; Kentucky rarely needed to seek a player. "Every high school player in Kentucky had the image of playing for Kentucky," said Russell Ellington, who lettered as a Wildcat in 1935 and 1936. "They thought it was something special to play for Rupp." In those days, tryouts were legal, and Rupp would invite forty or fifty boys to Lexington each week during the spring and summer. Most players paid their own way; some hitchhiked, but most rode into town with family, friends, boosters, or alumni. Cliff Barker and Bud Robertson and two friends who owned motorcycles rode double from Yorktown, Indiana. Rupp kept the best players and sent the rest to other state schools, helping to make basketball strong throughout the commonwealth. He also held preseason tryouts that were open to all male members of the student body. When asked about his method of selection, Rupp would point to the top of his office door, which was seventy-four inches high. "If they do not duck their heads when they enter," he said, "I don't even shake their hands." He also favored big hands, big feet, and broad butts.

University aid was unavailable to athletes before 1935, technically, at least. Before that, the players waited on tables, painted fences, and did other odd jobs that the coaches lined up for them. Rupp opened a service station near the campus to provide jobs, but he abandoned that effort when the receipts did not match the gallons of gas pumped.

Lack of financial aid got in Rupp's way from the start. In the new coach's first week at Kentucky, Birkett Pribble told him about a fine high school player from Walton. John "Frenchy" DeMoisey, 6-foot-5, had scored fifty points in a game against Butler and forty-five in a regional game against Paris. Before school started, Rupp drove the seventy miles to Walton, where DeMoisey was working on a road gang. They sat in the shade on a creek bank, and Rupp invited him to become part of a brand new system of basketball. DeMoisey planned to attend Trinity College—as a minister's son, he would receive free tuition, and the school had promised him a job. Rupp failed to get the commitment he wanted, but he didn't give up. Returning to Walton a few days later, he made the first great recruiting pitch of his career. Tuition for a semester at Kentucky was $31.50. If DeMoisey could raise that amount, Rupp would find someone to pay for the second semester.

When Rupp held his first spring practice in 1931, word leaked out that the Wildcats were working on a shot that would revolutionize the game of basketball. DeMoisey had developed a hook shot since high school, but in spite of his great potential, the sophomore was far down on the list of centers when fall practice began, and Rupp turned the youngster over to one of his assistants. "Frenchy was as green as they come in the beginning," Rupp said. "I put Len Miller in charge of him and concentrated my efforts on several other centers who were ahead of him." Not for long.

George Yates was supposed to start at center, but the captain-elect was injured playing football and would miss the season. Aggie Sale moved from forward to center, but he was back at his old position for one practice, when DeMoisey scored twelve points against him in ten minutes. The other starting forward, Darrell Darby, had been Ellis Johnson's teammate on Ashland's 1927 national championship high school team, but he had played sparingly as a Wildcat. With Yates out of action, the players elected Jake Bronston captain, but he left the team when the university declared him ineligible. "It was a game of musical captains," Rupp said. "We solved that situation by naming Ellis Johnson to that position." Johnson started at guard with Charles Worthington. Howard "Dutch" Kreuger was a valuable front-line substitute.

Minor injuries had handicapped Sale and Johnson the preceding year, but both were healthy when the new season began. Sale was a diamond in the rough, in need of just a little polishing. "Aggie would shoot off balance, falling down, or sitting on the floor, if he had to," George Yates said. "Mauer would not have permitted that. Adolph did not care how you shot the ball as long as it went in the basket." Rupp said Sale was one of few players who could miss a shot on one side of the basket, rebound, and put it in on the other side. That season, Kentucky opened with Georgetown College, coached by Carey Spicer. Spicer lacked the personnel to employ the fast break taught by Rupp, and the Wildcats won 66-24. Harry Lancaster scored nine points for Georgetown.

DeMoisey scored fifteen points and Sale thirteen in a 34-32 victory over Carnegie Tech that brought UK attention on a national scale. "My team is strong," Tech coach Ralph Hogan said. "At least it's as good as anything around Pittsburgh, and Kentucky beat us." Rupp could build on that.

Berea and Marshall were easy victims, and the Wildcats took a 4-0 record into the holidays. DeMoisey missed the next five games while making up a deficiency in a sociology class. While sitting out the games, he spent his spare time learning to shoot the hook shot with his left hand. Rupp shifted Sale into the pivot and moved Kreuger into the vacated forward spot. The Wildcats did not miss a beat. They defeated Clemson twice, Sewanee, Tennessee, and Chattanooga and were 9-0 when DeMoisey rejoined the team. Sale blocked five shots in the one-point win over Tennessee— Rupp said it was his best game. With DeMoisey back in the lineup, the Wildcats defeated Washington & Lee 48-28, but the next night he and Johnson came in twenty minutes late from a movie.

Rupp was waiting for them. He chewed out team captain Johnson, because the important Vanderbilt game was next on the schedule. As for DeMoisey, Rupp told him he wouldn't be needed against the Commodores. But Johnson promised that the two of them would score thirty points against Vanderbilt if Rupp let them off. Reprieved, DeMoisey scored twenty-nine points and dazzled the Nashville fans with his hook shot in a 61-37 rout. One writer called it "a whirling dervish job that looked like an accident, but wasn't." Johnson, meanwhile, sank one free throw. "I see you kept your promise," Rupp told Johnson. Kentucky was 14-0, one game away from a perfect regular season, when Vanderbilt came to town for a rematch. DeMoisey and Sale played with the flu, and Vanderbilt won 32-31.

In Atlanta, the Wildcats beat Tulane by fourteen points in the opening round of the Southern Conference tournament and led North Carolina 42-41 with one minute remaining in the next game. The Tar Heels missed a desperation shot, but the ball bounced back toward the foul line, and Virgil Weathers spanked it handball fashion into the basket. With two men guarding him, Sale scored twenty points. Rupp was critical of how the tournament was run and threatened not to return. "If my boys are undefeated next season, I won't take them there," he said. "We would have everything to lose and nothing to gain." Johnson and Sale made the all-conference team, and Sale was All-America. He led the team in scoring with 235 points in seventeen games. With fifteen wins and two losses, Rupp's two-year record at Kentucky was 30-5. John Mauer had been 22-11 at the same stage.

Before the 1932-1933 season, Kentucky and twelve other schools quit the Southern Conference and formed the Southeastern Conference. Other charter members were Alabama, Auburn, Florida, Georgia, Georgia Tech, Louisiana State, Mississippi, Mississippi State, Sewanee, Tennessee, Tulane, and Vanderbilt. The new league got Kentucky away from such powerhouses as North Carolina and Maryland, and with Dave Lawrence of Corinth, Jack Tucker of Cynthiana, and Bill Davis of Hazard joining Sale, Johnson, DeMoisey, Darby, and

Yates on the varsity in 1932, Rupp and the Wildcats were ready to dominate the SEC.

Lawrence, a two-time all-state tournament player had led little Corinth to the state championship as a junior in 1930, and his desperation shot beat St. John's Military Academy for third place in the national high school tournament in Chicago. Lawrence was making thirty-five cents an hour digging a ditch under a railroad bridge, slogging in the mud and getting a headache from handling dynamite, when Rupp recruited him in the spring of 1931. There were some fences that needed painting in Lexington, the coach told him, and the pay was seventy-five cents an hour. The conversation lasted fifteen minutes, and the next day, Len Miller brought Lawrence to Lexington, got him a room, and put him to work on the football field. Rupp did not speak to the recruit again until the first day of practice. Tucker and Davis joined the team after Rupp's tryout sessions that fall. Rupp had never contacted Tucker, didn't even know he was in school until he came out for basketball. Davis also made the team the hard way, but he ended up starting with Johnson in the backcourt. DeMoisey was at center, with Darby and Sale at forward.

Kentucky's fourth game was at Chicago, a homecoming of sorts for Rupp, who had come a long way from the little-known high school coach he'd been at Freeport. Before the opening tip-off against Georgetown, he had modeled a new suit for press row; after a sharp pirouette, he boasted, "Look, new from head to foot and all brown." Rupp's cockiness rubbed off on his players. DeMoisey asked Chicago sportswriters what the scoring record was in the gym where they were to play. Told the mark was twenty points, he promised to break it. True to his word, DeMoisey tossed in crazy hook shots from all angles, scoring twenty-four points to lead the Wildcats to a 58-26 victory. After benching his high scorer late in the game, Rupp told the big city writers that breaking records was fine, but he wasn't happy that Chicago had scored so many points.

The Wildcats returned home with a 4-0 record and Ohio State coming to town. It was a mess. Ticket holders couldn't get through the mob at the gym entrance, and several people received minor injuries. Officials had to delay the start of the second half to remove spectators from the floor. Despite the home-court advantage, the Wildcats were no match for the powerful Buckeyes. Wilmer Hosket, a 6-foot-5 center, dominated the boards and scored fourteen points, and Ohio State won 46-30, the biggest margin of defeat for a Rupp-coached team to date.

Next on the schedule was a trip to Omaha, Nebraska, to play Creighton. Travel budgets were limited in those days, and when a team made a long trip, the coach tried to line up other games along the route; often the visitors would even play back-to-back games against the same school. The first time Kentucky had brought in a team from afar was in January 1930, when Creighton came to town for consecutive nights. Each game drew a capacity crowd, but by the time Kentucky covered expenses and paid Creighton its guarantee, there was almost no profit. The contract called for Kentucky to make a return visit to Omaha the following year, but with Depression-era budgets still tight, the schools put the series on hold. This was the payback, with the teams splitting two games. The Wildcats then won ten of eleven games to go 16-3 and enter the first SEC tournament as the favorite.

In Atlanta, the superstitious Rupp sent a student manager to grab the left-hand bench, where the Wildcats had sat when they won the first game of the 1932 Southern tournament. They sat there all the way to the championship of the 1933 tournament. But the way Aggie Sale played, the Wildcats would have won if their bench had been in the parking lot. With the senior center-forward leading the tournament in scoring, Kentucky coasted past Mississippi, Florida, Louisiana State, and Mississippi State—only LSU came within thirteen points. Sale was named the tournament's outstanding player, and DeMoisey and Johnson joined him on the all-tourney team. Sale earned All-America honors for the second year in a row, and the Helms Athletic Foundation named him the college basketball player of the year.

Milerd "Andy" Anderson caught Rupp's eye when he led Covington to the semifinals of the 1932 state tournament. Anderson was not a natural shooter, but he was a hustler, and he became adept at running the Kentucky offense. By his sophomore year, Anderson was a starting guard.

Having had success with his early in-state recruiting efforts, Rupp began to look north. Nearby Southern Indiana contained a rich lode of high school talent just waiting for him to mine. He could leave Lexington early in the morning, visit a boy, and be home in time for dinner.

Rupp welcomed invitations to speak at banquets and coaching clinics in the Hoosier State. While driving to a clinic in Jeffersonville, Rupp gave a ride to a tall boy standing on a street corner. The young man was Garland Lewis, the star of the local high school team, and he was waiting for Purdue basketball coach Ward "Piggy" Lambert. "That's all right," Rupp assured him. "Piggy is a friend of mine. He won't mind. Hop in." In fact, Lambert had reason to mind: in the time it took Rupp to drive to the gym, Lewis decided that Kentucky was the right place for him. He would play three years of solid basketball for Rupp.

The Wildcats carried an eight-game winning streak left from the previous season into the 1933-34 campaign, and Rupp seemed less concerned about the teams on his schedule than about competition from within the Lexington campus. The UK football team had won its first four games, but when the Wildcats lost four of their last five games, Harry Gamage resigned as head coach and was replaced by Chet Wynn. Wynn was a graduate of Notre Dame, teaming with George Gipp, Frank Thomas, and Johnny Marhardt in one of Knute Rockne's most famous backfields. He had coached Auburn to a conference championship, and the Lexington media were still calling him the savior of the football program when the basketball season began. That in itself was enough to rankle Rupp, but worse, Wynn had also been hired as the school's athletic director—he was Adolph's boss. The Wildcats started the season 6-0, but attendance was down for the first time in five years. Rupp blamed it on all that football talk.

Neville Dunn, sports editor of the *Herald*, wrote a set of New Year's resolutions for Rupp. He should:

> 1. Equip his chair with a friction-proof pillow to save the seat of his pants from wear and tear when the score got too close for comfort.
> 2. Keep the letter and spirit of the law regarding sideline coaching by resisting the temptation to shout instructions to his team.

3. Not tell coaches whose teams defeated his—at least to their faces—that they were the poorest aggregation he ever saw and that their victory was just dumb luck.

"What does he (Dunn) know about basketball?" Rupp asked. "I always suspected he was a football man."

Rupp predicted Kentucky would go undefeated in the SEC. Although DeMoisey had the flu, the Wildcats defeated Sewanee 55-16, and he came back with twenty points in a 44-23 win over Tennessee. He fouled out with nine minutes to play against Alabama, but Kentucky managed to come from behind in the last five minutes and win 33-28. In the home finale against Vanderbilt, DeMoisey scored twenty-five points in twenty-seven minutes—the Wildcats won 47-27 and were 16-0. Only the conference tournament in Atlanta stood in the way of Rupp's first undefeated season.

Kentucky's first-round foe was Florida, which had a mediocre team that year. Jack Tucker predicted a twenty-point Kentucky win followed by a big steak dinner. But when the Gators scored the first six points, the crowd got behind them, booing each call that went against Florida, cheering every whistle against Kentucky, and shouting at the top of their lungs when a Wildcat went to the free throw line. Florida increased its lead to ten points. Kentucky rallied within two, but the Gators held off the Wildcats and won by six points. Denied his perfect season, Rupp threw a tantrum, blasting everybody in sight and taking close aim at the tournament itself. "I see no reason to end the basketball season in February just so some of these schools can start spring football practice early," he said. "Someday they are going to wake up and realize that basketball is here to stay."

Chapter Eight

Earning a Reputation

y the 1934-35 season, writers were calling Rupp the most hated person in Dixie. He earned that distinction the hard way, criticizing practically everything about basketball in the South: the schools and their untrained coaches, who were mostly assistants in football; the red-neck fans, imcompetent officials, substandard arenas and slow-down basketball. When Ned Irish invited Kentucky to play New York University in one of a series of six doubleheaders scheduled at Madison Square Garden, Rupp welcomed the opportunity to get away from Lexington. Rupp, who had spent four summers at Columbia University, loved New York. It was the big time. The bright lights didn't excite him, but there was always somebody around who liked to talk basketball. Whenever he went to a coaches meeting, the New York contingent would hustle him to a bar, buy him a few drinks, and listen to his tall tales.

Garden basketball was a natural for Rupp, who was eager to match his sharpshooters against the best in the Big Apple. He also wanted to press the basketball team's advantage in Lexington, where the football team had won only half of its ten games.The NYU game was part of Kentucky's toughest schedule to date. The Wildcats would play Tulane twice in New Orleans and travel to Chicago before their trip to the Garden. The nonconference schedule also included games at Maryland and Michigan State, as well as Creighton's return to Lexington. It was the beginning of what would become know as the Wildcats' Modern Era.

Rupp built what he considered his most powerful team yet around Leroy "Cowboy" Edwards, a 6-foot-5, 215-pound center from Tech High in Indianapolis. Rupp found out about Edwards through George Keogan, the Notre Dame coach. Edwards was as big and tough as they came, Keogan told Rupp, but he might have a hard time staying in school. When Rupp got a commitment from Edwards, surprised Indiana coaches wondered how long the big guy would last at Kentucky.

Edwards arrived at Lexington in the middle of the night, waking Rupp at 12:30 a.m. Rupp sent him next door to a fraternity house, where Edwards stayed for ten days. He was too tough for the frat boys to handle, and they were glad when the school found him a new home. Edwards brought along a high school buddy named Jack Cronin, who carried the Cowboy's books and did his studying for him. Cronin was nicknamed "The Shadow" because everywhere Edwards went, his buddy was right behind. Cronin kept Edwards in line for Rupp, who knew the big guy was in love and homesick.

Edwards had adopted a hook shot after watching a touring pro team from Texas play in nearby Martinsville, and that shot would eventually carry him to the pros. He scored four hundred points in sixteen games for Len Miller's undefeated 1933-34 freshman team— the best UK frosh team to date. The Kittens also featured Warfield Donohue and Ralph Carlisle. Donohue was a 6-foot-2 guard from St. Xavier High School in Louisville. Carlisle had played for Kavanaugh Academy, a prep school in Lawrenceburg, Kentucky, that had produced UK All-Americans Paul McBrayer and Aggie Sale, as well as Fred "Buzz" Borries, an All-America halfback at Navy.

Carlisle was a shooter and driver who had developed his layup style out of necessity—goals in the Kavanaugh gym were near the wall, and players learned to jump high for the basket. Carlisle had been coached in the game's fundamentals first by Earle D. Jones and then by Paul McBrayer. Jones later had an outstanding career at Maysville High School. McBrayer, who had been an All-America guard under John Mauer the year before Rupp arrived at Kentucky, returned to Lexington in 1934 and later became the head coach at Eastern Kentucky.

Edwards scored twenty-four points in an 81-12 laugher against Oglethorpe. Or maybe laugher isn't the right word: late in the game, Dave Lawrence stole the ball twice and went in for layups, but he missed one of them. Rupp met him at the gate and raised hell all the way down the steps. "Adolph was really bloodthirsty," remembered Lawrence years later. "He wanted every point he could get."

Kentucky held Tulane to three field goals in a 38-9 rout, then jumped to an eighteen-point lead before a Tulane player finally slipped free for a basket. "Who in the hell is guarding that man?" Rupp shouted, bringing down catcalls from the New Orleans fans. The Wildcats romped again at Chicago, winning 42-16 as Edwards outscored the opposing center 26-0 in spite of the home team's roughhouse tactics in the pivot. One reporter said Chicago used everything but lariats, bludgeons, harpoons, and blackjacks on Edwards—and that would be a good preview of New York.

The Original Celtics had taught Rupp all he knew about the New York style of play. The Celtics were a touring professional team, featuring players like Dutch Dehnert, Nat Holman, and Joe Lapchick. They had come to Alumni Gym, where coach Dave Kerr conducted a clinic for a thousand people, talking about his team and showing films of the Original Celtics. Dehnert, one of the biggest men Rupp had seen on a basketball court, was so huge that he could play in front of his man, screening him from the play in progress. Dutch utilized the pivot to feed the cutters, as an aid to teammates under pressure, and to protect the ball until the cutters got free. When defensive guards overplayed him, he would pivot away from them, and drive to the basket. "I didn't have a great knowledge of how the play should be executed, but I had some players I wanted to develop into good pivot men," Rupp said. "There was much basketball to learn from the Original Celtics, and I would stay until the wee hours of the morning talking to them."

When a strong pivot man stationed himself inside the free throw line and crowded back with the ball, the defensive man had only one option: hold him and hack him. Rupp contended that officials should not permit a method of defense against the pivot man that would be a foul against any other player. He also noticed that the screening rules were interpreted differently from one section of the country to the next—what Rupp considered a screen, for example, New York called a block. Southern and Midwestern officials gave the offensive player a right to his place on the floor, but in the East, the offensive player was blocking if he got in the way of a defensive man.

News of Kentucky's decisive victory at Chicago caused a buzz in New York—apparently, the sportswriters acknowledged, the Wildcats were more than just a bunch of barefoot boys from the sticks. Both teams were undefeated, and the media billed the UK-NYU game as a battle to decide the national championship.

The Wildcats arrived at the Lexington train station ready to live up to the writers' hype—all except Ralph Carlisle, who discovered that he'd forgotten his uniform. He took a taxi back to Alumni Gym while railway officials delayed the team's departure. Uniform in hand, he boarded the train—then turned around again to retrieve the suitcase he had left in the station. "I'm taking a bunch of country boys to the big city," Rupp said. "I hope they won't embarrass me."

Once in New York, those country boys were greeted by Ned Irish—and by more newspaper reporters than they had ever seen. Rupp kept the writers busy, though. He told Paul Gardner of the *American* that many of his boys had never seen a train before coming to New York, and some had dribbled their first basketball after arriving at Kentucky. Another writer asked whether Rupp could suggest any changes in the game. "Sure, take the net off," Rupp said. "Just leave the hoop on and raise it five feet." A player later asked Rupp if he was serious. "Hell, no," he bellowed, "but anything for a column."

The Kentucky delegation checked into their headquarters at the Victoria Hotel, where Rupp was escorted to the largest press conference he had ever seen. Rupp downplayed the notion that the teams might decide the national championship so early in the season, and he made a radical proposal: the top college teams from each section of the nation should meet in a postseason tournament to determine who should wear the crown. Not only would such a tournament put an official stamp on the heretofore mythical and much-disputed championship, Rupp argued, it would also increase interest in the sport throughout the country. Maybe it would even bring about a more uniform interpretation of the rules. Rupp wasn't the first to propose a national tournament, but he gave the idea extra attention by suggesting it amid the UK-NYU hype. Four years later, the national tourney would debut.

The only large permanent basketball arena in town was at Fordham University, but it was unavailable for Kentucky's practices. Irish took them to the Hudson Guild, a community gym with a small court, but Rupp refused it. Finally, the Wildcats worked out on a large court in the NYU Physical Building. Once in the Garden, the players had to contend with a huge, oval-shaped floor that workers put down a few hours before a game and pulled up afterward to make room for the next event. The quality of the playing surface was so inconsistent that dribbling was a risk. The arena also featured the first glass backboards the Kentuckians had seen.

NYU had played Notre Dame in the first game of the doubleheader the week before, and John Murray and Frank Lane had officiated. Murray was a former manager of the Original Celtics, and George Keogan had insisted on Lane—the general manager of the Cincinnati Reds—to assure the Irish an even break. Fans in the Garden booed Lane often, especially when Irving "Slim" Terjensen, the Violets' center, fouled out. Notre Dame still lost 25-18, and Keogan warned Rupp to bring a non-New Yorker to officiate. Rupp got Dave Walsh to work with Murray, but he still came away convinced Kentucky had gotten the worst of the calls.

The game matched teams employing entirely different systems of play. The Violets played the Eastern game—fast break, a quick cut, and a flick-in. The Wildcats' deliberate offense and set plays were foreign to Manhattan court circles. Kentucky's slowdown attack was as much by necessity as design: every inside screen in the opening minutes brought a referee's whistle. Edwards drew three quick fouls, and Rupp was at a loss. At halftime, he asked Murray to explain. "You know what you're doing," Murray replied, "and it isn't legal." Rupp told his players to discard the screening plays and just do the best they could.

But while the refs were taking away the Wildcats' offensive scheme, they were letting NYU get away with murder, at least as Rupp saw it. To neutralize Edwards, Terjensen and Irwin "King Kong" Klein pushed, shoved, and muscled him away from the basket. Each time Edwards made a move, one of the big bruisers would clobber him, once knocking him ten feet off of the floor. "It was a wrestling match every time the ball went in there," Dave Lawrence remembered. "They were just knocking and banging and trying to take the ball away from each other." Still, the visitors stayed close. With a minute to go, New York's Sidney Gross scored to tie the score at 22. The Wildcats were running a set play when Murray called Edwards again for an illegal screen. Gross sank a free throw, and with Edwards on the bench with his fourth foul, the Violets controlled the center tap and ran off the remaining seconds.

"There is no excuse for calling a foul like that," Rupp complained after the game. "I don't mind losing a game, but I just hate to give them away." Grabbing a newspaper reporter he said, "That's a foul, but anything went when they had the ball. I can't understand why it's a foul when one of my boys moves toward the basket on a screening play, and it isn't a foul when a New York boy drapes himself over the back of one of my country kids and hugs him around the arms."

Rupp claimed that with neutral Western Conference officials, Kentucky would beat NYU by 30 points on any court, and he wasn't the only one who thought Kentucky had been robbed. An *International News Service* story said the better team had lost, and Lewis Burton of the *American* said New York simply couldn't handle Edwards legally. In the *Herald-Tribune*, Irvin T. Marsh called the Wildcats one of the greatest teams ever to hit town.

Even Howard Cann, the NYU coach, recognized the injustice. According to Tom Meany's story in the *World-Telegram,* Cann came into the UK dressing room and told Rupp, "Adolph, I have nothing to do with selecting the officials. I hated to see it end that way." Irish apologized to Rupp, but he later backed the officials. Murray continued to insist that the blocks taught by Rupp were illegal, at least according to the interpretation taught officials in the East. The controversy raged for the remainder of the year until the rules committee finally acted, making clear the distinction between legal screens and illegal ones. At the same time, the committee adopted the three-second rule to force the pivot man away from the basket without subjecting him to defensive mayhem.

Of course, some coaches thought NYU's advantage in the Garden wasn't just limited to rules interpretations. "It was great to have eighteen thousand people in there to see a ball game," Rupp said, "but the only way they could maintain interest in basketball was to have the New York teams winning." When he was asked later what had happened in New York, Rupp deadpanned, "I really don't know, but while riding back I turned on the radio. A broadcast came on from one of the churches in New York. The minister used as his text, 'He was a stranger and they took him in.' That's all I know about it."

After the Garden loss, the Wildcats won nine straight games before losing to Michigan State at East Lansing. In late February, Edwards scored thirty-four points in a 63-42 win over Creighton, breaking Frenchy DeMoisey's Alumni Gym record. The SEC had abandoned its annual tournament, so Kentucky and LSU shared the conference title. Edwards was a consensus All-America and the Helms Foundation's Player of the Year, and Lawrence joined him on the All-SEC team. The Wildcats' Andy Anderson was selected as the best guard to play that year in Madison Square Garden.

Ending the 1934-35 campaign with a 19-2 record, the Wildcats had become a force on the national scene. Tucker and Lawrence were leaving, but Edwards, Donohue, Anderson, and Carlisle formed a good nucleus for the upcoming season. Edwards—who still pined for the gal he'd left behind—was the key. Rupp, hoping to keep an eye on his lovesick star, urged Edwards to stay in Lexington and participate in coaching clinics over the summer. Edwards declined the invitation. He went home to Indianapolis, and not only did he marry his sweetheart, he refused to return to Kentucky without some financial guarantees. Rupp's reply burned the telephone line.

Some of the players offered to pay living expenses for the newlyweds if Ed came back to school—fortunately, Rupp never heard about that. Edwards worked and played AAU ball for a rubber company in Indianapolis, and the following season he joined the Oshkosh All-Stars, a professional team in Wisconsin. Thirty-five years later, Rupp would still call "Big Ed" the best pivot man he had ever seen.

Ironically, the fall of 1935—when Edwards made his pitch for under-the-table money—was when the Southeastern Conference began to permit scholarships. But like most SEC schools, Kentucky gave very few basketball grants at first— many of the best basketball players attended school on football scholarships. Rupp split up his scholarships, giving partial grants to lesser players and full rides to the stars. Kentucky could house and feed the players for about three dollars a week. Tuition was free, leaving only the only cost of books.

Joseph "Red" Hagan was the best newcomer to the varsity that year. Hagan, a Louisville prep, had planned to attend Xavier University. After one week at the Cincinnati school's football camp, he returned home for his clothes. The next morning, Kentucky alumnus Reed Miller came by the Hagan home and told Red to hop in; they ended up at Lexington, where Hagan agreed to play football for the Wildcats, eventually becoming team captain. For Rupp's team, he started as a sophomore, and more than once the 6-foot-2 player found himself in the pivot.

Kentucky played another brutal schedule in 1935-36. Before the season, Pittsburgh coach H. C. "Doc" Carlson had told Rupp the Panthers needed a game en route to the Sugar Bowl, and Kentucky agreed to host that game. Pittsburgh's perpetual-motion Figure 8 offense had made Carlson famous throughout the nation. The Panthers gave the defense no time to get set, sometimes moving the ball around for several minutes without taking a shot, then suddenly going full speed to the basket.

On the way to New Orleans, the Panthers also scheduled games with Butler and Xavier. Rupp and Len Miller scouted the Butler game, which the Panthers won handily. When the UK coaches got back to their motel, Rupp could not sleep. "Get the car," he told Miller. "I have work to do." Arriving in

Lexington at 4 a.m., Rupp still could not sleep. He got up, diagrammed Carlson's offense, and decided for the first time to abandon his man-to-man defense. Instead, one defender would make an automatic switch on the cutter—a zone concept, although he wouldn't admit it.

The move frustrated the Pittsburgh players, and the Wildcats raced to a 22-2 halftime lead en route to an eighteen-point victory. The next morning, Adolph and Esther took goodies to the train station for the Pitt players. Carlson, who had attached small elephant pins to each player's jacket—so they would never forget—asked Rupp to pose for a picture, which would be another reminder of what had happened in Lexington.

The Wildcats found themselves in Madison Square Garden playing NYU again on January 8. Over Rupp's objections, Jack Murray officiated the game, but even the Wildcats coach might have admitted that without Edwards his team had no chance against the bigger and more talented Violets. NYU won by 13.

After losing to NYU, the Wildcats defeated Tulane twice, Michigan State, and Tennessee. When they lost to Vanderbilt in Nashville, it was Kentucky's first regular-season conference loss in four years. They followed with a pair of victories over Alabama, and after the second one, Joe Hagan grabbed the basketball and ran with it to the locker room. When Rupp demanded the ball, Hagan whipped it to him.

"That will be all for you," Rupp said, and he had athletic director Chet Wynn suspend Hagan from the team. When the Wildcats prepared to leave for the next game, against Notre Dame at South Bend, Hagan was at the railway station—just to see his teammates off, he said. "Well, as long as you're here, you might as well make the trip," Rupp said, "because it will be the last one you make anyway." Kentucky fell behind by fourteen points with Hagan riding the end of the bench. Suddenly Rupp pulled out a piece of paper and waved it at him. "Son, I just got a telegram," he said. "They have lifted your suspension; you can go in now." Despite Hagan's six field goals, the Irish won 41-20.

The once-mighty Wildcats lost two more games, at Tennessee and to Creighton at home—Kentucky's first loss at home in forty games. The Wildcats finished 15-6, Rupp's worst record in six years.

The returning starters in the 1936-1937 season were seniors Ralph Carlisle, Warfield Donohue, and Joe Hagan. Jim Goforth and J. Rice Walker were the reserves who had seen action the preceding year. Among the sophomore hopefuls was a New Yorker who had written Rupp after seeing Kentucky play NYU in the Garden in 1935. Bernie Opper brought the recommendations of Clair Bee and Nat Holman down to Lexington. Another soph, Fred "Cab" Curtis, who played for Jimmy Armistead at East Nashville High School in Tennessee, had been making thirty-five cents an hour at the Carter Shoe Factory in Nashville when Rupp offered him a scholarship. The pay was good for the time, but bed-lasting shoes made his hands so sore he could not even scratch. When Nell Jones, his future wife, put Curtis on a bus to Lexington, he wore a new $10 suit and a new pair of shoes. "Hell, Armistead said you needed help," Rupp said. "Your clothes are better than mine."

The Wildcats were 5-0 in the new season when they played Notre Dame in the Jefferson County Armory at Louisville, Kentucky's first appearance in Louisville during Rupp's tenure. The game was played before 6,352 people, the largest crowd ever to see a game in the state. Officials called thirty-three fouls, many of them the result of a slippery floor that sent players crashing into one another. The Irish, captained by Ray Meyer, won 41-28, but Rupp marked it down as another lesson learned. He would be back.

The Wildcats went on a 7-2 run, then lost to Alabama 34-31— their first loss to the Crimson Tide in six years, and their first home loss of the season. Bama coach Hank Crisp had promised Rupp that he would beat him if it was the last thing he did. Kentucky finished 14-5, a second straight subpar regular season by Rupp's high standards, and Wildcat fans wanted to know what was wrong.

Redemption came in the revived conference tournament. Curtis had started the regular-season finale against Xavier in place of Carlisle, but Rupp returned Carlisle to the lineup in the second half of the tourney opener against LSU. Carlisle hit five of seven one-hand push shots as Kentucky won 57-37. Then he scored sixteen points in a 40-30 win over

Georgia Tech, and the Wildcats went on to beat Tennessee 39-25 for their second SEC tournament title. Carlisle and captain Donohue were first team All-SEC, but Larry Shropshire, sports editor of the Lexington *Leader*, reported that most of the discussions at the tournament were about football. That only strengthened Rupp's objection to the event.

Before the 1937-38 season, the rules committee eliminated the center jump after every basket, a change Dr. Naismith predicted would make basketball a racehorse game. If so, who better to take advantage than a team from the Bluegrass State?

Rupp underwent surgery during the off-season for a spinal ailment that apparently went back to an injury he had suffered when he was an assistant football coach in 1932. The surgeons also corrected a hip maladjustment. During a thirty-one-day hospital stay, Rupp lost fifteen pounds.

Then he missed the season opener with a cold. Paul McBrayer used sixteen players in a 67-33 romp over Berea. He started sophomores Jim Goodman and Harry Denham at forward and Layton "Mickey" Rouse at guard. Rupp had invited Rouse to Lexington for a tryout after meeting him at a Ludlow High School basketball banquet. Rouse hit three of four shots against the varsity and was offered a partial scholarship—a full ride would depend on his performance rating. The veteran starters were Homer Thompson at center and J. Rice Walker at guard. Walter Hodge was out for the season with a football injury.

With Rupp back on the bench—and shuffling the lineup—Kentucky beat Cincinnati and Centenary before meeting Pittsburgh in the Sugar Bowl. The team planned to fly to New Orleans—it would have been the first air trip for a UK squad—but Rupp thought the $1,300 fare too steep.

Pitt was the Eastern Intercollegiate League champion, and Carlson came South with one of the best teams in the school's history, but Kentucky's defense frustrated the Panthers in a UK 40-29 win. After the game, Carlson gathered up some sweat clothes and dumped them at Rupp's feet. "Here, take these," he said. "You've taken everything else."

But the Wildcats were in a giving mood on a trip north, losing at Michigan State, Detroit, and Notre Dame. Back home, they had a meeting and Rupp demanded to know what was wrong. Was it a case of somebody not passing the ball? He wanted a heart-to-heart talk. Tub Thompson said, "Coach, I just think you're calling us too many SOBs." Rupp replied, "Well, I'm going to say this. If you don't like it, you can turn in your uniform and go back to where you came from."

The Wildcats righted themselves and were 9-4 when Marquette came to Alumni Gym, where a capacity crowd showed up for the first meeting of the schools. It was an important game for the Wildcats: the Warriors had beaten Notre Dame, and Kentucky had lost to the Irish.

It came down to the final twelve seconds tied, Kentucky with the ball. During a timeout, Rupp told his players to take the last shot and win or go into overtime. Hagan got the ball far out on the floor and tossed up a two-hand set shot. Rupp sat with head bowed, hands over his eyes as the ball arched higher. "I thought it took a thousand years to come down," Hagan said. "Then I saw it go through the hoop." As the crowd carried Hagan off the court, Governor Chandler came onto the court and drove a nail to mark the spot of what was at the time the longest goal in UK basketball history: 48 feet, 2 1/4 inches.

Winning their final three games, the Wildcats took a 13-4 record into the conference tournament at Baton Rouge, but in the opening round, Tulane's Paul Pare hit a shot with seconds remaining as the Green Wave upset Kentucky 36-34. Rupp hated the tournament more than ever. When UK President Frank L. McVey scolded Rupp for blaming his tournament loss on the officials, Rupp replied that if the university would provide a gym that didn't double as a dance floor, the team would not need an excuse. Two weeks before the tournament, Chet Wynn had resigned as athletic director and football coach, and in a reorganization of the athletic department, the AD's position was separated from the coaching job. Rupp and Bernie Shively were top candidates for the position; Shively was selected unanimously. More than fifty years later, Ruth Shively would claim Rupp wanted the job so he could "put football in its place," but Rupp said he backed Shively all the way.

Rupp built his 1938-39 team around Opper, who became the second out-of-state player elected captain of a Wildcat basketball team. (The first was Fred Fest, the 1923 captain from West Virginia.) Outstanding newcomers were Lee Huber and Keith Farnsley. Huber was the best high school tennis player in Kentucky, twice the state singles champion, and Rupp recruited him with help from Professor H. H. Downing, the UK tennis coach. They gave him a partial scholarship that consisted of food and tuition. Farnsley, a forward from New Albany, Indiana, stepped into a starting berth at forward with Cab Curtis. Bernie Opper and Mickey Rouse were the guards. Marion Cluggish and Homer Thompson shared playing time in the pivot. Carl Combs, Stan Cluggish, Don Orme, Carl Staker, and Waller White were Rupp's "Lost Battalion," the "Z-Squad"—they practiced with the team, but they didn't play in games.

The Wildcats won their first four games before losing to Long Island University in Madison Square Garden. Opper later called that LIU team, led by Irving Torgoff, the best he played against in college. After beating St. Joseph's in Philadelphia, the Wildcats lost 42-37 to Notre Dame in Louisville. Rupp was winless in four outings against the Irish, but he was getting closer.

Next came Tennessee and a special challenge for Rupp: his first meeting with John Mauer, the man he had succeeded at Kentucky. Mauer had left Miami of Ohio to coach the Volunteers, and he brought his team to Lexington as a heavy underdog despite a 5-2 record that matched Kentucky's. The Vols won 30-29. In the years that followed, Mauer would remember that game as the one that secured his standing at Tennessee. A loss to Alabama gave Rupp his second three-game losing streak in two years, but Kentucky rebounded with eleven straight wins, including a 36-34 double-overtime victory over Tennessee at Knoxville.

The Volunteers were hosts for the SEC tournament, and they met Kentucky again in the championship game. Tennessee was ahead 18-11 when Opper hit three field goals and rallied the Wildcats. Opper finished with thirteen points, and UK won 36-28. When he left the court, the crowd of three thousand gave him a standing ovation. "I never thought I would see this in Knoxville," Rupp said. Opper was named All-SEC and All-America.

Members of the 1939-40 Wildcat team exemplified a welcome trend in college athletics: genuine student-athletes. Team captain Mickey Rouse and Harry Denham were honor students in premedicine. Carl Staker was one of the highest ranking engineers and a member of the student legislature. Jim King rated high in the College of Agriculture, as did Carl Combs in the school of journalism. "I know they are a group of smart boys," Rupp said. "Now let's see if they can play basketball."

Play basketball they could, but not quite up to usual Kentucky standards, taking a 12-6 record—including another close loss to Notre Dame, 51-47 at South Bend—into the conference tournament at Birmingham. Some observers thought Rupp was slipping.

The Wildcats breezed past Vanderbilt in the opening round, but struggled to beat Tennessee 30-29. Kentucky was leading by two points in the closing minute when Huber and Rouse rebounded a shot into Tennessee's basket to send the game into overtime. "My hand hit the ball just as Mickey went up," Huber said, remembering Rupp's thundering response: "Gawd, now you're making it for them." Huber redeemed himself in the waning moments of overtime, though, making a steal and setting up Farnsley for a left-handed hook shot that won the game.

The Wildcats were such a heavy favorite to beat Georgia that fewer than six hundred fans turned out to boo them in the championship game. A 51-43 victory over the Bulldogs gave Rupp his fifth title in seven tournaments played, his answer to those who thought he was slipping. Rouse earned all-conference honors and would have his number retired later by Rupp. The next year the tournament moved to Louisville, where it would remain through the 1951-1952 season.

In December 1940, Lee Huber was captain of the basketball team and the most popular man on campus. Rupp expected great things of the senior guard—and of the team as a whole. Graduation had taken Mickey Rouse, Marion Cluggish, and Harry Denham, but some good players were coming up from Paul McBrayer's undefeated freshman team.

The first setback came when Cliff Barker, the leading scorer for the frosh, got married and joined the Army Air Corps. Huber was excellent in the early going, but the star guard tailed off after a case of the flu.

Center was also shaping up as a problem. Rupp had to juggle the starting lineup all season long. He used five forwards: Keith Farnsley, Walter White, Ermal Allen, Lloyd Ramsey, and sophomore Milt Ticco of Jenkins. Sophomore Mel Brewer shared the pivot with Jim King, and Huber's mates at guard included Carl Staker and two more sophomores, Marvin Akers and Ken England.

Kentucky made another trip to Manhattan that year—Manhattan, Kansas, where they salvaged a victory over Kansas State following losses to Nebraska in Lincoln and to Creighton in Omaha. Rupp encountered two innovations on that western trip—fan-shaped backboards and the molded ball—that were standard equipment in the Big Six. He replaced the rectangular backboards in Alumni Gym as soon as the Wildcats got home.

Kentucky took a 5-2 record into a Sugar Bowl matchup with Indiana. The Wildcats traveled to New Orleans by train, while Indiana flew into town from the West Coast. The Hoosiers were so airsick after the flight that coach Branch McCracken canceled the first practice session. A Sugar Bowl record crowd of 7,500 saw Indiana, the defending NCAA champion, hold off Kentucky 48-45 behind Herm Schaefer and Bill Menke. The Kentuckians had attracted such a large following in their two previous Sugar Bowl appearances that they received a noisier ovation as runner-up than did Indiana as champion, and Huber was greeted by such a wild demonstration when he received his individual trophy that officials had to halt the ceremony. Later, the Sugar Bowl would name Huber to its all-time team, along with Bob Cousy of Holy Cross, Paul Arizin of Villanova, Bob Davies of Seton Hall, and Ed Macauley of St. Louis University.

Huber and Ticco had played in the Sugar Bowl with a touch of the flu, and both checked into the Good Samaritan Hospital immediately upon arriving home. Almost everyone else on the squad had a cold. On the day before Kentucky played Notre Dame in Louisville, Ticco left the hospital, but Huber stayed behind.

Still, the walking wounded Wildcats held their own against their nemesis. The scoreboards in the Jefferson County Armory read 47-47 at the end of the game, but Rupp and the four thousand fans in the arena knew something was wrong when the scorer called the referee to the sideline. The official scorebook showed Notre Dame with one more point. After ten minutes of heated wrangling, the officials gave the Irish the point and a 48-47 victory over the Wildcats.

"It is inexcusable," Rupp said. "I'm afraid that if such an error occurred in Lexington, the governor would be compelled to call out the militia to put down the civilian riots." Rupp's outburst did not go unnoticed in New York, where Everett Morris of the *Herald-Tribune* called Rupp a "popper-offer." Something was always happening to Rupp, Morris said, and the voluble gentleman never missed a chance to get his opinions into print.

The Wildcats lost three of their next five games, then put together a seven-game winning streak. One of the losses was to Tennessee at Knoxville, "Heckler's Row"—the fans in the far end zone galley just above the visitors' bench—had taken a special dislike to the Kentucky coach. They went into action the minute Rupp brought his boys onto the floor and kept up a steady stream of hooting, howling, and chanting aimed at Rupp. He complained that the practice was not sportsmanlike, but the hecklers said he had brought it on himself by deploring the lack of color in Dixie basketball. When Rupp was ill, Paul McBrayer coached the Wildcats to victories over Vanderbilt and Hank Crisp's Alabama team.

The decision to move the tournament to Louisville proved a wise move for the SEC, but Kentucky didn't profit right away from the home-state advantage. The Wildcats beat Mississippi, Tulane, and Alabama, but John Mauer had his Volunteers ready for them. The sportscaster Lindsay Nelson, a graduate of Tennessee, told Ben Byrd, author of *The Basketball Vols,* how ballhandling magician Bernie Mehen's favorite trick drove Rupp up the wall:

> Bernie was a master of the hidden ball trick. With those great hands of his, he could handle the basketball as though it were a baseball. He would move it around, slip it around his legs, and then fake a pass or shot; and his defensive man would go straight up in the air. Well, he did that about three straight times in this game, and the last time Rupp, who had taken about as much as he could stand, jumped up off the bench and pointed to the ball, which was firmly between Bernie's legs. "There it is, dammit," Rupp yelled, and it broke the place up.

With two minutes left, Tennessee led by two. Gilbert Huffman stole Kentucky's inbound pass and drove for the basket, drawing a two-shot foul. He made the first one and chose to take the second one out of bounds, which was an option in those days. Tennessee hung on for a 36-33 win and its second SEC championship. Kentucky still put three players on the All-SEC team—center King and guards Akers and Huber, but it looked like Rupp's domination of the South was at an end. He told friends not to bet on it. And no one had any idea what the 1941-42 season held in store.

Chapter Nine

Victory Garden

When the Japanese bombed Pearl Harbor on December 7, 1941, Rupp was forty years old and a poor prospect for military service because of a back problem dating back to 1937. Legend has it that he sat out the war, raising a victory garden on the two hundred-acre farm he bought in 1941 and scouring the back roads of Kentucky for basketball talent. That was only half-true, but it made a good story.

According to Bob Sparks, the victory garden never took root. Sparks offered to plow the plot if Rupp would help put in the garden. "Are you suggesting that I work with a rake and a hoe?" Rupp asked. "Old Mother Nature has been good to me, and I can't smack her in the face with a garden hoe." Instead, Rupp promoted War Bonds and appeared at any function or cause that helped the war effort, including coaching his team in benefit games for the Navy Relief Fund.

Sparks thought they should preserve some food, so he bought a bushel of peaches and suggested that they take them to the cannery at Lafayette High School. After eating the three overripe peaches in the batch, they canned the rest. Just before midnight, Rupp called Sparks and said he had made the greatest deal of his life. It was bigger than anything the financially astute coach had done before. On the way home from the cannery, he had stopped at the A&P grocery just out of curiosity. In Aisle 5, he found a can whose label showed a girl holding a peach. The can cost thirty-nine cents. Rupp compared that with the product from Lafayette. The can was shiny, but it bore no label, no pretty picture. Rupp knew the peaches inside were fine—they'd eaten the "rotten" ones and canned the good ones—but when he figured the cost of the sugar, the cans, and the peaches, he came up with forty-two cents a can, and that didn't include all the valuable time spent on the project. "I've called H. J. Heinz and made a deal with him," Rupp said. "He is not going to coach basketball, and I am not going to can any more peaches."

At the start of the 1941-42 season, Rupp thought he had the makings of a good team, but the war put quite a dent in his program. Ken England was a senior in military science. Ermal Allen was five months from a second lieutenant's commission. Lloyd Ramsey would receive his commission in June. Marvin Akers, Vince Splane, and Milt Ticco were juniors in a military advance course. Rupp had scheduled teams from the Big Ten, Big Six, and Ohio conferences, as well as some strong independents.

On the eve of the attack on Pearl Harbor, the Wildcats opened with a 35-21 win over Miami of Ohio, the schools' first meeting since John Mauer had left Kentucky to coach the Redskins. At Columbus, Ohio State held off Kentucky 43-41 when Ticco missed a shot under the basket near the end of the game; Rupp suggested that the Buckeyes award him a varsity letter.

During the next three games, Marvin Akers played so well that *Look* magazine named him to the All-America team for December, a high honor for someone who once preferred to play in the band than on the hardwood. Akers was a sophomore at Jeffersonville High School in Indiana when Frank Barnes, the school's basketball coach, saw him hit a shot from midcourt during a gym class. When Barnes invited him to try out for basketball, Akers said he would rather play the trombone. Three years later, Akers was following Jeffersonville grads Tub Thompson and Garland Lewis to Lexington.

During the Xavier game, Rupp signaled Allen to run play No. 5. When the defense sagged to prevent such a play, Allen called another play. Rupp took him out and asked what the hell he was thinking—why hadn't he run No. 5? Allen tried to explain why he thought the play would not work. "I don't care if we're playing the University of Jerusalem," Rupp bellowed, "that play will work." Allen returned to the game, ran No. 5, and the Wildcats scored.

Allen bailed the Wildcats out after Xavier appeared to have the game locked up, possessing the ball and a 39-38 lead with eight seconds to go. After the Musketeers were whistled for traveling, Allen drew a foul with four seconds on the clock. Allen had ice water in his veins, Rupp said; he swished two free throws in the time it took the coach to take a breath.

"It was like sitting in the electric chair, strapped and ready for the executioner to throw the switch," Rupp said, "and a fellow dashes in and tells us we've got a reprieve." Later Rupp asked Allen why he shot the free throws so quickly. Allen, who was an excellent golfer, replied that he wouldn't waste time standing over a four-foot putt for a dollar, either. "That's just for one dollar," Rupp said. "These free throws are for my job."

Ticco scored twenty-six points against Xavier, but he suffered a leg injury that put him out of action for the rest of the season. Wartime priorities nearly put the whole team out of action the next week when the army commandeered a train that was to take the Wildcats to Tennessee. Rupp finally arranged for fourteen spaces on a sleeper car and four berths on a Pullman, and at the last minute railway officials brought a compartment car from Cincinnati. War may have been hell, but the Wildcats made that trip in style. At Knoxville, a slick floor handicapped the speedy Wildcats, who lost 46-40 to the Volunteers. Tennessee officials were apologetic, but Rupp, upon hearing that there had been a student dance in the gym the night before, fumed that schools in the South needed to get their priorities straight.

Tennessee *had* struck one blow for Southern basketball, though—a 36-33 win over Long Island University in the Sugar Bowl, snapping a twenty-three-game Violet win streak. Dixie was doing something about basketball, and Mauer and Tennessee were among the leaders— on two basketball scholarships a year. Rupp, meanwhile, said he was going to "buzz over these Bluegrass highways like a hornet" looking for basketball players. "If it looks like my tires won't hold out," he said, "I'll thumb a ride or borrow a bicycle."

Mexico and Georgia were easy victims at home, but the Wildcats lost to Alabama and Notre Dame on the road. The Wildcats were leading Notre Dame 27-21 when Carl Staker fouled out. The Irish rallied and won 46-43. Thirty-seven fouls were called, 22 on the visitors, in George Keogan's seventh straight victory over Rupp, who took note of the Irish home-court advantage: "We come out to practice, and after a while Notre Dame comes out on one end of the floor, and the band comes out on the other end and starts playing that Notre Dame fight song. Before long, my boys are humming the thing. How can you beat them then?"

Kentucky avenged both the Alabama and Tennessee losses, but the Volunteers finished first in the SEC standings. Experts predicted a UK-UT final in the conference tournament at Louisville. The Wildcats defeated Florida and Mississippi before getting a scare against Auburn. Trailing 18-11 at halftime, they rallied behind Jim King to tie the score at 28, and King hit a one-hand shot from the side to put Kentucky ahead to stay.

In the other bracket, though, Alabama upset Tennessee to advance to the championship game. Attendance for the final was 8,500—the largest crowd ever to see a basketball game in the South up to that time—and they got a good show. Thirteen points from Ken England and 12- for-13 accuracy at the free throw line made the difference in a 36-34 Kentucky victory. The Wildcats claimed their sixth championship in eight tournaments played, and the tournament drew 16,412 paid admissions to the Jefferson County Armory, 3,584 more than in 1941.

After the game, Earl Ruby, sports editor of the *Courier-Journal*, approached Rupp with a proposition to play a postseason game in Louisville against the Great Lakes Naval Training Station for the Navy Relief Fund. Rupp was all for it: not only would it be a patriotic gesture, it would also get his boys ready for an expected bid to the NCAA tournament. A superstitious Rupp decreed that the frayed nets in the UK gym should remain on the goals until after the NCAA tournament.

Someone pointed out that the Wildcats wouldn't play at home again until December. "What difference does that make?" asked Rupp.

Two days before the exhibition game, the Wildcats had a good practice session. Rupp leaned back comfortably in his chair, blew cigar smoke in the air, and told Alex Bower of the *Herald-Leader* his favorite dream:

> I'll have a squad of ten centers, twenty-six guards, and thirty forwards. There will be a coach for each position and a scout to go around and look over the opposition. I'll be the head coach. We'll have two ball teams—one for home games and one for the road. We'll pack that field house every night at two dollars a head. At the end of the season, we'll win the NCAA tournament with one team and the NIT with the other. Then we'll throw the two together at Soldier Field in Chicago for the national championship. That will draw about eighty-seven thousand people at ten dollars a head. Saint Peter promised that I can coach both teams when I get to heaven.

Former Wildcat All-American Lee Huber was one of many stars on the Great Lakes team, which had won thirty-one of thirty-six games that season. Dick Klein scored fourteen points and the sailors won 58-47 before a crowd of nine thousand; the game netted $5,800 for Navy relief. Four nights later, the Wildcats made their first NCAA appearance, meeting Illinois in the Eastern Regional at New Orleans. Illinois featured three sophomores—Ken Menke, Andy Phillip, and Gene Vance—who had led them to an 18-4 record. A year later the "Whiz Kids" would post a 17-1 record, then go to war.

Kentucky played its best game of the season and defeated the Illini 46-44, as Milt Ticco, Carl Staker, and Marvin Akers combined for thirty points. The Wildcats were no match for Dartmouth, which combined speed and finesse to hand Kentucky a 47-28 defeat in the second round—the Wildcats' worst loss since that 41-20 trouncing by Notre Dame in February 1936.

As the war effort expanded, the impact was felt more and more on the home front. Sugar got scarce, tires got scarcer, and gasoline rationing went into effect. A nationwide push for food production brought about the Victory Garden movement, and Rupp, in spite of his reticence to take a hoe to Mother Nature, acquired the nicknames "Squire" and "Old Victory Gardener."

The 1942 football season was one week away when Rupp hung an eighteen-pound country ham in the Alumni Gym equipment room, in sight and smell of any visiting newspaperman. The press corps and others started a "We Want A Piece of Adolph's Ham-on-Him Club." Earl Ruby told *Courier-Journal* readers who wished to join the club to contact Rupp at the university. Once again, Rupp had upstaged the football folks.

By August, the Southeastern Conference had sent two hundred players and twenty-five coaches and support personnel to the armed services. Kentucky had contributed fifteen players and four coaches to the cause, including Paul McBrayer, who entered the Army. McBrayer's departure opened a door for Harry Lancaster, who was with the UK Physical Education Department and had become a regular at Wildcat practices. Lancaster scouted some opponents for Rupp that season and helped him coach the team the following year. After Lancaster joined the Navy a year later, Rupp asked his friend Lyman Ginger to assist in scouting and coaching. As dean of education, Ginger had little time to spare, but he agreed to help Rupp an afternoon or two a week on one condition:

"Adolph," he said "I can't take any money for this. I already work for the university."

"Oh, I hadn't planned to pay you," Rupp said.

Ginger would go to the gym after working hours, and Rupp would hand him an outline of his duties for the day. One afternoon, Rupp asked him to tutor Jack Tingle on layups. Tingle had learned to go under the basket and hook the shot back, and Rupp wanted him taught to shoot driving straight at the basket. Ginger worked with Tingle many afternoons until the player was perfect in practice. Before the opening game, Rupp said, "Lyman, I bet you that Tingle shoots the way he always has." Ginger acknowledged that changing a boy's habits was hard to do once he was in college. At the first opportunity, Tingle drove under the basket and hooked in a shot. Rupp turned to Ginger, who was sitting at the end of the bench, "Lyman, did you see that?" Ginger replied, "I most certainly did." "You didn't teach him a damned thing," Rupp said.

Most colleges felt the war's impact, particularly once the Army began to draft eighteen-year-olds. Vanderbilt, one of the first schools to discontinue football, suggested that athletics be held on an informal, nonscholarship basis until the end of the war. Basketball was hit hard by gasoline rationing, as high school coaches arranged schedules to reduce travel and colleges began looking closer to home for games. But no nationwide movement to eliminate scholastic sports ever emerged, because many Americans— including President Roosevelt— believed the country needed the games to furnish entertainment, bolster morale, raise relief funds, and condition prospective fighters.

And Rupp was doing exactly that. To Army trainees on the UK campus, Rupp had the same status as a captain, though his exercise sessions more likely made them think of him as a drill sergeant. John Duocomes, a native of New Hampshire, came to Kentucky in 1943 from Fort Bragg, where he had completed basic training. A former high school track star, Duocomes thought he was in excellent physical condition—until he met the Baron.

Once Rupp took the trainees to a tobacco warehouse and said he would show them what calisthenics were all about. He drew a big circle and had them duck-walk inside it for an hour. When a trainee standing at attention took a swat at a bee, Rupp put him on report. "He was a madman," Duocomes said in a 1993 interview. "I wanted to kill him; so did the other guys."

Off the exercise field, Rupp was quick to give military personnel a hand—and free tickets. When W. S. Duvall and a friend were on furlough, they asked him for seats for a game with Alabama. "There's liable to be a fight break out during the game," Rupp said as he handed them the tickets. "I want you two to be sure to get down near the floor, since we'll need all the help we can get."

The *Leader* reported that fall planting was well under way on Rupp's newly acquired acreage and that he expected a good crop of basketball players. He would build around veterans Brewer, Akers, and Ticco, filling in with sophomores Kenny Rollins and Muff Davis and freshmen Paul Noel, Tom Moseley, and William Hamm, who were eligible under a wartime ruling. Rollins, the leading scorer for Wickliffe High

School, became a Wildcat via Rupp's tryout system after Western Kentucky coach Ed Diddle decided he was too small. "I don't know that I've sensed a greater feeling than when he told me I was one of the five" to make the cut at tryouts, Rollins said in a 1975 interview. "Perhaps winning a gold medal in the 1948 Olympics equaled it."

Heading into the Notre Dame game, Kentucky lost to Indiana and Ohio State, both in Alumni Gym. The Wildcats would not lose another game at home until January 1955, when Georgia Tech broke the streak at 129 games. But that remarkable streak was in the foggy future; the streak that mattered now was seven straight losses to the Irish, who brought a 6-0 record into Freedom Hall. George Keogan told Rupp it was one of his best teams, and when Notre Dame built a ten-point lead, it was a familiar script. But Akers hit a two-hand set shot from midcourt, and Ticco lofted a push shot from the side to start a UK rally. There were nine minutes left to play when Akers hit another long shot to tie the score 49-49. Akers fouled out with seventeen points, and Ticco followed with sixteen, but the Wildcats maintained their momentum. Rollins fouled out, too, but this was Kentucky's night: 60-55.

Rupp had sent both Lancaster and Ed Lander, a former player, to scout the Irish, without letting either know that the other would be there. Lancaster's report on the Notre Dame offense proved to be a key in the victory—and may have been a key to Lancaster's future with Rupp's program. "They beat us seven times in a row, but we kept trying," Rupp said, "I learned something every time we played them."

Sadly, he would learn no more from Keogan, who died later in the season, days before a Chicago Stadium double-header that matched the Irish against Great Lakes and Kentucky against DePaul and its 6-foot-10 center George Mikan.

The Wildcats came in with a five-game winning streak. Mikan was so adept at blocking shots that the Wildcats failed to score a field goal in the first six minutes of the game. Rupp said Mikan goaltended twenty UK shots—a legal maneuver until the NCAA rules committee outlawed it before the 1944-45 season—and the Blue Demons won 53- 44. A medical examination of Brewer revealed that the UK center played with an arm muscle that had been severed in the previous game against Alabama.

Kentucky encountered an old problem in that game; the officials in Chicago were now calling his screens blocks. Nick Kearns, a veteran Midwest official, argued that the fans were booing the wrong guys: "They're pouring it on the officials when they ought to be letting the coaches have it. Here I am with the ball, and you're on my team. I go to pass to you, and Charlie is standing over there. I give you the ball and cut over and charge into Charlie. That's blocking, plain and simple. The crowd lets out a yell when the whistle blows, and the coach, the guy who has been teaching his team that very tactic for three months, jumps up and begins to scream. It's the coaches they ought to boo." Kearns said screening and blocking were taught by too many coaches, and he seemed to be pointing a finger at Rupp.

Fans at Western Kentucky were pointing a finger in the same direction, demanding a chance to play the Wildcats. Rupp had never been enthusiastic about promoting in-state rivalries. After Kentucky beat Georgetown 41-12 in the traditional opener in 1933, Rupp had said playing the Tigers was like shooting squirrels in Woodland Park. Enough of that tradition: the Wildcats would play their neighbors no more. And the Wildcats refused to schedule a series with the state's other marquee program, Louisville, until the 1980s.

The WKU bid got as far as the general assembly. Reportedly, Rupp and Western coach Ed Diddle didn't get along, but Barney Ballard of the Associated Press said the two coaches may have hoodwinked the fans. He pointed out that Diddle did a thorough job scouting DePaul for Rupp, and that the UK coach had helped Western get into some national tournaments. And the crowning achievement of the Wildcats was placing Leroy Edwards at first-team center and Aggie Sale on the honorable mention list of the AP's All-Time All-American team. Diddle and Rupp were the South's representatives on that board. Ballard wrote, "Some of us clucks who wanted to see the 'Toppers and 'Cats play this season wouldn't be surprised now at seeing Diddle out on Rupp's estate helping plow his victory garden."

The Wildcats' only SEC loss that season was to Alabama at Tuscaloosa. Late in the season Kentucky roughed up Tennessee's Dick Mehen in Alumni Gym and beat the Volunteers for the second time. Two weeks later the teams met in the conference tournament final, and John Mauer, knowing that Rupp would try the same strategy again, urged Mehen to fight fire with fire.

The Wildcats were going after Mehen early in the game when he swung what Mauer called the meanest elbow he had ever seen, catching Mel Brewer square in the mouth, and he went down to his knees. Mehen got the ball and scored. Referee Dan Tehan acted as though nothing had happened. When Mauer saw Tehan at the hotel after the game—a 33-30 Tennessee victory—he asked whether the ref had seen Mehen throw the elbow.

"No, and I didn't see the Kentucky man roughing him before he threw it," Tehan answered. "I can't watch those guys all the time; they have to learn to take care of themselves."

The Wildcats again closed the season with a loss to Great Lakes at Louisville. A year later, Kenny Rollins would be a member of the Navy team. Rupp also lost Marvin Akers, Mel Brewer, and Milt Ticco to graduation and sophomore starter Muff Davis to the military. In 1943 Kentucky suspended its football schedule, but the athletic council spared basketball when Rupp promised that he could put together a team that would not embarrass the university.

Rupp went home to Halstead, where he planned to visit 6-foot-5 twins who had led Winfield High School to the finals of the state tournament. Bob and Clarence Brannum were as rough and tough as they come. They arrived in Lexington on May 28, 1943, shortly after their seventeenth birthday. In their first halfcourt game, the Brannums were being knocked around until Bob stopped the action. "Nobody is calling fouls," he pointed out to his brother, "So let's go get them." Later Bob told Tevis Laudeman of the *Courier-Journal*, "We started cleaning house. We bounced those guys around good." When Bob looked around, he saw Rupp smiling.

The Brannums were among fifteen freshmen on the 1943-44 UK team. Other key frosh were Jack Tingle, a 6-foot-3 forward from Bedford, Kentucky, and Jack Parkinson, a 6-foot long-shot artist from Yorktown, Indiana. The sophomores were Wilbur Schu, 6-foot-4 forward from Versailles, and Tom Moseley, a 6-foot-3 guard on Lexington Lafayette's 1942 state championship team. The Army had rejected Tingle because of a crushed right elbow received in a fall from an apple tree when he was a child. The injury kept him from bending the elbow, but not from shooting. When Tingle was a boy, his mother hung up an oat box in the dining room; that was where he learned to shoot a jumper with practically no arch on it.

Once Tingle asked to borrow Rupp's car to visit his sick mother. A sympathetic Rupp agreed, later calling Mrs. Tingle to wish her well. The player's healthy mother was surprised and ashamed of her son's ruse, but Rupp assured her that he understood the situation, and that she needn't worry. Soon after, the state police stopped Jack at Frankfort with the happy news that his mother had made a swift and complete recovery. And, by the way, Mr. Rupp wanted his car back, pronto.

Perhaps because of immature stunts like that, Rupp declined to name a captain for the young squad, whose roster seemed to change almost weekly. Don Whitehead, a 5-foot-10 forward from Evansville, Indiana, and Walter Johnson, a 5-foot guard from Mt. Sterling, Kentucky, left for the Navy midway through the season. Buddy Parker, a 6-foot guard-forward from Lexington, would get out of the Navy in time to play in the SEC tournament a season's end. "You'd start to build a team, and the first thing you knew a boy would be drafted," Rupp said. "It got so I felt as I was running a kindergarten."

In early December, seven teams canceled games with Rupp's "Kindergarten Kids." Georgia Tech coach Dwight Keith said that the athletic director, Bill Alexander, did not want his Navy trainees to miss classroom work because of long trips. "Somebody ought to blast that guy," Rupp said. "He hauled his football team all over the United States last season, but he can't even get to Lexington for a weekend."

In an opening 51-18 breather against Fort Knox, Bob Brannum led all scorers with eleven points, starting a string of thirteen straight games in double figures. He had fifteen points in a 54-40 win over Berea's Navy V-12 trainees. Star of that Berea team was Joe Holland, a 6-foot-4 forward from Benton, who had attended Kentucky briefly before entering the Navy. Rupp took a chance on Holland, offering him a scholarship knowing that he had applied for the V-12 program. The Navy accepted Holland, who told Rupp he had to grab the opportunity. Rupp said his scholarship would be waiting after the war.

The Wildcats finished December 7-1, ringing out 1943 by defeating St. John's 44-38—their first win in Madison Square Garden—before a record crowd of 18,371. Tingle had scored only twenty-nine points in the first seven games, but he hit double figures for the first time against the Redmen. Kentucky started the new year with a 55-54 win over Notre Dame in Louisville, as Johnson scored fifteen points, and Brannum fourteen. Irish center Mark Todorovich wheeled around Brannum for a layup and tied the score 52-52, but seconds later Brannum intercepted a pass from Johnny Lujack—who was rarely picked off as the Irish's Heisman Trophy- winning quarterback. Fouled driving for a layup, Brannum sank the game-winning free throw, but Rupp still fussed at him for letting Notre Dame tie the score.

Because of the cancellations, that was one of only three January games, and the Wildcats won them all, then continued to roll through the opposition in February, including a 51-40 victory over Illinois, avenging their only defeat. Kentucky waltzed through the SEC tournament, winning three games by an average of more than twenty points and placing Brannum, Parkinson, and Tingle on the all-conference team. As a reward for their 17-1 season, the Wildcats received their first bid to the first National Invitation Tournament—in those days a much bigger deal than the NCAA tourney.

Kentucky met Utah in the opening round at Madison Square Garden. Vadal Peterson had introduced the Utes to the jump shot, which was something new to the Wildcats, whose coach would be one of the last to adopt it. Rupp told his players to warm up as usual, but to pay attention to the Utes' shooting style. He would then tell them how to stop the shot. And with Parkinson scoring twenty points and Brannum eleven, Kentucky won 46-38 over a team that would go on to win the NCAA championship.

In the second round Kentucky twice led St. John's by eight points but couldn't hold on. Wade Duym's free throw with a minute and a half to play gave the Redmen a one-point lead, and referee Pat Kennedy gave St. John's the ball after he accidentally got in the way of Tingle, who was trying to keep the ball inbounds. Don Weir's layup sealed a 48-45 St. John's victory. After the game, Schu and Tingle argued with Kennedy, but Rupp told them it was an argument they could not win.

In a consolation game, Oklahoma State's 7-foot shot-blocker Bob Kurland held Brannum scoreless for the first time in his career. But when the UK center passed off to teammates, they banked the ball home against Kurland. Tingle scored eighteen points and led the Wildcats to a 45-29 win that gave them a 19-2 final record. That year, Bob Brannum became the youngest-ever consensus All-American. After the season, the Brannums joined the Army. After they were discharged, Bob would return to Kentucky and Clarence would attend Kansas State.

For taking a group of players fresh out of high school and directing them to nineteen victories in twenty games, Rupp became the tenth coach elected to the Helms Athletic Foundation's Collegiate Basketball Hall of Fame. "The initial move in assembling a basketball team or any other undertaking is to understand the problems involved," Rupp said. "Then it is necessary to get the right kind of material for the purpose and to instill a winning complex." Talking about defeat, he believed, bred defeat. The foundation also added the 1933 UK team to its list of all-time champions.

During the off-season, Rupp sought the youngest players possible to keep his program going, hoping to keep them at least a year before Uncle Sam came calling. His reputation as a speaker was the entree he needed as a recruiter of high school talent. The Brooksville High School team, featuring Al Cummins and the Cooper brothers, Clyde and Warren, was undefeated until Olive Hill upset them in the quarterfinals of the state tournament. Named to the all-tournament team were Cummins and three UK players-to-be: senior Alonzo Nelson of Madison and juniors Ralph Beard of Male and Wallace Jones of Harlan. Rupp wanted Cummins and one of the Cooper boys. After speaking at their banquet, he signed the entire starting five. Unfortunately, Cummins got his draft notice three weeks before the season started, and Clyde Cooper had to quit due to academic problems.

Rupp went into Ohio to speak at the Martins Ferry High School banquet, hoping to land Alex Groza, a 6-foot-5, 167-pound stringbean who had led his team in scoring and into the state tournament semifinals two years running. A two-time all-stater, Groza scored a state-record 628 points as a senior. Floyd Baker, the Martins Ferry coach, told his good friend Rupp about the skinny center, who seemed to be the right person at the right time to replace Bob Brannum.

"Adolph had a few beers with my dad, and they had a big time," Alex later recalled. Groza's father was a miner and millworker of Hungarian descent who had come to Martins Ferry in the mid-1920s. He invested his savings in a poolroom, which he later converted to a tavern. Alex and his brothers, John, Frank, and Lou, grew up above the tavern. John, who starred in three sports at Martins Ferry, played freshman football at West Virginia before transferring to St. Thomas (now Scranton University). He was the first Groza to play basketball in Madison Square Garden. Frank also starred in three sports as a prep and later played one year of minor league baseball. Lou and Alex played basketball together on the 1941-42 Martins Ferry squad, but "the Toe" was better known for football, starring at Ohio State and becoming an All-Pro tackle and place-kicker for the Cleveland Browns.

Alex wanted to follow Lou to OSU, but the Buckeyes didn't recruit him, so he was among the thirty players who accepted an invitation to Rupp's annual tryout. "They put us up at the Phoenix Hotel and had the tryout on Friday and Saturday. To my knowledge, I was the only guy he invited back." Groza accepted a Kentucky scholarship—the only one he'd been offered. Returning Wildcats included Tingle and Schu at forward and Parkinson and Moseley at guard. Rupp dismissed Moseley when he failed to report one night for an extra practice, and John Stough, a freshman from Montgomery, Alabama, replaced him in the starting lineup.

Moseley was the only player Harry Lancaster ever saw Rupp lay a hand on. Moseley talked back to Rupp during halftime, and the coach was still fuming after the team went back out on the floor. "Harry," he said, "go get Moseley and bring him back. I'm going to slap the piss out of him, and if he raises a hand, you clobber him." Rupp raised hell with Moseley and then slapped him. The player hesitated, glanced at Lancaster, turned away, and went back out onto the floor.

A few days before the opening game Groza passed his Army exam; he was to report in three weeks. He scored forty-four points in four UK victories, and two days before Christmas, undefeated Kentucky met undefeated Ohio State in Alumni Gym.

"I remember playing Ohio State," Groza said, "because I was ready to show them they were wrong about not wanting me." He squared off against 6-foot-8 Arnie Risen, a taller and more experienced center from Williamsburg, Kentucky. Groza outscored Risen 16-14, and Tingle and Parkinson scored fifteen points each as Kentucky won 53-48 in overtime. Buckeye coach Harold Olsen cornered Groza after the game and asked why he hadn't come to OSU. Nobody had asked him, Groza replied, and it was too late now.

Groza got his induction notice and went home to report to his draft board, but he was able to join the Wildcats on an eastern swing, scoring fourteen points in a victory over Wyoming in Buffalo and twenty-seven—including the game-winning shot—in a 45-44 win over Temple. The Wildcats arrived in New York City ranked No. 1, but they fell behind Long Island U. 44-29 in the second half. Rupp started to send in Alonzo Nelson for Tingle, then changed his mind and yelled to Buddy Parker.

"You mean me?" a surprised Parker asked.

"Yes, you," Rupp said. "Hustle in there and take over for Tingle—snap those guys out of it." Parker scored a quick goal and sparked one of the most thrilling rallies ever seen in the Garden. With fans screaming, the Wildcats sent the game into overtime tied at 59, then outscored LIU by ten points in the extra period. Groza scored twenty-five points; Parker had only that single field goal, but it was a big one.

After hitting twenty-five again in a win over Ohio University, Groza went home for a visit while Kentucky beat hapless Arkansas State 75-6. His pre-Army swan song would be a game against Michigan State in Lexington.

"I'll never forget it," Groza said in 1975. "My train back to Lexington was a few minutes late. They picked me up, rushed me to the gym, brought me out at halftime, and presented me a key to the university and farewell gifts." He knew he was a Kentuckian for life. By the time Groza dressed, the game was ten minutes old; he scored two points in the first half, and the Spartans led at intermission. In the second half, Groza scored twelve points, and Kentucky romped 66-35. Two days later, he reported to the Army. His replacement was Kenton "Dutch" Campbell, a 6-foot-4 freshman from Newark, Ohio. John Mauer asked why Rupp should miss one guy when he had thirty. "You don't replace a Caruso with a barbershop singer," Rupp replied.

Without Groza, Kentucky lost 35-34 to a Tennessee program that had sat out the previous season. Paul Walther, a lean and knobby freshman from Covington, Kentucky, accounted for twenty-one points with his looping left-handed shots.

The game was the roughest Rupp had ever seen. The Tennessee band joined the football players and other hecklers on a stage behind the UK bench, and every time Rupp opened his mouth, the band played and the hecklers blew horns. When a Wildcat stepped to the free throw line, the crowd would yell, "Miss It! Miss It!" The racket was so loud that the timer's buzzer couldn't be heard at the end of the first half, and the officials counted a late Tennessee basket.

Midway through the second period, a Tennessee player started twisting Parkinson's neck. Both teams took up the fight, with the substitutes and three hundred fans joining in the melee. Some semblance of order was restored, and the game was tied with one minute to go, when Tingle drew a technical foul for protesting an out-of-bounds call. "Hell, friend," he said, pointing to a UT player, "it hit that guy on the head." Tennessee made the free throw and won the game.

Another late call proved costly against Notre Dame. With Kentucky trailing by a point, Tingle drove the length of the court for a layup, but Frank Gilhooley grabbed his shirt-tail, and the foul call nullified the goal. Tingle made one of two free throws to tie the game, but Johnny Dee, a future Notre Dame coach, scored the deciding field goal in a 59-58 Irish overtime victory. The Wildcats lost one other regular-season game, to Michigan State 66-50 at East Lansing.

When Tennessee came to Lexington, fans talked of revenge, but Rupp reminded them that they should treat the

Halstead High School, where Rupp enrolled in 1915.

Rupp was a member of the University of Kansas National Basketball Championship team in 1922.

Rupp's first team at Freeport High School (1926-27).

Rupp's first UK team—the 1930-31 squad.

Adolph with son Herky in 1942.

Rupp with President Truman and Fred Vinson, a native of Louisa, Kentucky, who was Chief Justice of the U.S. Supreme Court.

Adolph Rupp holds his first national championship trophy while Kenneth "Tug" Wilson, representing the NCAA at Madison Square Garden in 1948, pins a special medal on Alex Groza, who was the outstanding player in the tournament.

Rupp and his good friend Hank Iba shake hands before the 1949 NCAA championship game held in Minneapolis. Kentucky won 46-36.

The 1951-52 AP and UPI champions: Skippy Whitaker, Bobby Watson, Billy Evans. Standing— Rupp, Frank Ramsey, Lou Tsioropoulos, Cliff Hagan, and Shelby Linville.

Rupp and longtime assistant Harry Lancaster in action.

Adolph, Happy Chandler, and Esther, circa 1958.

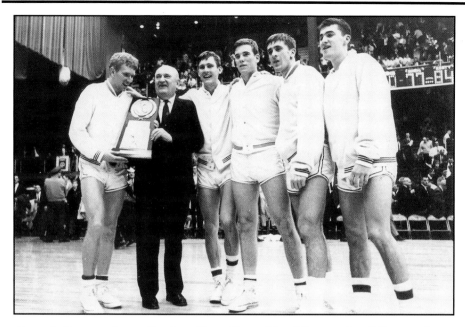

Rupp's Runts—Larry Conley, Tom Kron, Thad Jaracz, Pat Riley, and Louie Dampier.

Rupp cuts UK's 1,000 victory cake after defeating Florida 88-67 in Memorial Coliseum in January 1969. Watching Rupp's actions are Capt. Phil Argento, Thompson R. Bryant, a member of UK's 1905-06-07 teams, and Wylie B. Wendt, manager of the 1906 team.

Rupp with two Kentucky greats from the late '60s, Mike Pratt, left, and all-time UK scoring leader, Dan Issel.

Rupp with All-American Cotton Nash.

Ceremonies at the Basketball Hall of Fame, April 13, 1969, when Hall of Famer Howard Hobson unveils the Honors Court plaque of inductee Adolph Rupp as program chairman Edward Steitz looks on.

Tom Payne becomes the first black to sign a basketball grant-in-aid with the University of Kentucky. Rupp and Payne's parents signed the grant. Assistant coach Joe B. Hall is on the right.

Rupp's last UK coaching staff— (left to right) Dickie Parsons, Joe B. Hall, Gale Catlett.

Rupp with his legendary University of Kansas basketball coach, Dr. F. C. "Phog" Allen.

Adolph Rupp was presented a blue chair at halftime of the UK-Kansas game dedicating Rupp Arena in December 1976. The Wildcats defeated his alma mater 90-63. Rupp refused the game ball because the 'Cats were "doing so well with it."

Volunteers as guests. Kentucky's revenge took the form of a victory, and the Wildcats beat UT again in the final of the conference tournament. Campbell, Parkinson, and Tingle made the All-SEC team.

The NCAA district committee invited Kentucky to meet Ohio State in New York. Campbell held Arnie Risen to nine points, but the Wildcats lost 45-37. During the tournament, betting activity was heavy despite a close watch at the Garden. Rupp thought the newspapers were wrong in publishing the odds, which almost everyone could quote. The office of the New York district attorney was on the lookout for Lexington's Ed Curd, who was one of the biggest bookmakers in the country. His operation was no secret to most Lexingtonians. Rupp knew Curd because he donated to the Shriners Hospital for Crippled Children.

Five days after the loss to Ohio State, the Wildcats defeated Tufts College to finish 22-4. Rupp had 244 wins, 61 losses, and eight conference championships in fifteen seasons. The 1944-45 team had scored 1,464 points, eclipsing the school record set four years earlier. The *Herald-Leader* said it might be years before another Kentucky team matched that offensive output. "Just wait until next year," Rupp said.

But while the games went on at home, the reality of the war was brought home to Lexington. Five former Wildcats— Mel Brewer, Kenny England, Jim Goforth, Walter Johnson, and Jim King—would not return. Rupp was visiting in the England home in April 1944 when the family got the word that Kenny died of wounds received while crossing a minefield in Italy. As commander of the country's only ski troop, he received bronze and silver stars. King was co-pilot of a B-24 that went down over Germany. Goforth, who also held bronze and silver stars, lost his life to machine gun fire during the Battle of Saipan. Brewer died in the invasion of France. Johnson's ship was returning home from Guam after delivering atomic bomb supplies, when the Japanese torpedoed it. "What can you say?" Rupp would muse later. "It's just those tragic things that you have to remember with the good times."

As the war neared its end, Rupp was grateful that the university had kept basketball going throughout the hostilities, and he would soon have more reason to appreciate the program's continuity. If UK basketball had been suspended, Bob Brannum would have missed out on his freshman season and probably would have followed his twin to another school after the war. Jack Parkinson and Jack Tingle would have missed that first year of varsity experience and might also have been tempted to cast their lots elsewhere. Alex Groza probably would have gone from high school directly into the Army, where his fine play would have attracted the attention of many college coaches. Rupp would not have been able to recruit, train, and stockpile many fine young players who would leave the service and return to Kentucky as mature adults. Rupp had indeed tended his wartime "Victory Garden," and the harvest was at hand.

Chapter
Ten

Postwar

W orld War II ended in September 1945, but there was no peace in the office of UK president Herman Lee Donovan. The university had to do something about the school's football program. People had gotten tired of losing all the time, and the wolves were howling at Donovan's door. Their gripes and complaints extended from the general public all the way to the governor and the general assembly. If Donovan couldn't do something about the situation, he'd be looking for another job.

His first move was to incorporate an organization called the UK Athletics Association to replace the old athletic council. The new group wasn't bound by the $5,000 a year state constitutional salary limit, and it could cut the red tape that tied up equipment and travel budgets. Donovan laid it on the line to prominent business and professional people: Kentucky was ready to build a first-class athletic program, but the school needed money—at least $100,000— to do it. Backers immediately started a statewide campaign to raise that amount.

Athletic director Bernie Shively was filling in as football coach basis after Ab Kirwan had resigned at the end of the

1944 season, when the Wildcats had gone 2-6. Shively didn't feel that UK could compete in the SEC with the limited support it was giving football. Besides the old problem of securing good players, there was also the rivalry between the football coach—any football coach—and Rupp. Kentucky's 1945 football team went 2-8, a season salvaged only by the play of George Blanda. The freshman quarterback from Pennsylvania was a deadly passer and averaged almost forty yards a punt.

Basketball was also one of Donovan's immediate concerns, and the need for a new arena was evident. The university grew so rapidly after the war that fans could no longer fit in Alumni Gym. A larger facility would get the state tournament back to the UK campus, where many felt it belonged. The general assembly had allocated $400,000 to replace the old arena, but that was before the war, when buildings cost less.

Rupp was eager for the first postwar season, but he had some military business to take care of first. He left Lexington in August 1945 for Paris—with a stop in New York, where the Army made him a colonel and gave him the proper uniform— to lay the groundwork for a sports program that he would help install.

When Harry Lancaster, whose Navy softball and baseball teams were preparing to play the Third Army in Reims, France, reported to the USO commander in Paris, he was flabbergasted to find Adolph in the major's office. Rupp wore khaki—Eisenhower jacket, garrison cap, the whole works. He jumped up, shook Harry's hand, asked where he was staying, and if he had any bourbon.

"I'm staying in a damn place, Pig Alley, that doesn't even have a bathtub, and I don't have a change of uniform," Rupp complained. "How in the hell can we win a war this way?" Lancaster shared bathtub and bottle with his old friend. The next day Lancaster met John Bunn and Frosty Cox, two coaches traveling with Rupp. The three wanted to make a trip to the PX in Paris.

"I told them I could get in," Lancaster wrote in his book "but they would have to have special papers." "To hell with that," Rupp said. "We're over here on special business—we'll get in." When Rupp was stopped at the door, he asked to see the officer in charge. Rupp made his case with the colonel and soon was ushered in. When he came out, carrying an armload of brown shirts, socks, ties, handkerchiefs, and underwear, Bunn and Cox asked, "What about us, Adolph?" Rupp laughed and told them they were on their own.

That was the last Rupp would see of Lancaster for a year, but they corresponded throughout his Navy service, and when Harry returned after the war, the Baron had a job waiting for him. When Lancaster had joined the Navy, Rupp had told him that he didn't want McBrayer back. Lancaster and others suspected that Rupp thought McBrayer was after his job.

Some thought Rupp had never gotten over McBrayer's perfect record with the Wildcats when the head coach missed three games with illness in 1940-41. Others say Mac had outlived his usefulness to Rupp. When McBrayer came looking for his old job back, Rupp sent Bernie Shively to the Kentuckian Hotel to tell him the bad news. Rupp and McBrayer remained bitter enemies afterward.

In March of 1946, Lancaster would return to the UK Physical Education Department, and later that year, Rupp hired him as a full-time assistant. They would form a perfect coaching team for twenty-three years, though the relationship would be tested after Lancaster became the school's athletic director in 1968.

The ETO-MTO track meet in Frankfurt, Germany, was an early stop on Rupp's tour. There he ran into former UK football players Phil Cutchin and Noah Mullins and several other Kentucky boys who were among the twenty-seven thousand GI's in attendance. Thirty-eight generals were there, too, including George S. Patton. Rupp thought it peculiar that all those Yanks would spend a pleasant Sunday afternoon watching a track meet in the hotbed of Nazism. He would always remember that afternoon.

Rupp helped install a three-part program for U.S. servicemen all over Europe:

1) mass athletics, with participation voluntary and open to all men;

2) competitive athletics, including league tournaments, meets, and matches, involving all echelons of command, and culminating in theater championships and intertheater championships;

3) exhibitions that would send outstanding individuals and teams on tours of hospitals,and command posts.

Rupp set an early example of the latter approach, and clinics featuring his cadre of coaches were immediately popular. Sergeant Harry Taylor, a UK football letterman, wrote that some of the fellows were still talking about "that coach from Kentucky." Rupp said, "I am glad I had an opportunity to come over here and help in some small way with this program. The point is, the boys have an opportunity to play, and that means a lot."

When he arrived back in the States on October 20, Rupp discarded his uniform and refused to have his picture taken in it. He would continue to wear khaki, but only on the basketball practice court.

Opening practice for the 1945-46 season drew forty-three young athletes to Alumni Gym, but one of Rupp's prize recruits was missing. Before his mission to Paris, Rupp had received commitments from two of Kentucky's finest high school players—Ralph Beard of Louisville Male and Wallace Jones of Harlan. Beard was the image of an All-American boy. A UK media guide described him as the "perfect Wheaties ad." His mother said he started shooting baskets when he was a baby, using his potty for a goal. When Ralph began to walk, she attached a basketball goal to the wall of the family garage. But Beard, a four-sport star, had injured a shoulder in the fourth game of the Wildcats' football season, and then when a coach made disparaging remarks about the team, the freshman, discouraged and homesick, went home to Louisville, where he planned to play for the Cardinals. Rupp brought Beard back to Lexington, and the two sat down in his office for a long talk. Many years later, Beard would recall the coach's last words: "Son, I can't keep you from going to UL, but I will tell you one thing: we here at the university will not cancel our schedule."

"Wah-Wah" Jones was a 6-foot-4, 205-pound multisport star who came to Kentucky with more credentials than any high school player before him. At Harlan he had played four years of football, four years of baseball, and five years of basketball, starting in the eighth grade. During his last four seasons, he played in the state basketball tournament and set a national high school scoring record of 2,398 points.

Rupp started Jones in the pivot, Beard and junior Jack Parkinson at guard, and freshman Joe Holland and junior Jack Tingle at forward. They won their first seven games, including a 73-59 decision over St. John's in the Garden—the first time a team had ever scored more than seventy points against the Redmen. St. John's best player was Harry Boykoff, who was 6-foot-9 and weighed 280 pounds. Bernie Opper had recommended him to Rupp, and Boykoff had been ready to attend Kentucky, but his mother had urged him to stay home. He made All-America at St. John's.

While the basketball team rolled on the hardwood, the drive for football funds reached its goal—with help from an unlikely source, as Rupp let boosters auction off donated tobacco at halftime of the Ohio U. game, netting $600. The committee deposited $113,000 in the bank, and the university went on a bear hunt. Actually, Kentucky tried to land a "name" coach before looking at the younger men available for the job.

The name of Paul Bryant kept popping up. Just out of the Navy, Bryant had posted one winning season at the University of Maryland when Kentucky signed him to a five-year contract. For the next eight years, the Bear and the Baron shared the UK spotlight.

Rupp thought the sportswriters had been unfair to him when they accused him of dominating UK athletics and suppressing football. "I was boss of basketball, and I never did interfere with other athletics at UK," he said many years later. "I have always wanted to see UK have a great football team." He thought the writers were trying to drive a wedge between him and the new coach before they even met, but the initial meeting between Rupp and Bryant did not produce the expected fireworks.

Back from road victories over Tennessee and Georgia Tech, Rupp dropped by Bryant's office to shake hands and offer the basketball staff's cooperation. "I have two excellent basketball prospects for you," Bryant said. "By gosh, that's fine," Rupp said. "I have a list of good football prospects for you, and I'll turn them over to you in the morning." Two nights later, when the Wildcats played Notre Dame in Louisville, Bryant was there to interview two high school football players from the area. He got some attention by securing a commitment from Lee Truman—a third cousin to President Truman.

On the court, Notre Dame not only stopped Kentucky's winning streak at six but also humiliated Ralph Beard before the home folks. With Johnny Dee guarding him most of the time, Beard failed to score. He felt like jumping off a bridge. "Maybe that was the best thing that could ever have happened to you," Rupp told him. "Everything happens for the best, you know." Back at home, Kentucky defeated Georgia Tech, and Rupp gave his starters the day off. Before going to the farm, he appeared with Bryant on a program honoring the Georgetown High School football and basketball teams. The two coaches seemed to be getting along fine, but some people thought they were putting on a front.

Good news greeted Rupp after the Wildcats drove home in a snowstorm from Paducah, where they had defeated Vanderbilt: Ralph Beard had failed his military induction examination because of a speech impediment. Kentucky defeated Tennessee at home and Ohio on the road before closing the season at home with an 83-40 win over Xavier—the most points ever scored by a UK team.

Kentucky dominated the SEC tournament. Four Wildcats—Beard, Jones, Parkinson, and Tingle—made the all-conference team. Big crowds and a sold-out final convinced SEC schools that basketball could be a paying proposition, and they asked Rupp to help build up their programs by playing more games with league schools. He was happy to cooperate.

Rupp was socializing in the team reception room during the tournament when someone came in and told him Jack Tingle was drinking beer in the hotel bar. He thanked the informant and eased him out the door. Then he gave Bob Sparks and Cecil Bell time to get Tingle out of the bar before he went looking for him.

"He is a senior and I am going to win the NIT with him," Rupp said. "If I kick him off the team, I can't win it." Sparks and Bell hustled Tingle out one door just as Rupp came in the other.

New York's invitational tournament had become so popular that 49th Street had to be closed to traffic as basketball fans stormed the Garden for tickets. Extra mounted police kept the fans orderly. Windows opened at 9 a.m., but lines had begun forming at 5; 10,000 tickets were sold in the first hour. Postwar basketball was a booming business.

Jones, Parkinson, and Tingle scored in double figures to lead Kentucky past Arizona 77-53 in the first round. Against West Virginia, the Wildcats broke the fourteenth and last tie with eight unanswered points in the final two minutes to win 59-51 and advance to the final against Rhode Island.

Rupp predicted that if Kentucky held Rhode Island to forty- five points, it would win the championship game. The prediction reflected Rupp's deep belief in the importance of statistics. As far back as 1933 he had designed a set of charts that kept track of shots, turnovers, and fouls—a forerunner of the charts common today. Wildcats fan George Hukle refined the chart that recorded field goal attempts, recording the shots on a diagram of a basketball court. Small circles designated the location of all shots attempted during a game, and a blackened circle indicated a successful shot. Hukle was a modest, soft-spoken man who had started following the Wildcats in 1914. Since that time, he had seen almost every game played in Lexington; and for most of the period he kept team stats just for amusement.

During the 1940-41 season, he started keeping statistics on individual players as a hobby. In 1943, Rupp became more than casually interested in the figures Hukle had been compiling for three seasons.

"I looked at them and discovered things about my players that I never knew before," Rupp said. "If there are questions from the players about the starting lineup, I just show them the shooting averages." Hukle began traveling with the team in 1945 and would be a fixture at the scorer's table for twenty-seven years.

So Rupp knew his stats well enough—both offensive and defensive—that he could confidently predict a victory if the defense could hold Rhode Island to the designated level. But that was a tall order: Ernie Calverley alone averaged 26.7 points for Frank Keaney's squad. "I'm leaving this guy Calverley up to you," Rupp told Beard. "I want him stopped." Beard, who had held his man scoreless in the Arizona game and limited his West Virginia opponent to four free throws, shrugged his shoulders, put four pieces of chewing gum in his mouth, and told Rupp not to worry.

The score was 45-45 with forty seconds to go when Beard drove for the basket, stopped suddenly, and caused Calverley to run into him. With thousands of fans screaming, Beard calmly sank the winning free throw for his thirteenth point, five more than Calverley scored. The players carried a smiling Rupp to the dressing room. He predicted—inaccurately, as it turned out—that no Kentucky team would ever equal the record of that squad: twenty-eight victories in thirty games, conference and NIT titles, and a new team scoring record of 1,821 points. Parkinson earned All-America honors by scoring 339 points to break Leroy Edwards' UK record by five.

That spring Lexington showed its appreciation with a "Rupp Day." Baseball commissioner "Happy" Chandler was among those in attendance at a testimonial dinner. Ned Irish was also on hand to praise Rupp for his role in developing basketball in the South and Midwest. Rupp, Irish observed, was one of the first coaches to take his teams to other sections of the country, fostering interest in intersectional basketball. Touched by the praise, Rupp said, "The object in life is to strive for success and try to win. As long as I am coach at the university, I am going to try to win every game we play." He would come close: over the next four seasons his teams would win 130 of 140 games.

Jack Parkinson received his induction notice in the spring, but Kenny Rollins arrived home from the Navy, and Bob Brannum and Alex Groza wrote to say that they would be returning to Kentucky. After completing infantry training, Groza had been among eight thousand soldiers at Fort Hood waiting for combat duty. He was cleaning his gear when an officer approached and asked whether he would like to stay and play for a basketball team that was being organized. The answer was obvious. When the others shipped out, Groza remained behind. He was assigned to the Medical Corps and worked in a hospital. SEC fans familiar with UK teamwork would not have been surprised to learn that the officer who kept Groza stateside was Bob Brannum.

While in the Army, Groza grew two inches and gained seventy pounds. When he was discharged, he caught a plane from San Antonio to Birmingham, then a train to Lexington. Rupp was waiting for him on the platform, but Groza strolled right by him unrecognized. Then Groza walked back and said, "Coach." Rupp's puzzled look quickly turned into a big grin.

"He liked what he saw," Groza remembered. "I was 6-foot-7 and weighed 238 pounds."

Also back in school was Cliff Barker, who had spent sixteen months in a prisoner of war camp after his B-17 was shot down over Germany. "We made our own facilities and just messed around," he said. "You always had to have something to occupy your mind." He passed the time by fooling with a basketball. Palming and rolling the sphere from hand to hand and finger to finger, he developed an uncanny ballhandling magic. Rupp held him out of action in 1945-46 so he could become accustomed to campus life.

Rupp ran the football all-star game that fall, and there was no hint of friction with the Wildcat coaching staff, which seemed to enjoy his wit and stories. Bryant's first UK football team won seven games that season—the most wins by a Wildcat team since the 1912 squad finished 7-2.

After two weeks of unofficial drills, Rupp opened practice on October 16. Returning from the previous year were Jack Tingle, Muff Davis, Joe Holland, Dutch Campbell, Malcolm McMullen, Ralph Beard, Buddy Parker, and Rudy Yessin. Wallace Jones would join them when football ended. Bob Brannum, Cliff Barker, Al Cummins, Alex Groza, Jim Jordan, and Kenny Rollins had returned home from the military. Dale Barnstable and Jim Line were promising freshmen. Rupp had a problem that many coaches would envy: too many good players. There was no way he could keep them all happy. Fighting for the center position alone were Brannum, a former All-American; Campbell and Jones, each with All-SEC credentials; and Groza—who would beat out his all-everything rivals for the starting spot. Eventually the Baron divided the players into two squads. He had nineteen players on his A Squad; Harry Lancaster coached twenty-three on the B squad.

After the NIT clincher, Beard had asked Rupp to list his weaknesses so he could work on them during the summer, and the Baron was eager to oblige:

1. You made only 49 of 117 free throw attempts. That is less than 50 percent. You must improve that by at least 20 percent.

2. You have a tendency when you start the offense to make the first pass to the left forward. This is natural

because it allows you to make the pass with your right hand. Work on a pass with your left hand to the right forward.

3. I have noticed that you miss your crip shots when you use your left hand. That fits in with weakness No. 2, because you favor going in on the right-hand side.

4. Work on driving in and using a jump one-hand shot near the free-throw line.

Beard did his homework and quickly claimed one starting guard position in the fall, but the other one was up for grabs. The winner was Rollins, who had started for Rupp in 1942-43 and came home polished and matured by three years of service basketball. Tingle, team captain and a three-time All-SEC player, and Holland, who had started occasionally the previous year, claimed the starting forward spots, but many of Rupp's "cast of thousands" would make their presence felt.

Barnstable had been discovered by Milt Ticco in Germany. "I have been playing with a boy who I think could help the UK basketball program," Ticco wrote to Rupp, adding a P.S.: "My basketball shoes are worn out; could you please send me another pair?" Rupp wrote back and closed with his own postscript: "Milt, don't you realize there has been a war going on? As a result, it has created a severe rubber shortage and therefore I am unable to send you the shoes. However, I am interested in you sending me the boy."

Rupp would later remember this group as a "dream team," one that played straight basketball but was better equipped to the task than some. He had players suited to his style of play—they could rebound and run, they had brains and spirit. He once had been forced to "shake the bushes," but now, he said—with just a trace of exaggeration—"Every starter came unsolicited."

Rupp used fourteen players against Wabash but couldn't keep down the score. The 96-24 victory was a UK single-game scoring mark. The previous record of eighty-three points had been set four games earlier in a sixty-five point romp over Texas A&M. The Wildcats were 11-0 and riding a twenty-six-game winning streak when they played Oklahoma A&M in the Sugar Bowl. Rupp took fourteen players to New Orleans— almost three whole teams—but deciding who should stay at home was tough.

Hank Iba's Aggies played a slow-down game, keeping their hands on the ball two-thirds of the time. A Sugar Bowl-record crowd of nine thousand saw A&M win 37-31. "Tough luck, Coach," a UK fan said to Rupp. "Don't call me Coach," he screamed. "A team that makes only twelve points in the second half has no coach."

Back in Lexington, Rupp attributed the loss to the strenuous schedule, with trips to the Atlantic and the Gulf of Mexico. Some critics thought he drove the players too hard; others said they got too much publicity and were jealous of each other. Rupp finally took the matter to some of the more mature players, who told him there was a leadership problem. He agreed to let the players choose a captain, and they elected Kenny Rollins. The Wildcats rebounded from the Sugar Bowl loss to win ten games in a row, including a 54-39 victory over Tennessee and a 60-30 rout of Notre Dame. John Mauer called Kentucky the best team he had ever seen. Beard avenged his embarrassment at the hands of the Irish the previous year, scoring seventeen points and holding All-American Kevin O'Shea to two.

DePaul snapped this streak, 53-47 behind eighteen points from Ed Mikan, in the season's biggest upset. Still, the Wildcats were 27-2 and a heavy favorite to win the SEC tournament, even though the tourney presented Rupp with his biggest challenge—trimming his roster to ten players. The Wildcats followed form and placed five players—Beard, Jones, Holland, Rollins, and Tingle, native-born Kentuckians all—on the All-SEC team. In Louisville, the Wildcats defeated Temple 68-29 in a post-season game. Wallace Jones got his second start of the season and his first at forward. He would remain there in place of Tingle throughout the NIT.

The Metropolitan Basketball Writers named Navy coach Ben Carnevale their first Coach of the Year with nineteen of twenty-five first-place votes. Beard beat out Don Barksdale of UCLA for the Gold Star Award, but with the Wildcats ranked No. 1 in every poll, Rupp felt slighted by the New York writers—he had thought they were his friends. No longer the jolly Baron who had entertained the writers in the past, his remarks at their annual luncheon were blunt and cutting.

When asked why he had left Brannum home, Rupp said the boy just wasn't good enough to make the team. "If any of you coaches are interested," he said, "his telephone number in Lexington is 682." Brannum said he told Rupp before the Temple game that he was not going to New York and that Rupp asked him to stay out for practice. "Maybe I'm not as good as the boys he took in my place," Brannum said, "but I made plans some time ago to leave the university and go to another school." Rupp later admitted that he had approved Brannum's plan to transfer. Brannum went to Michigan State, where he would play an excellent game against his old teammates the following year.

Suddenly Rupp was no longer the darling of Gotham sportswriters. When Kentucky struggled to a 63-62 win over Long Island U. in the opening round, they accused him of poor use of his strong bench. The Wildcats defeated North Carolina State 60-42 to gain the finals against Utah, which played the slowdown game that Kentucky hated. The Utes' star player was Wat Misaka, born in Utah of Japanese parents. He held Beard without a field goal, and Arnie Ferren and Vern Gardner scored fifteen points each in Utah's 49-45 victory. Larry Shropshire of the Lexington *Leader*, reported that the crowd of eighteen thousand roared most for just one more basket— everybody seemed to have a bet on the margin of victory. Gambling on point spreads was a dark cloud on basketball's horizon. Warning signs were everywhere, but few paid them any mind.

Groza and Beard earned All-America honors. Beard was *True* Magazine's "Player of the Year" and the outstanding player to appear in the Garden all season. The little guard was so dejected after losing to Utah that he did not stick around to receive his trophy. Again he asked Rupp how to improve his game. Beard was a slashing, driving type of player, but Rupp said he must learn to shoot long shots. That meant changing his entire technique, since every two-hand shot he took revolved to the right because of too much right-hand pressure. Six hours after arriving home, Beard was on the gym floor shooting his long shot. He practiced it at least three days a week all summer long, taking approximately five hundred shots each session. Beard would return the following season as one of the deadliest outside shooters in the nation.

Kentucky finished with a 34-3 record, by far the most victories in school history. At the annual banquet, Rupp called it the team of the century. "If anyone is to be blamed for loss of the final game in the national tournament," he said, "I will take the blame." He praised the seniors, Tingle and Parker, and said, "Wherever you go, the night will never be so dark that I won't help you if you need help."

During that first postwar year, the sports boom hit the Blue Grass State. Bryant's arrival helped the university presell all its permanent stadium seats, and the best Kentucky football team in years played before one hundred thousand fans. Increased student enrollment and the small capacity of Alumni Gym limited the sale of basketball tickets. The university admitted the public to six of the seventeen home games that year, scheduling three of those "public" games during the semester break.

In April of 1947, the university broke ground across from the football stadium for a new field house—the first "House that Rupp Built." One month later, the university signed Rupp to a ten-year contract—his first pact since arriving in Lexington. During the season, some Louisville businessmen who were trying to secure a professional basketball franchise, had offered Rupp $15,000 annually to coach the team. "I'm too busy," he said. "Come back in April." When April came, he told the group that he planned to stay at Kentucky. He had taken the Wildcats job "on approval," refusing a contract until he could establish whether he liked Kentucky and Kentucky liked him. Now, seventeen years later, it was official.

Chapter
Eleven

Fabulous Five

A 60-59 loss to Temple in Philadelphia on December 28, 1948, started a string of events that led to the formation of Kentucky's most famous basketball team. The Wildcats had dispatched their first seven foes with such ease that they seemed invincible. As the season got under way, Rupp had moved Cliff Barker into the starting lineup with Ralph Beard, Kenny Rollins, Alex Groza, and Joe Holland. Wah Jones was coming out of football season with a foot injury. He was the missing piece to the puzzle.

The Wildcats were en route to Madison Square Garden when they stopped off in Philadelphia. Rollins, the best UK free throw shooter, missed a foul shot that would have tied the game near the end. Beard played only ten minutes because of a sore ankle; Jones didn't play at all. Even after a 52-40 victory in the Garden over St. John's, Rupp was seething about the Temple game, about the shattered dreams of an undefeated season. He knew he had the horses to go all the way—they were a combination of seasoned veterans and brilliant youngsters, and they had the best coach in the country. He could hardly wait to get them back to Lexington.

It was the Christmas season, but the UK coach was no jolly Santa Claus. "Rupp was a terror, a bear, a tiger in practice the following week," Joe Holland said. "We had not seen him like that." It was a relief to travel to Omaha to play Creighton.

During the game, someone threw a pass over Dale Barnstable's head. Rupp rushed onto the floor and raised hell with the passer. When he came back to the bench, Holland said, "Dammit, Coach, if you'd get off our backs, maybe we could play." Buddy Parker grabbed Holland and tried to shut him up.

Rupp turned and said, "You mean the referees, don't you, Joe?"

"No, dammit, Coach, I mean you."

"I'll see you in my room after the game," he said.

Alex Groza recalls that the players helped persuade Rupp not to dismiss Holland from the team. As it was, the coach gave Holland a blistering lecture. "I can't have this," he said in one of his milder moments. "It is a rebellion." Holland had to apologize both to Rupp and to the team.

"I drove a nail in my coffin," said Holland, who was afraid that "it was the end of my basketball career at Kentucky." In fact, he never regained his starting position, but Holland was too good to let go. After letting him sit for four or five games, Rupp started using him off the bench.

Holland was not the only Wildcat tired of being harassed by Rupp. Other players told Rollins they had had it. He called a meeting and reminded them that if they planned to play professional basketball, "The best record you make here will mean the best money you will make in the pros. Carry on for yourselves," he added, "not the coaches." They got the message.

Kentucky's next game was at home against Western Ontario. The Wildcats were in charge from the start, but at halftime Rupp followed his usual routine: storm into dressing room, hang up jacket, use the bathroom, and raise hell.

"Who in the hell is guarding No. 10?" he yelled from the urinal. Cliff Barker confessed his guilt. "Well, by Gawd, get on him," Rupp said, "He's scored the only two damned field goals they've got." That was the only time in Harry Lancaster's memory that the team got up enough nerve to laugh. Even Rupp laughed.

Two nights later, all the pieces came together. The Wildcats were in Oxford, Ohio, to play Miami at the start of a six-day road trip. Rupp stood in front of the team and named a new lineup: Wah Jones and Cliff Barker at forward, Alex Groza at center, and Kenny Rollins and Ralph Beard at guard. Thus was born the Fabulous Five. They would be the yardstick for all future Wildcat teams.

Each man had a role in the group. Kenny Rollins was the playmaker. A good shooter, he was content to set up the other players. Harry Lancaster said he had the best mind of any UK player ever. He was a defensive specialist who always guarded the opposing team's best scoring guard. That kept the high-scoring Beard from fouling out. "We were never rattled," Rollins said. "We went into many games on the road that demanded poise, and we always kept it." It was hard to rattle seasoned war veterans.

Ralph Beard's attributes were speed, aggressiveness, shooting ability, and desire. Rupp, who ordinarily disliked dribblers, praised Beard as the fastest dribbler he had ever seen. Beard was deadly when driving for the basket or shooting long set shots. He was also a ball hawk who delighted in stealing the ball and zipping down the floor for a layup. When Beard ran, Rupp claimed that you could smell the rubber burning. Lancaster said Beard made the soles on his basketball shoes scream and that his shoes left black marks on the floor. He said that Beard was the best ballplayer he had ever seen. Kentucky was a guard-oriented team with the second guard carrying the scoring load. It was the old second guard-around offense reborn.

Alex Groza was small for a center by modern standards, but he was a giant in 1947-48. He was the leading rebounder, the leading scorer, and the heart and soul of the team. "Exceptional quickness allowed him to go around anyone who played him tightly," Tevis Laudeman said. "Marvelous timing around the basket made him a strong rebounder; he had delicate touch on his shots." His best shot was a right-handed hook.

Cliff Barker, at 27, was the old man of the group. Barker was not a good shot, but Lancaster called him college basketball's first great passer. During his early months as a

POW, Barker's group would go from camp to camp playing other teams. As Barker improved his passing skills, he lost his shooting touch, but he was content to feed the other players and guard the opponent's best forward. His passing was effective both on fast breaks and in Kentucky's pattern offense. Groza credits much of his scoring success to Barker. "He did not even look when he passed me the ball," Groza said, "because he knew I would catch it."

Wah Jones was 6-foot-4, strong as an ox and aggressive as a lion. Teammates marveled that such an easygoing person could be such a killer on the boards. He would clobber an opponent going up for a rebound, pick him up, apologize—and clobber him again the next time a shot went up. "Wah knocked people around," Harry Lancaster said. "He hurt people." When Lancaster ran into Leo Barnhorst, a former Notre Dame star who had played against the Fabulous Five, Barnhorst said: "You guys used to talk about Groza being tough. Groza never hurt you; Jones would leave you black and blue and white."

Jones downplayed his contributions. "I guess I was mostly a rebounder, but I set up other plays, too," he said. "Groza got everything that came to his side of the basket, but when it came to my side, I guess I did all right." Jones' specialty was a long, overhead shot from the side. He practiced it diligently under Rupp's prodding. It helped him make All-America, along with Beard and Groza.

Things might have been different for the "Five" if Joe Holland had kept his mouth shut. Perhaps he would have been one of them.

After the Miami game, Bob Brannum was waiting for the Wildcats at Michigan State. "He knew all our plays," Al Cummins said. "When we ran the guard-around, there he was." Brannum outscored Groza 23-10, but Kentucky won 47-45. On the last night of the year, the Wildcats defeated DePaul 68-51. Two nights later, they lost to Notre Dame 64-55 in South Bend. Never before had a Kentucky team tackled such a tough road schedule, and the Wildcats would not lose again that season. They won their next eighteen games, including the Southeastern Conference and the NCAA tournaments. A late-season highlight came against Tennessee in Alumni Gym, where Beard hit a shot from 51 1/2 feet with one second remaining in the first half. That beat the previous long shot of 48 feet, 2 1/2 inches set by Joe Hagan in 1938. Kenny Rollins drove a nail to mark the spot.

Defending national champion Holy Cross entered the NCAA Eastern playoffs on a nineteen-game winning streak. Their leader, sophomore guard Bob Cousy, had scored twenty-three points in a 63-45 win over Michigan and had mystified the Wolverines with his dribbling and passing. Crusaders fans festooned the Garden with banners. Hanging from the balcony was a bedsheet on which was painted: "COUSY—THE GREAT-EST." Another sign billed him as "Best Player in the World." "We'll see about that," Rupp said, turning to Rollins. "Kenny, he's your man."

"We studied his moves and Barnstable and I talked about what we would try to do," Rollins recalled. "We never knew which way he would go." They decided to keep him in the center of the floor because he did most of his shooting from the sides. Rollins shut down Cousy, who scored only three points, all on free throws, before Dale Barnstable relieved Rollins. Groza scored twenty-three points, and the Wildcats won 60-52. Someone brought Rollins the sheet proclaiming Cousy the greatest.

Baylor was Kentucky's unlikely opponent in the NCAA final, having rallied from seventeen points down to beat Washington and then come from behind again to beat Kansas State. The Bears' center, 6-foot-3 Don Heathington, was no match for Groza, and they had no forward as big and strong as Jones. Five minutes elapsed before the Bears scored their first point. Kentucky led 7-0, 13-1 and 24-7 on the way to a sixteen-point triumph.

Rupp called that squad the greatest team ever assembled in college sports. He locked the dressing room door, hung up his coat, and told them, "You've done everything you've been asked to do. You won your own SEC tournament, and you won the NCAA championship. You've kept training and made many sacrifices, and I thank you from the bottom of my heart." There were tears in his eyes. He turned to Groza, who had scored thirty-three points: "You undoubtedly played the great-est game at center that has ever been seen in the Garden."

It was an Olympic year, and the Trials were to start the following week in the Garden. The eight-team field included college and AAU squads. More than eighteen thousand fans saw the championship game, as the Phillips Oilers, led by 7-foot Bob Kurland, finally stopped Rupp's rampaging Wildcats 53-49. Beard scored twenty-three points, but Kurland held Groza to one field goal, and Barker received a broken nose midway through the first half. The five starters from each of the finalists made the Olympic team, along with four other players. Coach of the winning team would be the head coach, and the losing coach would be his associate. Rupp was not eager to play second fiddle to Bud Browning, but he had to live with it.

When the Wildcats returned home, an estimated fifteen thousand fans met them at Blue Grass Field, parading the team through town on fire trucks while Rupp rode in the back seat of an open convertible driven by the mayor. Banners proclaimed Kentucky the greatest collegiate basketball champion of all time. Most schools in the area dismissed classes for the occasion. Warner Brothers' *Pathe News* recorded the festivities. Phog Allen spoke at a victory banquet sponsored by six local luncheon clubs. The Kansas coach praised his former student and the Wildcats for an outstanding season. He also warned that gamblers throughout the country sought to control the outcome of basketball and football games. Allen said colleges and their conferences should do more to protect their athletes from those leeches. Rupp seemed unconcerned; after all, his boys were champions and could do no wrong.

That summer Kentucky and the Oilers played three exhibition games to raise money for the Olympics Fund. In the first, Don Barksdale led the Oilers to a 60-52 victory before six thousand fans at Fairgrounds Pavilion in Tulsa. In the second, the Wildcats were trailing by one point with time running out during the second overtime. Rupp told Holland and Rollins to double-team the ball. Rollins batted the ball into the hands of Holland, who scored a layup that won the game for Kentucky 70-69. Phog Allen rushed onto the floor and grabbed a microphone. "The Kentucky boys fought their hearts out," he said, "and I never saw a greater exhibition of basketball in my life." The third exhibition game was held in Lexington, on a temporary floor constructed over the football field, fulfilling Rupp's longtime dream of basketball in an outdoor arena. Fourteen thousand spectators saw the Oilers beat the Wildcats 56-50. Net proceeds from the game were $25,000, and in addition, Wildcat fans had contributed enough money to send Barnstable, Holland, and Line—three Wildcats who had played as much that year as some of the starters—to the Games in London.

After the flight to London, the U.S. basketball players stayed at a Royal Air Force camp in Uxbridge. They toured Scotland by bus, visiting six Scottish cities and playing exhibition games wherever they could find a court. Edinburgh had the only wooden floor they saw on the trip. More than twelve thousand Scots cheered them as they played in the open air arena at Princess Park.

Mr. and Mrs. Earl Ruby were among those accompanying the Americans. Earl was sports editor of the *Courier-Journal* from 1938 until 1968. At age 90 in 1994, he still had fond memories of Rupp and Scotland. As the head coach, Bud Browning was supposed to do the talking, Ruby said, but somehow Rupp got the job. At every stop, the lord mayor would make a flowery speech and give mementos to the visitors. Rupp would reply in kind, extolling the virtues of Scotland and its people.

"With that twang in his voice, Adolph was uproarious," Ruby said. "Half of them laughed with them, half laughed at him." Once during a high tea in Edinburgh, Rupp ran out of mementos. He dug into his luggage and found a key with a thermometer on it. "Adolph told of the wonderful treatment he and his boys received in the small towns, the ancient inns, and the metropolis of Edinburgh," Ruby said. The lord mayor cried.

Throughout the trip, the Oilers made fun of the Wildcats and the respect they had for Rupp. When boarding the bus, the Oilers would line up and wait for Rupp. Then they would goose him up and down the aisle as he looked for a seat. It horrified the Kentucky boys, Earl Ruby said, but soon everybody, even Rupp, was laughing.

London cared little for basketball, and Harringay Arena was almost empty for most of the games. Ralph Beard said the opponents were no better than a good YMCA team back home—except for Argentina, which led the Americans by seven points at halftime. Browning and Rupp put in a new "unit" system for that game, starting Wildcats Groza, Jones, and Rollins, along with Ray Lumpp of NYU and Vince Boryla of the Denver Nuggets. They were ahead 14-3 when Browning sent in the second unit—Oilers Gordon Carpenter, Lew Beck, and R. C. Pitts, plus Don Barksdale of the Oakland Bittners and Jack Robinson of Baylor. That group passed the ball wildly and played porous defense. Returning for the second half, the starters tied the score at 37-37, and it was 55-55 with three minutes to play. Rollins and Carpenter sandwiched free throws around a layup by Robinson, and the U.S. team prevailed despite a long Argentine buzzer beater. That was one of the few times in Rupp's career that he had failed to scout an upcoming opponent. He would make that mistake again seven years later.

Mixing players from the AAU and college ranks failed in Scotland, and it failed again when the coaches tried it in the first three games of Olympic competition. But when they settled on one unit from each division, alternating the fives to keep everybody happy, the Americans breezed through the remaining games. The United States defeated France 65-21 in the gold medal game. When the basketball champions received their Olympic medals in Wembley Stadium, it was the proudest moment of Rupp's life.

Chapter
Twelve

Shaving Glory

As the 1948-49 season got under way, Rupp was on top of the basketball world. He seemed to have conquered all. Hints of an early retirement to the contrary, there was no way would he leave that bunch of good boys to someone else. The Fabulous Four—Barker, Beard, Groza, and Jones—were stars who could survive the loss of their Fifth, Kenny Rollins, who had joined the Chicago Stags. Rupp had seasoned Dale Barnstable to replace Rollins, and John Stough would also see much action at that position.

True, there had been some defections. Al Cummins, dissatisfied with sitting on the bench of the "best team in the country," had transferred to Michigan State, and Joe B. Hall moved on to Sewanee to play for Rupp's friend Lon Varnell. But the Wildcats were still deep, with forwards Walt Hirsch and Jim Line providing firepower as Rupp's top reserves. Rupp had also picked up some help from the UK football team—Al Bruno, a 6-foot-3 sophomore end. After seeing Bruno play for the championship intramural basketball team, Lancaster had asked him to join the varsity.

"All I want you to do is bang on the big boys," Rupp instructed the gridder. "I want you to get tough on Alex." Some assignment. Bruno recalled years later, "Groza used to knock the hell out of me. He was four inches taller." Still, Bruno played well enough to make the cut for the postseason tournaments.

Rupp was popular in the Bluegrass State, but he was hated everywhere else in the South, as well as in the North, and— particularly after he'd alienated the New York reporters—in the East. If he had played more games in the West, they probably would have joined the club. He was "King of the Hill," and everybody was eager to knock him off the throne. When the Helms Athletic Foundation named him "Coach of the Year," he was asked the secret of his success. "That's easy," he said, making no attempt to feign modesty. "Good coaching."

The Wildcats won their first eight games, including one each in Boston and New York, where the cheers had turned to boos. At Boston Garden, Cliff Barker and Bob Cousy got into a shoving match that brought Rupp and Holy Cross coach Buster Sheary onto the floor. An official told them to get their behinds back on the bench. After Wah Jones fouled out with five minutes to go, boisterous Crusader fans kept daring him to turn around. When Jones finally did, the man hit him in the face with a wadded cigarette package. Jones grabbed the man by the shirt and punched him. The man's friend came roaring to the rescue, but Lancaster decked him. As the Wildcats walked off the floor 52-48 victors, they needed a police escort to their dressing room.

At Madison Square Garden, Kentucky held St. John's to nine field goals and defeated the Redmen 57-30. New York writers praised the Wildcats, but they ignored the gambling that went on throughout the game. Betting on the point spread had become a way of life in the Garden.

Sugar Bowl officials did themselves proud when they matched Kentucky and St. Louis, two of the best teams in the country. St. Louis, the defending NIT champion, had declined to play in the Olympic Trials or the match might have come about sooner. St. Louis' Ed Hickey taught a slow-down offense and tenacious defense. Sportswriters billed the game as a matchup of two of the best centers in the nation, Groza versus

"Easy" Ed Macauley, a 6-foot-9 All-American. Macauley had been Most Valuable Player in the NIT and Helms Player of the Year; Groza was MVP in the NCAA and the sportswriters' Player of the Year.

Groza, with thirteen points, and Macauley, with twelve, were an even match, but Lou Lehman scored seven points in the last five minutes to give St. Louis a 42-40 victory. Hickey called Wah Jones the best UK player and said the key to the Billikens' victory was the defensive work of Marv Schatzman, who held Jones to one field goal.

Looking over game statistics, Rupp was disappointed with Groza's point total. Neither Beard nor Barnstable had the playmaking ability of Kenny Rollins, and somebody had to get the ball to Groza more. Rupp moved the 6-foot-2 passing wizard Barker from forward to guard and switched Barnstable to the frontcourt. Kentucky went to a center-oriented offense, giving Groza more control of the game.

The Wildcats beat Bowling Green 63-61 in a game reporters called the greatest game ever played in Cleveland. Rupp was less enthusiastic. His boys had played poorly, but he was at a loss to understand why. (Note: some Wildcats later admitted shaving points in that game) His solution was to get his boys back to Lexington and work their butts off. The scrimmage sessions were brutal. With all that talent split between two teams, some of the best games in the nation were played in the afternoons at Alumni Gym, before a critical audience of one.

The narrow escape over Bowling Green sent the Wildcats on a twenty-one-game winning streak. In the last seconds of a game against Vanderbilt, with Kentucky winning by thirty-one points, Barker hit a shot from 63 feet, 7 1/2 inches, breaking Beard's short-lived Alumni Gym record.

The Wildcats were 29-1, ranked No. 1 in the country, and Rupp could see his chance to fulfill a long-standing goal: to be the first coach to win both the NIT and the NCAA tournament in the same season. Kentucky went into Chicago heavily favored to beat Loyola, which was 25-5. Loyola's center, Jack Kerris, was big and slow— what Harry Lancaster called a "mule" player: you could run him three miles a day for ten years, but you'd never win the Kentucky Derby with him. Groza figured to eat his lunch.

To everyone's surprise—or almost everyone's—Kerris not only outscored Groza 23-12, but he fouled him out in the process. Instead of trying to block Kerris' shots, Groza seemed to back away. Kerris fronted him on offense and Groza did not move enough for Barker and Beard to get the ball to him. Jones fouled out midway through the second half, and Groza and Hirsch soon followed suit. Beard scored only two points in the first half but came back to finish with fifteen. The Wildcats lost 67-56 in a stunning upset.

In analyzing the shocker, writers suggested that the Wildcats had held back and had let the game get away from them. Rupp had no clue and offered no excuse—his boys were flat, they hadn't hustled, and they hadn't fed Groza in the second half when Kerris was playing with four fouls. Asked whether he had given them those instructions, Rupp blurted, "Good Lord, didn't you hear the whole bench yelling at them?"

Rupp and Lancaster went to their room early, drank some bourbon, and tried to figure out what had gone wrong. Why wouldn't Groza move? Rupp kept asking. Why wouldn't he try to get open when they were all yelling at him? The answer would come two years later—a painful answer: some of the Wildcats were shaving points.

Rupp couldn't wait to get those boys back to Lexington. He would work their butts off. That solution had seemed to work after the St. Louis and Bowling Green games, but he was up against a tougher foe than he knew. Lancaster was closer to the players, but he, too, was blind. He later recalled that Rupp took them to the woodshed that week, practicing them tough and hard.

"I mean we really worked out," Lancaster said. "I showed no mercy." Nobody thought to lecture them about the evils of gambling, but it was too late for lectures anyway. Rupp benched Barnstable, replacing him with Line. The Wildcats were a determined bunch when they returned to New York for the NCAA tournament. Rupp had whipped them into shape physically, but he had lost some of them mentally.

First in Kentucky's path in the Eastern playoffs was Villanova, whose Paul Arizin had scored eighty-five points against Naval Air Material Center earlier in the season. Arizin scored thirty against Kentucky, and Groza matched that total despite sitting out most of the second half with foul trouble. The final score—85-72, Kentucky—set tournament marks for most points by one team and most by two teams. Kentucky passed brilliantly in a 76-47 second-round win over Illinois. Each of the seven players Rupp used had at least one assist—Jones had five—and sixteen of the Wildcats' thirty-one field goals were layups.

The championship game was in Seattle, at the University of Washington's Edmundson Pavilion. It was the first campus site for an NCAA title game since Northwestern played host to the first tournament final in 1939. Hank Iba's Oklahoma A&M Cowboys advanced to the championship by beating Wyoming 40-39 and Oregon State 55-30, and observers looked forward to the matchup of "Red Hot" Rupp and "Deep Freeze" Iba. But Rupp turned the tables on his friend: Kentucky slowed the game down to the Aggie pace and controlled it so artistically that A&M went without a field goal for a twelve-minute stretch.

Iba believed that Bob Harris, his 6-foot-7 center, could contain Groza, but the Wildcats doubted it. "Get the ball to Groza," Lancaster said. "Harris can't handle him." Hank was wrong; Harry was right. Jones would drive across the circle to lure Harris out, then pass to Groza breaking for the basket. Groza fouled out with five minutes to go after scoring twenty-five points. Harris fouled out with seven. The Wildcats stalled for a 46-36 victory. In winnng the tournament, the Wildcats set twenty-two NCAA team and individual records. MVP Groza scored eighty-two points. In his interrupted tenure at Kentucky, he had rewritten the SEC record book on scoring.

Wildcat Appreciation Day on April 4, 1949, was the biggest and noisiest celebration ever held in Lexington. Twenty-five thousand faithful fans turned out to cheer a thirty-seven-unit parade through an eight-block downtown area and then on to the campus. Main Street was a solid mass of humanity. Faces filled every store window. Rupp had used only seven players—the four seniors, Barnstable, Line, and Hirsch—in the Final Four games, and only those players won letters, slighting five others who made the tournament trips. The university retired the jersey numbers of Barker, Beard, Jones, Groza, and Rollins—the Fabulous Five.

For two years the 1949 seniors had been planning a barnstorming tour. Fans would pay for the privilege of seeing their heroes in action. Joined by Holland and Rollins, they called themselves the "Kentucky Olympians." The players asked J. R. "Babe" Kimbrough, sports editor of the *Herald*, to handle the business details of the exhibition tour. The tour drew overflow crowds throughout Kentucky and parts of West Virginia. No one had thought of including Rupp in the deal, and he seethed at reports of the tour's financial success.

While the players were barnstorming, teams in two professional basketball leagues courted their services. The four seniors and Holland decided to remain together as a unit, forming a National Basketball League entry called the Indianapolis Olympians, with Kimbrough as the general manager. The players owned all the common stock, and Indianapolis businessmen bought thirty shares of preferred stock at $1,000 a share. The Olympians named Barker, the oldest player, as their coach, making him the first man to step from a college classroom to the position of head coach of a major league basketball team. Barker had never coached any type of basketball team, but the players had confidence in his ability. They did not even consider asking Rupp. Rupp's friend Maurice Podoloff, president of the rival Basketball Association of America, offered Groza $16,000—$6,000 for signing and $10,000 for his first year's salary. Groza accepted the offer, but later returned the contract and the money. Rupp had lost another round.

That fall, the Kentucky football team won eight games and accepted an invitation to the Orange Bowl in Miami. The Sugar Bowl again invited Rupp to bring his Wildcats to New Orleans. Al Bruno, caught in the middle, made the mistake of telling a radio announcer that he liked basketball. Bryant put him on the spot.

"Al," he said, "I understand you like that roundball."

"I do, Coach," Bruno replied. "I like all sports, but right now football is my love."

"You'd better say that," Bryant said, "because there's no other way you're going to Florida." That ended Bruno's basketball career at Kentucky, and Rupp had lost another round.

The National Collegiate Athletic Bureau certified Kentucky as the nation's most successful major college in the combined 1949 basketball-football campaign, but four years earlier, a fault-finding firm declared that athletics at the school had become professional in nature. It advised governor Simeon Willis to put the UK sports program on an "amateur" basis. There was no way the governor could tackle the Bear and the Baron over such an issue. Both were more powerful than he— which just confirmed the auditors' suspicions.

Chapter
Thirteen

Wall of Shame

T he departure of the Fabulous Four brought joy to the college basketball world. Other teams suddenly wanted to play Kentucky, but Rupp ignored those who had ignored him. The Southeastern Conference had adopted a fourteen-game league schedule, leaving only twelve available nonconference games.

The lone returning starter was Dale Barnstable, who would move back to guard. Seasoned reserves Jim Line and Walt Hirsch could handle the forward positions. Rupp expected sophomore Bill Spivey, his first 7-footer, to play the pivot. Several hopefuls from Harry Lancaster's undefeated freshman team would fill in the gaps, along with a couple of junior college transfers who would be eligible the second semester.

Spivey came to Kentucky from Warner Robins, Georgia, where his father was a civil service worker at nearby Fort Benning. The gym was a USO building that was also the site of dances and other functions. Spivey was a junior in high school before he knew it was possible to earn a college scholarship by playing basketball. That was the spark he needed: he averaged twenty-two points as a junior and twenty-nine as a senior. Rupp invited the boy to a tryout after reading about him in an *Atlanta Journal* article written by Ed Danforth, a UK alumnus.

The 6-foot-10 1/2 Spivey weighed only 165 pounds, and had a limited range of shots. Rupp was impressed by his height but put off by his lack of coordination. The baron gave him a scholarship because he was tall and managed to dribble the length of the floor. Rupp also chose Guy Strong, Bobby Watson, and C. M. Newton from that 1948 tryout. He rejected Mark Workman because of his attitude. Workman would become an All-American and one of the nation's leading scorers at West Virginia.

That summer Rupp enrolled Spivey at Kentucky, found him a job at a drugstore, and set about trying to put some meat on his bones. One of Spivey's duties at the store was changing bulbs in the ceiling lights, and Rupp would tell everybody the boy did it without a ladder. The coach set Spivey up with free passes to a theater across from the drugstore, but there was a catch: whenever he went to a movie, he had to stop first at the drug store, drink a milk shake, and get his theater ticket signed. He carried two trays through the UK cafeteria line at each meal. The skinny kid was eating three or four orders of mashed potatoes and drinking four quarts of milk a day.

Spivey practiced with the Olympians when they trained for the exhibition game on Stoll Field. Vince Boryla showed him how to shoot a hook shot, and Groza taught him head fakes. Spivey later called Groza the cleverest pivot man he ever saw. When Rupp and the Olympians left for England, Lancaster took charge of Spivey. At the train station Rupp noticed that Spivey was five inches taller but only half as broad as Groza. "Harry, put some meat on that boy's bones," he said. "I don't care if you force feed him."

Every afternoon, Lancaster worked with Spivey and Whitey Pearson in Alumni Gym, working their butts off in that sweat shop for two or three hours. Spivey learned to pass, dribble, fake, slide back to the basket, and shoot a hook shot. Each week, Lancaster wired Rupp a progress and weight report on Spivey. When he reported that Spivey's weight had reached 185 pounds, Rupp wired back, "I know Spivey can eat, but can he play basketball?"

As the 1949-50 season opened, the only position open was a guard spot opposite Barnstable. At times Rupp started Strong, Len Pearson, or Lucian "Skippy" Whitaker, but in the end, he would finally settle on Watson, who had been a cab ride away from playing for Alabama. Although Watson had made the *Courier-Journal* All-State team, Rupp had doubts that the 5-foot-10 guard could help Kentucky. Lancaster invited him to the tryout, but the Crimson Tide offered him a scholarship, so he boarded a train for Tuscaloosa. When no one was there to meet him and he had difficulty getting directions, he got back on a train for Lexington. By the second semester, Watson had earned his scholarship and was captain of the freshman team.

Kentucky opened with a 84-61 win over Indiana Central, as Jim Line scored thirty-seven points. After he fouled out with two minutes remaining, he received a five-minute standing ovation. The Wildcats took a 4-1 record south for the Sugar Bowl, beating Villanova 57-56 in overtime to move into the title game against Bradley. The Braves, with Bill Mann, Paul Unruh, and Gene Melchiorre, had lost to Kentucky's 1949 national champions by only ten points the preceding year. Spivey scored twenty-two points, Line nineteen, and Whitaker thirteen to lead the Wildcats to a 71-66 victory. Rupp told them, "Boys, I'm proud of you. You've won the Sugar Bowl, something the Fabulous Five never did. We've been riding around since before Christmas with a bunch of kids in diapers and winning games."

At Knoxville, Tennessee snapped a seven-game UK winning streak when Art Burrus outscored Spivey 28-12. The Wildcats lost at Georgia on January 17 and at Notre Dame on January 19. Then they won eleven consecutive games, closing the Alumni Gym era with a 70-66 win over Vanderbilt. During the streak, Spivey scored forty points against Georgia Tech, breaking Groza's SEC record of thirty- eight. In that last game in Alumni Gym, the Wildcats trailed Vanderbilt by twelve points at halftime before Rupp cajoled them into a better effort.

"Boys," he said, "a man spends a lifetime compiling a record, and in one given night a group of bums like you are about to tear it down. If it looks like we're going to go down in defeat tonight, I want you to know that I am personally going to do something to this facility before the game is over and before you get out of this gym." They got the message—and Kentucky's eighty-fourth consecutive victory on the home floor, a national record. The Wildcats left Alumni Gym for Memorial Coliseum with a record of 262-25 in the old arena.

Spivey scored thirty-seven points in a 95-58 romp over Tennessee in the championship game of the SEC tournament. Although he broke Groza's single-game tournament scoring record, he placed second to Burrus on the all-tournament team. Rupp's stubbornness prevented the Wildcats from competing for their third straight NCAA championship. The District 3 selection committee, chaired by Art Tebell of Virginia, wanted a playoff between Kentucky, 25-4, and North Carolina State, 24-5, for the district's tournament slot. The Baron pointed out that Kentucky was fourth in the most recent Associated Press poll, compared with N. C. State's ninth. The Wildcats had defeated No. 1 Bradley and Villanova in the Sugar Bowl, and Villanova had beaten N.C. State on the Wolfpack's floor.

"North Carolina State agreed to play Kentucky anyplace, anytime," Tebell said, in explaining why N.C. State was given the berth, "but Kentucky declined and asked to be selected outright." Rupp felt the defending national champions deserved that right. The negative publicity directed at the NCAA over the Kentucky snub would help bring about a new format in the tournament in 1951. The field would double to sixteen teams, with two representatives from each district.

Kentucky accepted a bid to the NIT, and Rupp promptly predicted that his boys would win the tournament. His sophomore crop was better than the Fabulous Five at that stage, he said, and Bill Spivey would be better than Alex Groza. Gambling had become so prevalent at Madison Square Garden that some coaches refused to let their teams play there, but Rupp said that was "poppycock." He loved the big city, and so did his boys. They were always under his wing. He would vouch for them.

The Wildcats drew City College of New York in the opening round. CCNY, 17-5 and unranked, featured a look the

Wildcats weren't used to seeing: four black starters. The flu bug hit the Wildcats the minute they arrived in New York. Spivey was too sick to start, though he came off the bench to score fifteen points. With Ed Warner scoring twenty-six points, CCNY beat the Wildcats 89-50, the worst defeat of Rupp's career. CCNY coach Nat Holman said Rupp congratulated the winners in a gracious manner, but the Baron was anything but gracious in the Wildcat locker room. "I want to thank you boys," he said. "You get me selected Coach of the Year (by the New York Writers Association) and then bring me up here and embarrass the hell out of me."

During that summer, Rupp sent Spivey and some of his teammates to the Catskill Mountains to work in the resorts and play basketball. A gambler who called himself George— later identified as Eli Kay—took Spivey aside and offered him $500 to miss a few free throws when the proper time arrived. "George" told the UK center that some former and current UK players had been shaving points for years. Spivey mentioned the incident to his girlfriend, who was a singer at the hotel. She told him to avoid the gamblers— those guys played rough, she said. Shortly before the 1950-51 season, Kay came to Spivey's room in Lexington. Spivey claims that he ran Kay off, then asked Walt Hirsch whether he knew the man. Walt's face flushed. Kay would later tell New York authorities that he had involved Spivey in fixing games.

Still, Rupp couldn't see the gambling clouds on the horizon— all he could see were future All-Americans Frank Ramsey of Madisonville and Cliff Hagan of Owensboro. Hirsh, Shelby Linville, Spivey, Watson, and Ramsey were the starters; Hagan would play on the freshman team until becoming eligible for the varsity at the semester break. More than eight thousand fans attended the opening game in the new Memorial Coliseum. The sacrificial lamb was West Texas State. Kentucky won by thirty points. A week later, Purdue came to town to help dedicate the facility. This time eleven thousand were on hand and the Wildcats won by eighteen. They were 4-0 when Kansas came to town on December 16.

There was not an empty seat. Fans stood in the walkways, jammed the aisles, and sat on the floor. It was a battle for the No. 1 national ranking in the nation. It was a faceoff between Spivey and Clyde Lovellette, the two best centers in the nation. And to Rupp, it was a private battle. For the first time, he would go head-to-head with his old coach, Phog Allen, the winningest coach in the country—and he was nervous. That evening, Rupp held a gathering at his house. He and Allen did most of the talking. After watching the two of them, Lancaster understood where Adolph had gotten most of his mannerisms. It was one of the few times he ever saw Adolph intimidated by anybody.

I had a similar experience with Rupp in the summer of 1970. We were in Lawrence, where he was to receive an alumni award, and Dr. Allen was recovering from a stroke. Although he was an invalid, he was still a dominating figure. I had never seen Adolph so humble. I didn't know he could even be humble.

Rupp sent Lancaster to scout Kansas games in New York and Philadelphia. Lancaster noticed that Lovellette would spread himself out and play with his elbows wide, making it difficult for the defensive center to do anything until Lovellette had the ball. He thought Spivey was quick enough to step around to the side of Lovellette and swat the pass away. He returned to Kentucky with newspaper clippings praising Lovellette. The coaches would paste some clippings on Spivey's locker, and Spivey would tear them down. The next day, a fresh batch would be there.

"I kept ripping them off and looking forward to the game," Spivey recalled. "When time finally came, I felt as they had opened the cage door and let me out." During the game, Spivey slapped away eleven passes meant for Lovellette. He brought down the house when he picked up one of those deflections, dribbled the length of the floor, and dunked. That was the first time many of the twelve thousand-plus fans had ever seen a dunk. Thanks to Lancaster's scouting report, Spivey knew where Lovellette was going, and he made sure of being there first. Spivey outscored Lovellette 22-10 and fouled the Kansas center out with 13:33 to go. There were tears in the big guy's eyes. For the sake of comparison, Rupp removed Spivey from the game at the same time. He could afford to: the Wildcats were in control, en route to a 68-39 victory.

Kentucky had won six games in a row before falling to St. Louis again in the Sugar Bowl. They were leading the Billikens by two with twenty seconds to go when Hirsch threw the ball away, and St. Louis scored to send the game into overtime. Spivey hit a free throw and Hirsch missed two in the overtime. Ray Sonnerberg's field goal won it for the Billikens 43-42. Some gamblers claimed the game was so obviously suspicious that they could not get a bet down.

The Wildcats reeled off twenty-one straight victories, closing the season with a thirty-two-point win over Vanderbilt. They lost to the Commodores in the championship game of the SEC tournament, but under the new setup, the regular-season conference champion went to the NCAA tournament automatically, and Kentucky met Louisville in the opening round of the Eastern Regional at Raleigh, North Carolina.

Rupp had developed severe pain and swelling in his right leg, which required first a cast from the hip to below the knee, then a laced leather stocking. An eye ailment had also flared up. Rupp was having so many health problems that some thought he would retire if his boys won the championship. Lancaster was skeptical; he had heard that talk many times.

Hirsch was ineligible for the tournament because he was in his fourth season of varsity play, so Hagan took his place. Midway through the second half Kentucky trailed Louisville 64-60, but they rallied for a 79-68 victory. In the Eastern final at Madison Square Garden, Illinois pushed Kentucky to the limit, but C. M. Newton got a crucial steal that set up Shelby Linville for the winning goal with twelve seconds left, and the Wildcats prevailed 76-74. Spivey scored twenty-eight points and grabbed sixteen rebounds.

Kentucky advanced to the championship game against Kansas State, which had beaten Oklahoma A&M 68-44 in the semifinals. Rupp's friend Hank Iba told him that Kansas State was the best team he had seen all year. On the day of the game, Cliff Hagan was ill, and so was Rupp; both were on the bench, but Lancaster was running the team.

When Kansas State got a six-point lead, Rupp told the team doctor, "Hell, Hagan's the right temperature to play." Almost immediately, Hagan tipped in a missed shot and Kentucky began asserting itself under the basket. The Wildcats were down two points at halftime. Rupp told Hagan he was going to start the second half. Cliff reminded Rupp of that young wrestler back at Marshalltown. Hagan finished with ten points—Kentucky's margin of victory in a 68-58 final. Spivey finished with twenty-two points and twenty-one rebounds. Kentucky became the first school to win three NCAA championships.

"He convinced us we could do things we didn't know we could do," Frank Ramsey remembered. "We were just cogs in the wheel. We were country boys, impressed with what we read about other players and teams. He made us believe we were as good as anyone. He told us what he wanted done, and we did it."

In August, the Wildcats played a series of six exhibition games in Puerto Rico. The only unpleasant incident occurred when Rupp accused the Puerto Rican all-stars of dirty play and threatened to cancel the game scheduled for the next day. Coach Victor Perez said Rupp was the first American coach to criticize his team's sportsmanship. Three decades later, another American coaching legend would have an unpleasant experience in Puerto Rico, when Indiana University's Bob Knight was accused of assault.

The first hint of corruption in college basketball came in 1945, when Brooklyn College expelled five players who confessed to taking bribes to lose a game. The next revelation came in 1951, when Manhattan College star Julius Kellogg admitted that he had accepted money to control the point spread in a game. By the end of that year, authorities would disclose that between 1947 and 1950 gamblers had fixed at least eighty-six games in thirty-three cities and seventeen states. They named thirty-three players involved in the bribes and said there were more to follow.

During an appearance in Lincoln, Nebraska, Rupp told a reporter that gamblers could not touch his boys with a ten-foot pole. The Wildcats were under "constant and absolutely complete supervision while on the road." He said that they were watched particularly closely when in New York. But newspapers in Chicago and New York hinted that an investigation of UK players was under way. Arch Ward wrote in the Chicago *Tribune*, "The simmering University of Kentucky basketball scandal will hit the sports pages soon." Vincent O'Connor, the New York district attorney, said Rupp might have to eat his words.

In a Chicago speech, Rupp urged leniency for the players involved in the fix scandal. It was unfair to put the basketball players in the same category as the 1919 Chicago White Sox, who lost the World Series to the Cincinnati Reds.

"The Black Sox threw games," he said. "These kids shaved points. There's a difference. Why forever condemn a boy for his one mistake of a lifetime?" Rupp was in town to coach the College All-Stars against the Rochester Royals. Sitting in the stands were several of Rupp's former players, now members of Indianapolis Olympians. They were en route to Moline, Illinois, for an exhibition game. Investigators from the Illinois State attorney's office picked up Ralph Beard and Alex Groza outside the stadium after the all-star game. Kentucky authorities accosted Dale Barnstable away from his home in Louisville.

They turned the players over to New York authorities, who eventually charged them with involvement in Kentucky's 67-56 loss to Loyola in the 1949 NIT. The players admitted conspiring to undercut the point spread, thus enabling the gamblers who arranged the fix to win money. On April 30, 1952, they were placed on indefinite probation. Lon Varnell, the Sewanee coach, was sharing a room with Rupp in Chicago, and it fell to him to break the news to the Baron. Rupp was attending a wedding anniversary dinner when he called to tell Varnell that he'd be late.

"Adolph, I have some bad news for you," Varnell said. "You should come over to the hotel as soon as you can." Rupp could not believe the news. He had Varnell call the newspapers and radio stations to confirm the story. Varnell assured him it was true—and that it might turn out even worse than it seemed. "Oh, my God!" Rupp said. Then he stretched out on the bed and sobbed.

The first thing that went through Harry Lancaster's mind when he heard the news was "that terrible game against Loyola." When Rupp arrived home the next morning, the two sat down and talked. At first, they agreed that the charge must be untrue. Rupp brought up the Loyola game, and then they thought about the two one-point losses to St. Louis in New Orleans. The pieces began to fit. Weeks later, Beard and Groza came to see their old coaches. They echoed Rupp's defense in the Chicago speech: they hadn't thrown games, they had just tried to go above or below the point spread. Rupp was the sympathetic father at first, but not for long. The net soon trapped thirty-one players from seven schools who had conspired with the gamblers.

Attorneys for some other former UK players said that they had violated no laws and refused to let New York investigators interview their clients. Spivey withdrew his name from the team's eligibility list. Later, he testified before a New York grand jury, as did Hirsch and Line. Spivey didn't want to get his buddies in trouble, but his testimony differed from that of his former teammates. He insisted that his only error was in not reporting Kay's bribery offer to the authorities. Hirsch, Barnstable, and Line admitted to a New York grand jury that they accepted bribes to shave the points in two games, against DePaul on December 31, 1949, in Louisville, and against Arkansas on January 2, 1950, in Little Rock. They were not brought to trial because the games involved were out of the New York court's jurisdiction. Neither Kentucky nor Arkansas had laws against bribery in connection with sporting events.

Later Spivey stood trial in New York on a perjury charge. The jury voted 9-3 in favor of acquittal. Spivey had passed a lie detector test, but his basketball career at Kentucky was over. When he signed a contract with the Cincinnati Royals, other teams in the league objected, demanding that his name be in a hat to give every team a chance at him. Ultimately, Spivey never played in the NBA. He claimed that his accusers from New York cost him two or three million dollars.

When he was counting on Spivey, Rupp predicted that his Wildcats would be his best team, better even than the Fabulous Five. The 1950-51 squad had no catchy nickname, but even without Spivey, Kentucky went 32-2 and won SEC and NCAA titles. The 6-foot-4 Hagan played the pivot, 6-5 Shelby Linville and 6-6 Lou Tsioropoulos were the forwards, and 6-3 Frank Ramsey and 5-10 Bobby Watson were the guards. Billy Evans drew some starts at Linville's forward position, and Skippy Whitaker was a valuable swing man. The only losses in the regular season were by four points at Minnesota and by one to St. Louis in the Sugar Bowl championship. Ed Kalafat, a husky center, scored thirty points for Minnesota, and Hagan and Ramsey got into foul trouble. Against the Billikens, Bobby Watson lost the ball to Pat Partington in the closing seconds. Partington shot and missed, but substitute Tom Lillis tipped it in. Rupp told Watson that fans would always remember him as the boy who lost the Sugar Bowl.

In between the losses, Kentucky handed visiting St. John's its worst loss in 43 years of basketball, 81-40. Some UK fans had threatened to boycott the game if a black player appeared in the Coliseum, but Solly Walker, St. John's fine black player, got the warmest ovation of any of the Redmen.

The Wildcats won twenty-three straight games after the loss to St. Louis, and in the finals of the SEC tournament, Kentucky squeezed by LSU 44-43. Bob Pettit outscored Hagan 25-19, but Tsioropoulos made the winning layup with 1:43 remaining. The Wildcats easily defeated Penn State 82-54 in the Eastern Regional at Raleigh. They expected to do the same to St. John's, but Bob Zawoluk had other ideas. The 6-foot-7 center scored thirty-two points, and Jack McMahon added eighteen for the Redmen. Hagan scored twenty-two points, but he, Evans, and Tsioropoulos fouled out. With St. John's leading by six at halftime, shouts from the adjoining locker room interrupted coach Frank McGuire's instructions to his team. "I thought the walls were coming down," he said. "I never did give my halftime talk; we just listened to Rupp screaming at his players." St. John's won the game, 64-57.

After the season, there was still some untidy business to finish. Judge Saul Streit dealt suspended sentences to Barnstable, Beard, and Groza, then blasted Rupp and the University of Kentucky. He devoted eighteen pages of his scorching sixty-three-page statement to the UK coach. Among other things, the judge accused Rupp of aiding and abetting in the immoral subsidization of players. He said Rupp "failed in his duty to observe the amateur rules, to build character, and to protect the morals and health of his charges." The judge questioned Rupp's relationship with Ed Curd, Lexington's undisputed king of bookmakers. The Senate Crime Committee listed Curd's name at least twice in its investigation as the city's betting commissioner. Rupp admitted to the court that he knew Curd and had visited his home to solicit donations to the Shriners Hospital for Crippled Children. The Baron also knew that Curd operated a bookmaking establishment, but Rupp had not been in it. Gambling was not one of Rupp's passions. Curd on at least two occasions joined Rupp and others at meals in New York's Copacabana night club, but Rupp denied allegations by some of the players that he frequently called Curd to learn the point spread on UK games.

At first, Rupp had been sympathetic to Barnstable, Beard, and Groza, but their allegations changed all that. He "unretired" the numbers of Beard and Groza, and their All-American pictures on the Coliseum "Wall of Fame" disappeared one night. So did a big picture of the Fabulous Five and the All-SEC pictures of Jim Line and Walt Hirsch. It would take twenty years for Rupp to admit again that they had ever existed. Claude Hammond, a Wildcat football letterman, was president of the K-Men's Association in the mid-1970s. He and I convinced Lancaster and Rupp that those pictures belonged back on the wall. We quietly put them there. Barnstable and Beard made peace with the Baron. Lancaster said Groza never did.

It became evident that dismissal of Rupp would spare the school punishment by the SEC and the NCAA. Dr. Herman Lee Donovan stood by his friend Rupp, whom he called "an honorable man who did not knowingly violate the athletic rules." He believed Rupp's woes were due in part to his status as the best basketball coach in the country. In a surprise move, the Southeastern Conference barred the Wildcats from basketball competition for one year; three months later, the NCAA followed suit. At the time, it was the harshest penalty ever given a college sports program. Tennessee was the only school that voted in Kentucky's favor, and Rupp would never forget that. He also would never forgive Tulane and his former friend Cliff Wells, who was their basketball coach. Rupp said he would not retire until the people who said Kentucky could not play in the NCAA handed him the national championship trophy.

"Harry, by Gawd, we're going to make those bastards pay next year," Rupp told Lancaster. "By Gawd, we did," Harry wrote in his book.

Chapter Fourteen

Unbearable Pair

Paul "Bear" Bryant was the most successful coach in UK football history. His teams went 60-23-5 between 1946 and 1953, appearing in five bowl games and losing only one. Bryant's resignation was a shock to Kentucky, to its fans, and to the school's football-hating basketball coach. Rupp felt he had lost a good friend. He said Bryant left because he could not get Bernie Shively's job as athletic director, but Bryant would later say that the crux of the matter was a clash of objectives with Rupp. He was jealous of the prominence of Rupp and Kentucky basketball. If Rupp was going to stay, Bryant was going to go—it was that simple.

Rupp and Bryant were too much alike. Each wanted his sport to be No. 1. Bryant said you either liked Rupp or you hated him. "There was no middle ground. He had that abrasive way of talking and dealing with people, and if you didn't like it, you didn't like him." Their offices were side by side in Alumni Gym. Bryant heard Rupp tell his players, "By Gawd, you just walked into the 'pearly gates' of basketball." He would give them his speech about how good his program was, and

Bryant knew it was true. Bryant heard Rupp give that spiel to Forrest Tucker, a basketball player who later became an actor and a friend of Bryant's. "Only trouble is, son, you're just too damned short," Rupp told him. "I don't think we'll be able to use you around here." Rupp gave him a dollar and told him to get something to eat and catch a bus home.

In the *Bear Bryant Story*, Bryant tells of the time a faculty group was investigating the athletic department. They talked to him and the other coaches about finances and budgets, but when they got to Rupp, he gave them no opportunity to question him.

"By gawd, come on in here, I've been waiting for you bastards," he said. "I want to know what the hell happened to my basketball player over there in your English class. You expect me to take these pine knots and make All-Americans out of them, and I send you a B student and he's making a goddamn D!" Rupp knew well that a good offense is the best defense. The investigators got out of his office. Bryant made sure his office was on the other end of the hall from Rupp's when they moved into the new stadium. He wanted to be away from all the Baron's traffic.

Ruth Shively said there was constant tension between the two coaching giants. "They hated each other," she said, "only Bryant was more subtle. Each was afraid one would make a nickel more than the other. Bernie had to bear down on them all the time to keep the peace. They would go out in public, put their arms around each other, and pretend they were the best of buddies. Either would do his best to stick a knife in the other's ribs. It was no joy living with them. They took ten years off my husband's life." (Shively was sixty-four when he died in December 1967). Ruth had her prejudices.

C. M. Newton, named UK director of athletics in 1990, is in a good position to compare the two men. He played on Rupp's 1951 NCAA championship team and coached basketball at Alabama for Bryant in 1969. Interviewed in October 1993, Newton said that both coaches cared about their players, but they had a different way of showing it. Bryant was outgoing, while Rupp had a hard time expressing his feelings. Bryant worked to build loyalty; Rupp expected it. Bryant could practically kill his boys on the practice field and they would take up for him. Let Rupp do the same thing, and his players would bitch and moan. Say something about Bryant, and the football players would challenge you in a minute. That wasn't true of Rupp's players.

According to Newton, Bryant always took the blame for his losses, saying he hadn't prepare his players properly. Rupp was never at fault; if Johnny didn't guard his man, he heard about it, and so did fans tuned to Rupp's postgame radio shows. Bryant might feel the same, but he would not say so publicly. Rupp guarded his players jealously, trying to keep them away from Bryant. Wah Jones, who starred in basketball, baseball, and football, said it was OK with Bryant for him to play basketball, but he got the feeling that Rupp did not want him to play football. The Baron kept quiet, though, because of pressure from the football fans. After Wah Jones, no UK athlete with a basketball scholarship ever played football.

During the 1951 Sugar Bowl, Rupp and Bryant looked like best buddies. Bryant sat on Rupp's bench during Kentucky's 43-42 loss to St. Louis, and Rupp sat on Bryant's bench during the UK-Oklahoma game. That morning Rupp picked up Bryant in his hotel room and accompanied the team to the stadium, even listening in on the pregame talk. The Sooners were national champions and had won thirty-one games in a row, but Kentucky beat them 13-6 in one of football's biggest upsets. After the game, Rupp escorted Bryant through the mob. He hailed a taxi while Bryant waited in the locker room, and they had a drink together at the hotel. Bryant invited Rupp to a party that night.

Football and basketball were riding so high that the city of Lexington named a street in their honor. A portion of Euclid Avenue between Stoll Field and Memorial Coliseum became Avenue of Champions. Bryant and Rupp were all smiles at the ceremony dedicating the strip of concrete. That was only a few weeks before the investigators from New York would come to town.

The basketball scandal cast a shadow on all UK sports and caught two of Bryant's players in the backwash. Gene Donaldson was a guard with All-America potential, but the point shavers testified that a local architect had hired him for work he did not do. A merchant gave Chet Lukawski clothing. Both players had accepted gift certificates and bonuses from local merchants. The SEC suspended the pair and fined the university $500 for each violation. Brooklyn boy Nick Englisis brought down more scandal. Englisis had met Ralph Beard when both were on the UK football team. When Bryant became coach, Englisis quit football, eventually joining gambling forces in Brooklyn. The *Courier-Journal* published a picture of "The Greek" sitting on the UK bench during an SEC basketball game in Louisville. Rupp said he didn't remember Englisis' being there and claimed he didn't even know "The Greek."

Bryant, who already thought that basketball governed the university at the expense of football, felt that the basketball scandals kept many athletes from attending Kentucky. "Everywhere I went trying to sell the football program, it was 'basketball and Rupp, basketball and Rupp,'" he said, "I was jealous." Donovan hinted that Rupp would retire after the 1952 season, but when that didn't happen, Bryant tried to resign then and again before the 1953 season. He finally left for Texas A&M after his team finished 7-2-1 that year.

During his first year at A&M, Bryant lost nine games. The next summer, he and Rupp appeared at a clinic in Utah. Rupp got up and said—inaccurately—that Bryant had left Kentucky for a lot of money.

"You think he's down a little bit now, but I'll tell you, he *will* win," Rupp said. "He will win." Rupp predicted that within five or ten years, Bryant would be the top man. "Make no mistake about it," he said, "and don't forget 'Uncle Adolph' told you." He said opponents might as well "get your old buggies together and grease them up and go out and start recruiting, because he's gonna do it night and day and he's gonna beat you."

Bryant said he never appreciated Adolph until after he left Kentucky. When Bryant hired C. M. Newton as basketball coach, he recognized that Newton was in a position similar to what the Bear had faced with Rupp. Rupp claimed he never knew that Bryant was so jealous of basketball. "I was a professor at the university. There was no way for me to lose my job, and at the same time, I had no idea of resigning," he said in 1975. "My relationship with Paul was absolutely perfect."

After a year in exile, the Wildcats were back in the hunt, and they had their guns loaded. Led by the "Big Three"—Cliff

Hagan, Frank Ramsey and Lou Tsioropoulos—they were ready to give Rupp his first and only undefeated season. Their embittered coach would take no prisoners. There were rumors that he had installed a new scoreboard with room for three digits on the "home" side. It might have been a good idea, because the Wildcats would go over the century mark four times during the 1953-54 season.

During the year of banishment, the Wildcats practiced basketball every day. Far from letting up on a team that wouldn't get to take the floor for a year, Rupp acted like the Wildcats were preparing for an NCAA tournament. They ran the plays in their sleep. Three public scrimmages relieved the monotony. Those were among the best games in the nation, each played before a full house. Kentucky's seniors were bitter over being punished for things that happened while they were still in high school, and Rupp, well, he was just plain bitter.

All that changed on the night of December 5, 1953, when the Wildcats played Temple in the Coliseum. Lexington had a reason to live again. Thirteen thousand spectators—fifteen hundred of them standing—roared their approval, and Cliff Hagan gave them a night to remember beyond the UK's 86-59 victory. The 6-foot-4 center scored from all over the court, hooking shots in, batting them in, laying them in. When the smoke cleared, he had scored fifty-one points, one more than the previous SEC record, set by LSU's Bob Pettit against Georgia in 1952 and nine more than Hagan's own UK mark. Hagan had the best natural hands of any player Rupp ever coached. Rupp never appreciated his hook shot until Hagan hit four or five in a row against Temple. And whenever the Owls tried to zone him near the basket, Hagan scored from the outside.

Ramsey was a driver. In his book, Lancaster recalled a time Ramsey ran over somebody in practice. "Ramsey, by God," Rupp barked, "if the Maginot Line was in front of you and you had a basketball in your hands, you'd try to dribble through it. There must be some insanity in your family." The offhand remark hit close to home: Ramsey confided to Lancaster that he had an aunt with mental problems, and he asked Harry to tell Rupp that his comments hurt. "Hell, I knew it," Rupp said. "This just confirms my judgment." Rupp described Ramsey as "a big, powerful kid who would get the ball off the board and bring it down and ram the basket—an intelligent boy who developed every single day." The Boston Celtics, who drafted all of the Big Three, failed to get Ramsey to give up his final year of eligibility and join them, but he would later become the first great "sixth man" in pro basketball.

Tsioropoulos was an All-America high school football player who came to Kentucky in the fall of 1949. When the freshman basketball players began practice, he joined in on a lark. Paul Bryant came around a few days later looking for a football player. Bryant couldn't remember the name, but he asked Rupp if he'd seen a "big Greek kid with a prominent nose from Lynn, Massachusetts." After Bryant had left, Rupp called over the big kid with a big nose who knocked people around. He asked his name, and Lou pronounced and spelled it for him. Tsioropoulos never made it to the football side of the campus. Tsioropoulos was 6-foot-5, strong as an ox, and the team's best rebounder and defensive player. The way he rebounded reminded Harry Lancaster of Wah Jones, who left them black and blue.

The Big Three started every game that season. Rupp alternated the other positions between guards Gayle Rose and Linville Puckett and forwards Billy Evans and Phil Grawemeyer. The season's first rhubarb came at St. Louis, where the Wildcats sought revenge on a team that had edged them three times in the Sugar Bowl. (UK was shaving for at least one of those games) Rupp didn't like Ed Hickey, the successful Billiken coach, and before the game he told his players it was time to get even with "that little son of a bitch." When a St. Louis player fouled Tsioropoulos, the Wildcat pointed a finger at him. That brought the crowd to its feet, calling the visitor a "greasy Greek." Tsioropoulos fouled out with six minutes remaining in the game, and as the crowd roared, he held up his arm in a gesture of triumph and defiance. He had scored fifteen points and held St. Louis star Dick Boushka to ten, and the Wildcats had a comfortable lead.

The official timer for that game was Hickey's son, Pat, who was sitting next to Lancaster. He fired a blank cartridge to signify the end of each quarter. As the first quarter ended, Hickey placed the gun against Lancaster's right leg and fired. The wad from the blank hit Harry's leg, and it stung. Lancaster thought it was an accident, but he told young Hickey not to do it again. When Hickey told him to go to hell, Lancaster said he'd knock his ass off if it happened again. It happened again at halftime, and Lancaster slugged him. After the police restored order, they escorted Shively, Rupp, and Lancaster to the UK locker room. Shively persuaded them not to take Lancaster to jail, provided that he behaved during the second half. There was a new timekeeper for the second half. The Kentuckians were glad to get out of town with a 71-59 victory and no gunshot wounds.

In a move to capitalize on basketball's return, the university held its first invitational tournament that year. The four-team event was held while the students were home for the holidays. The other three participants were Duke, UCLA, and La Salle. Each visitor took home $10,000, making it the richest holiday classic in the nation. The Wildcats disposed of Duke 85-69 and defeated La Salle 73-60 in the championship game.

When Tulane came to campus, Kentucky was 10-0. Rupp posted newspaper clippings before the game that told how Tulane had voted to suspend the Wildcats. Pointing to Cliff Wells, he told his players, "He's on the floor now, the man that led the fight against you last year. For every blister, every bruise, every black eye, every tooth knocked out last year, that little runt of a coach owes you. Tonight, you pay them back for all of last year." The Wildcats defeated Tulane 94-43 and won the remaining thirteen games on their schedule.

Before the season there had been a hassle over where the Wildcats would play four of the required single conference games outside of their division. The season before its suspension Kentucky had gone to LSU, Mississippi, Mississippi State, and Tulane. Since UK did not play a schedule in 1952-53, Rupp thought those schools should come to Kentucky. The SEC schools voted in his favor, but LSU refused to play its game in Lexington, and the conference wouldn't force the issue. Georgia's Red Lawson agreed to an extra game with the Wildcats to help Kentucky fill its conference schedule. Kentucky beat the Bulldogs at Lexington 105-66 and at Owensboro 100-68.

Kentucky closed the regular season with a 68-43 victory over Alabama at Tuscaloosa. Before the game, Rupp said it was Kentucky's best team, but Tide coach Johnny Dee, the former Notre Dame player, accused Rupp of playing a patsy schedule and then calling Georgia names after Lawson had done him a favor. Dee compared Rupp's march through the South to taking a team of Canadians and forming a hockey league in Texas.

Rupp had every reason to believe his boys would give him a fourth national championship, but first they had to beat LSU in a playoff game in Nashville to decide the conference championship. The winner would get the league's NCAA bid. Then the NCAA dealt him another low blow: the Big Three were graduate students, and ineligible for tournament competition. He had little hope of winning an appeal, but they went ahead and played LSU just in case. On the afternoon of the game, Rupp was under a doctor's care at the hotel with heart problems. Bernie Shively brought him to the gym and supported him on the bench during the game. Kentucky was leading LSU by four points with six minutes to play when Rupp suffered more heart spasms, but he was determined to stick it out. Hagan and his future St. Louis Hawks teammate Bob Pettit fought to a standoff with seventeen points each. Late in the game, Billy Evans fouled out, and the UK cause seemed lost. But Frank Ramsey, who scored thirty points, came through in the end and the Wildcats won 63-56.

Rupp had his first undefeated season, but he was in danger of a deadly defeat. Shively helped him to the locker room, where the players voted 9-3 to accept the NCAA bid. The Big Three said no.

"I had hoped you would not vote to go and not to put this record in jeopardy," Rupp said. "If we can't play with our full team, we won't allow a group of turds to mar the record established in a large measure by our three seniors." They stayed home. Rupp had another mild heart attack in the taxi that took him back to the hotel. The world was closing in on him. He was glad to get back in bed. Hagan and Ramsey made All-America again that year, and the Helms Foundation gave Kentucky its final No.1 ranking, but without the Big Three, the House of Rupp seemed in danger of crumbling.

The Wildcats went 23-3 in 1954-55, but those three losses were significant. Kentucky was 7-0 and the top-ranked team in the nation when it played Georgia Tech in Lexington on January 8. The Wildcats had won 129 consecutive games at home, and UK fans were as confident as the players of No. 130.

There were three thousand empty seats in the Coliseum that night. John "Whack" Hyder's Yellow Jackets, young and unheralded, had just lost to lowly Sewanee. Rupp didn't even bother to scout them.

Some of the Tech players were familiar to Kentuckians. Bobby Kimmel was a little guard from Louisville. Lenny Cohen and Dick Lenholt had played in Tech's two lopsided losses to the Wildcats the preceding year. In the first half Kentucky trailed by eight points, but the home team finally managed to go ahead 58-55 with 1:30 left in the game. But Kimmel made two free throws, and as Evans was dribbling up the court, Joe Helms sneaked behind him, stole the ball, and hit a twelve-foot jump shot. That 59-58 loss ended a UK winning streak that had begun on January 4, 1943, with a wartime victory over Fort Knox. "From this time until history is no longer recorded, you will be remembered as the team that broke the string," Rupp scolded his players. "Even if you go on to win the NCAA championship, you must carry this scar with you the rest of your lives."

Evans and Puckett were the only returning regulars on the team. Jerry Bird of Corbin and Phil Grawemeyer of Louisville started at forward. Bob Burrow, a 6-foot-6 center, had scored two thousand points at Lon Morris Junior College in Texas.

Kentucky's other regular-season loss was also to Georgia Tech, 65-59 on New Year's Eve in Atlanta. "What a hell of a way to start the new year," Rupp said. "These turds are making me old before my time." The players felt fortunate that Rupp let them ride home on the team plane. After arriving in Lexington, some of the players went home overnight, although it was against team rules. A student manager told Rupp what was going on. The coach called a practice for the following day—Sunday, the day before the DePaul game.

The players hustled back and met at a service station near the campus. All agreed to quit if Rupp kicked any of them off the team. Rupp called a squad meeting and questioned the players about their whereabouts on Saturday night. Some of them lied to him, so he took away their tickets for the DePaul game. Linville Puckett said no tickets, no play, and nearly every player echoed his remarks. They walked out, leaving only Billy Evans, Dan Chandler, and Rupp in the room.

Evans was the good guy with the white hat. Puckett wore black. Rupp told Evans to talk to the players individually and tell them practice was at 3:15 that afternoon. Any player who was late need not bother to clean out his locker—Rupp and Lancaster would leave his stuff in the middle of Euclid Avenue. Then Rupp told Chandler to recruit some football players for the DePaul game. All the players except Puckett and Burrow, who was ill, reported for practice, as did six football players.

Puckett quit the team. "I enjoy participating in basketball as much as anybody in the world," he said in a statement. "However, basketball at Kentucky isn't regarded as a game, but as a matter of life or death, with resemblance of one going to war." He and Bill Bibb transferred to Kentucky Wesleyan College.

The Wildcats did not win the NCAA championship that year. They didn't even come close. Grawemeyer was out with a broken leg, and Evans was ineligible as a graduate student. John Brewer and Gerry Calvert were their replacements. Kentucky fought Marquette on even terms until the Warriors pulled away with six minutes to go and won 79-71. In the regional at Evanston, Burrow scored twenty-two points and Calvert nineteen as the Wildcats beat Penn State 84-59 for third place. Burrow made the NCAA All-Regional team. Evans later played with the Bartlesville Oilers and earned a gold medal with the 1956 Olympic squad. Rupp reached a milestone that season when the Wildcats defeated La Salle 63-54 in the UK Invitational. It was his five hundredth victory at Kentucky.

The following year, Rupp had the makings of a good team, but others were catching up with him, and a record of 20-6 was disappointing by Wildcat standards. The best player was Burrow, who teamed with two other returning seniors, Jerry Bird and Phil Grawemeyer, to give Kentucky the tallest front line in the SEC.

Kentucky lost to Temple and Dayton in Memorial Coliseum. Temple came in with a pair of classy black guards, Hal Lear and Guy Rodgers, who combined for forty-three points in the Owls' 73-61 victory. Burrow scored twenty-seven points against Minnesota in the opening round of the UK Invitational

Tournament, but he went down with an ankle sprain with 2:20 to go. That kept him out of action the next night against Dayton. Led by seven-foot Bill Uhl, the Flyers handed Kentucky its first UKIT loss, 89-74. Bird scored thirty-four points at center. Rupp played Bird and Burrow in a double pivot at St. Louis, the first change in offense since Rupp came to Kentucky. Gerry Calvert scored twenty-two points, and the Wildcats won 101-80.

Burrow left the game with 2:35 remaining in a 107-65 win over LSU, but when Rupp saw that he had forty-five points, he sent him back into the game. Burrow scored five more, but he fell one short of Cliff Hagan's record. Vanderbilt beat Kentucky 81-73 in their first meeting that year, as Kentucky natives Babe Taylor of Frankfort and Al Rochelle of Guthrie scored fifty-two points between them. Those Kentucky boys at other schools were beginning to annoy Rupp.

The first team to score one hundred points against Kentucky was Alabama. Johnny Dee had five players in their fifth year as students. The best was Jerry Harper, a center from Flaget High School in Louisville. When Kentucky and Alabama met on February 2 at Montgomery, their records were almost identical: each team had won seventeen games. Alabama was undefeated in conference play, and Kentucky had lost only to Vanderbilt. With Harper scoring thirty-seven points, Alabama beat the Wildcats 101-77.

"Back when I was playing," Rupp told his players, "we would have taken the ball and eaten it, chewed it up, and swallowed it before we would ever let them score a hundred points on us. You guys are like a slot machine. Something is set in there to make you click or not click. You've played the worst basketball I've seen and some of the best." Alabama went on to win the conference title but declined an NCAA bid because its seniors were ineligible.

Kentucky took Bama's place. The Wildcats went to Iowa City, where they demolished Wayne State 84-64 in the regional. The next night Kentucky came up against Iowa. Rupp assigned Grawemeyer to guard 6-foot-3 Carl "Sugar" Cane. Grawemeyer held Cane scoreless for the first fifteen minutes before Rupp gave him a rest. Cane hit two quick baskets, and Grawemeyer rushed back into the game. It was too late—Cane had his stroke going. He scored thirty-four points, three more than Burrow, and Iowa won 89-77. The sportswriters named Burrow to their All-America team.

Gerry Calvert was the only senior in the lineup when Kentucky opened its 1956-57 season. Junior Vern Hatton of Lexington was the other guard. The forwards were 6-foot-4 sophomore Johnny Cox of Hazard and 6-foot-3 John Crigler of Hebron, Kentucky. Ed Beck, 6-foot-7, was the center. Calvert and Beck were co-captains. The Wildcats opened with three wins before losing to St. Louis 71-70 in Lexington. Cox, called the best sophomore in the country by Ed Hickey, scored twenty points in that game and thirty-four in a 76-55 win over Maryland. In a loss to Duke, Blue Devil Bucky Allen stole the ball from Hatton and scored the winning bucket with twenty seconds to play. Calvert insisted that Allen almost knocked Hatton down.

That year, Kentucky won both the UKIT and the Sugar Bowl. In New Orleans, John Brewer stole the ball on a throw-in after a UK basket and scored the goal that beat Virginia Tech 56-55. Ed Beck scored sixteen points against VPI and ten points in a 111-76 win over Houston in the championship game, earning most valuable player honors. The Wildcats set five Sugar Bowl records: all-time high individual team score, highest winning team margin, and highest combined team total. The remainder of the season, they lost only two games. Tulane beat them 68-60 at New Orleans, and Mississippi State was an 89-81 winner at Starkville, as Bailey Howell, a 6-foot-7 sophomore, scored thirty-seven points. Howell was Beck's responsibility on defense, and Rupp was predictably perturbed by the future NBA star's output.

"Ed," he told Beck on the way to the locker room, "you will never make All-American, but you sure made one tonight."

Kentucky won its seventeenth conference title and played the Midwest Regional on its own court. Brewer hit all eight of his free throws late in the game to give Kentucky a 98-92 win over Pittsburgh. In the regional final, the Wildcats led Michigan State 47-35 at halftime. But Jack Quiggle scored twenty-two points, Johnnie Green dominated the boards, and the Spartans won 80-68.

Rupp told his team: "Forget about the game. You will never be able to play it again. Just remember one thing. At the start of the season, you were the twenty-second team in the nation. Tonight you are No. 3 because you gave me, your coach, more than you actually had. You gave more than your best."

Chapter
Fifteen

Fiddlers Five

T he 1957-58 Wildcats were Rupp's most experienced squad since the undefeated 1953-54 team. Vern Hatton and Johnny Cox were future All-Americans; Adrian Smith would play in the Olympic Games. Rupp seemed to have little cause to cast doubts on the team's prospects, but he did. He was sending out his most experienced team in years—but also the most baffling—to play what he called an awesome schedule. The December slate began with Duke at home and Ohio State at Columbus. The Wildcats next played Temple at home then traveled to Maryland, St. Louis, and Southern Methodist. In the first game of the UKIT, Kentucky played West Virginia for the chance to meet the winner of a game between North Carolina and Minnesota.

"Our boys might be good fiddlers, but we have a Carnegie Hall schedule," Rupp said. "We need violinists to play that competition."

Rupp knew that his players were better than he was admitting, but he needed thoroughbreds, not stud horses, to compete in the NCAA. He had four starters back from a 23-5 team: Cox and John Crigler, both 6-foot-3, at forward; Ed Beck, 6-foot-7, at center; and Hatton, 6-foot-3, at guard. All were seniors except Cox, a junior who had led the team in scoring the preceding year. Cox had the makings of a superstar, with an excellent one-hand jump shot, a deadly hook, and good rebounding skills.

Crigler was Rupp's blue collar worker—unselfish, strong on the boards, and happy to play tough defense. He was a poor outside shooter who made up for it by driving to the basket. Rupp tongue-lashed Crigler more than any player on the team. Once at Auburn, Crigler's man scored the tying basket at the halftime gun. Rupp fumed at him: "John Lloyd, 150 years from now there will be no university, no field house. There will have been an atomic war, and it will all be destroyed. Underneath the rubble there will be a monument, on which is the inscription, 'Here lies John Crigler, the most stupid basketball player ever at Kentucky, killed by Adolph Rupp,' because if you don't play better, I'm going to kill you."

Vernon Hatton, an elder in the Mormon Church, wouldn't take Rupp's abuse. Rupp once admonished him, "Play defense, you lazy thing." Hatton walked to the bench, sat down, and announced he was quitting the team. "Vernon, I have been coaching thirty years and I have never had a boy quit on me like this," Rupp said. But the Baron knew that Vernon gave 100 percent all the time. He could handle and shoot the ball, drive to the basket, and rebound. He came through time and again in clutch situations. Lancaster later wrote, "If I had to put a man on the line and my life depended on whether he made it or not, Vernon Hatton is the man I'd want to shoot it."

Ed Beck, who had been a consistent high school scorer at Fort Valley, Georgia, heeded Rupp's advice to give up shooting and concentrate on defense and rebounding. As a junior, he led the team with fourteen rebounds a game. The fifth starter, Adrian Smith, picked up the scoring slack when Vern Hatton was out with an appendectomy. The top reserve forward, Phil Johnson, also got some starts. Harry Lancaster said the strongest part of that team was that every starter specialized in a different phase of the game, and each sensed what he did best. Perhaps drawn together by the doubts about their ability, they became one of Rupp's closest teams.

Duke had the same starters who had defeated Kentucky by a point the previous year in Durham, and the Blue Devils had a one- point edge with less than three minutes remaining in the opener. But Hatton maneuvered for a layup and then hit three free throws to finish with twenty points and give the Wildcats a 78-74 victory. In a game dedicating Ohio State's St. John Arena in Columbus, Crigler scored twenty-two points and Hatton twenty to lead a 61-54 UK win. The Buckeyes did not get a single layup, and Beck held their 6-foot-7 center, Frank Howard, to seven points. Encouraged by that performance, Rupp said defense would be the key to a successful season.

The Wildcats returned home to meet Guy Rodgers and undefeated Temple. Hatton made a free throw in the closing minute to tie the score, and Smith missed a sixty-foot heave that would have won it. Rodgers canned a fifteen-footer to put Temple ahead 67-65 with three seconds to play in the extra period, and only one second remained on the clock by the time the Wildcats got time out.

"Well, Smitty," Rupp said in the huddle, "I guess we'll have to let you try another one." But Lancaster could see that Hatton wanted the ball, and he suggested that they let Vernon take the last shot. As the crowd filed out of the Coliseum, Temple's defense backed up to protect against a long pass under the basket and a quick tip. Crigler tossed the ball in to Hatton, who took the throw near the sideline at midcourt and lofted a two-hand set shot toward the basket. The ball clanged around the rim several times before dropping through. The fast-getaway fans hurried back to their seats when they heard the roar of the faithful. Temple tied the score 75-75 to send the game into a third overtime, but Hatton took control of the third, scoring six of Kentucky's last eight points for an 83-81 victory.

The following day, Hatton went to Rupp's office and asked for the game ball. Rupp said he didn't see why he should give someone a $35 ball just because he hit a forty-seven-foot shot with one second left on the clock. Rupp fretted about what the athletics board would do if it found out about the giveaway. "If you hadn't scored the basket, one of the other boys would have done the job," he said. "The play was one we had been practicing for occasions like that." As Hatton again contemplated quitting the team, Rupp pulled the basketball from under his desk and flipped it to him. "Congratulations, son. You sure are tough in the clutch," he said. "Tell your grandchildren about it."

The Wildcats were No. 3 in the polls when they lost to Maryland 71-62 at College Park. Then they beat St. Louis 71-60 and lost to Southern Methodist 65-64 before returning home for the UKIT. West Virginia featured Jerry West, one of the best players Rupp had ever seen. The Mountaineers led Kentucky 51-32 at halftime and held on to win 77-70—the first time in fifteen years that the Wildcats had lost two games in a row. The Wildcats won their next ten games before falling to Georgia Tech 71-52 in Atlanta.

That season the word *stall* became part of Rupp's vocabulary. "We decided it was going to be hard to outscore some of those good teams," Rupp said. "So we concentrated on keeping the other fellow from scoring." That meant hard work on defense and patience on offense. Kentucky held the ball during the last nine minutes of a game with Mississippi State. The Wildcats didn't take a shot from the field during that time, but they hit twelve of thirteen from the free throw line and won by ten points. After a loss to Loyola at Chicago—Hatton and Art McZeir traded clutch shots in the closing seconds, McZeir's winning it for the Ramblers 57-56—the Wildcats again put the stall to use against Vanderbilt. Kentucky used a ten-point free throw margin to win 65-61.

Crigler hit a long one-hand shot from the side with two seconds remaining to give the Wildcats a two-point victory over Alabama, but Auburn escaped with a one-point victory—its first in fourteen tries against Kentucky—when Cox bounced a last-second shot off the rim. Next came what Rupp called the best game of the season. Adrian Smith came off the bench and made nine buckets in a 77-66 win over Tennessee at Knoxville.

The Wildcats were 12-2 in the SEC, 19-6 overall, and they would play the NCAA regional on their home court. And there was more good news: Louisville was the Final Four site that year. The only bad news was those six losses—no team with that many setbacks had ever won the NCAA tournament.

Miami didn't have a prayer in the regional opener. The home-standing Wildcats got double-figure scoring from four players, led by Cox with twenty-three, in a 94-70 rout. Notre Dame, meanwhile, was 24-3 after whipping Big Ten champion Indiana for its twelfth win in a row. Tom Hawkins had scored thirty-one points against the Hoosiers, and Rupp, who wouldn't use a zone defense until eight years later, modified his man-to-man in an effort to stop the Irish star. Beck played behind Hawkins while Smith sagged at guard to front him. The defensive scheme held Hawkins to fifteen points, and every UK starter scored in double figures. Kentucky swamped the Irish 89-56—Notre Dame's worst defeat ever.

That year the road to the Final Four resulted in heartbreaks for some of the nation's top teams. West Virginia, first in both wire-service polls, lost to Manhattan in the first round of the East Regional. Second-ranked Cincinnati lost to Kansas State in the Midwest. San Francisco fell to Seattle in the Far West. The Wildcats, though, were in the Final Four for the first time since 1951—Rupp's Fiddlers had made it to Carnegie Hall. In Louisville, they faced a rematch with Temple. Seattle and Kansas State filled the other Final Four bracket.

The Owls were 26-2, losing to Kentucky and to Oscar Robertson's Cincinnati Bearcats. As they had in December, Kentucky and Temple played on even terms, and the game's outcome was in doubt until the end. Led by Rodgers' twenty-three points, the Owls were ahead 60-59 with twenty-three seconds remaining. In a timeout, Rupp told the Wildcats to get the ball to Hatton, and the clutch player responded again. He drove the lane and twisted under the basket for a layup. Kentucky was in the title game again.

Kansas State had a big front line—6-foot-9 Bob Boozer, 6-8 Jack Parr, and 6-8 Wally Frank—but it was no match for Seattle's Elgin Baylor. Baylor was a 6-foot-6 all-around performer who was averaging thirty points a game. He could fake, drive, shoot, and seemingly hang in the air at will. Against Kansas State, he put on one of the finest one-man shows UK scouts had ever seen, scoring twenty-three points and pulling down twenty-three rebounds in the Chieftains' 73-51 victory.

"Seattle made monkeys out of Kansas State," Lancaster said. "Baylor blocked shots in their faces, threw behind-the-back passes, and just took charge of the game." Lancaster and Baldy Gilb agreed they had no scouting report on Seattle. They told Rupp Kentucky couldn't beat the Chieftains. As Rupp and

Lancaster were trying to come up with a game plan, someone knocked on their hotel door. Outside was a man holding a roll of movie film. He introduced himself as Harry Grayson, coach at Idaho State College. Because the UK coaches had sent him films over the years, Grayson was there to return the favor— he would show them how to beat Seattle. (Grayson did not mention that Baylor had taken a football scholarship at the Idaho college and then transferred to Seattle after proving himself in basketball.)

Grayson said that the coaches' first task was convincing the Wildcats not to stand around and watch Baylor play. As the film rolled, Grayson pointed out that Baylor had trouble staying with a player who would drive on him. He felt the key to beating Seattle was to get Baylor in foul trouble. Rupp had the team manager get the players out of bed and bring them to the film room. After showing the film, Rupp and Lancaster explained the plan: Baylor would guard Beck, who would screen for Hatton and force Baylor to switch off. Then Beck would roll for the basket and get some easy points.

The plan hit an early snag: Seattle coach John Castellani put Baylor on Crigler, who hadn't scored against Temple. Rupp and Lancaster called a quick timeout and instructed Crigler to screen for Hatton and then drive for the basket. Seattle led by as many as eleven points early in the game, but the UK strategy was working. Trying to stay with the hard-driving Crigler, Baylor committed two quick fouls, and Crigler scored twice. Baylor committed his third foul near the end of the first half, which ended with Seattle on top by three points.

In the locker room, Crigler waited for the compliment he thought he'd earned. Rupp told him to wipe the smile off his face. "If you hadn't missed one of those free throws," he said, "we'd be behind them by two points instead of three."

In the second half, Baylor switched to guarding the UK centers. Hatton started driving the middle, forcing Baylor to switch and pick him up. Seattle led 44-38 when Baylor drew his fourth foul trying to block a shot by Don Mills, less than four minutes into the second half. Seattle went into a zone to protect its superstar. That was an invitation for Cox to shoot his one-hand outside shots and for Hatton to drive. Kentucky seized the initiative, tied the score at 56, and went on to win

84-72. Baylor scored twenty-five points and grabbed nineteen rebounds, but the Wildcats had kept him from winning the game single-handedly. Hatton had thirty points, Cox twenty-four points and sixteen rebounds; both made the all-tournament team. The unsung hero Crigler, meanwhile, ended up with fourteen points and fourteen rebounds.

It was an ugly duckling team, Rupp said. Not a single Wildcat made the all-conference team. "I didn't get a single vote for Coach of the Year, so I know it wasn't over-coaching," Rupp said. "Frankly, I didn't think we'd get this far." He said the Fiddlers as a unit played the best of any of the championship teams he had coached. The individuals had weaknesses; the team had few. "Our boys may not be violinists," Rupp allowed, "but they're good barnyard fiddlers."

Chapter
Sixteen

Shades of Gray

Rupp came from the Midwest to a town that had a life-size, bronze statue of Confederate raider John Hunt Morgan and his horse on the courthouse lawn. Old-line Lexingtonians still fought the Civil War, and they kept the "coloreds" in their place. During Rupp's first three decades at Kentucky, no one ever charged him with racism. He recruited only white players because it was the accepted practice. According to some administrators and alumni, black athletes would be welcome at the university but for the problems of housing, feeding, and protecting them—issues that provided a convenient crutch for implicit racism.

When Don Barksdale accompanied the Phillips Oilers to Lexington for that 1948 pre-Olympic exhibition game, his white teammates stayed in a hotel while Barksdale found shelter with a local black family. During the next three years, the Wildcats played against two fine black players on New York teams—Ed Warner of City College of New York and Solly Walker of St. John's. When St. John's paid Kentucky a return visit, there was concern for Walker's safety in Lexington. Rupp urged UK fans to treat Walker as they would any visitor, and there were no incidents.

But if Rupp's teams took on all comers, he didn't go out of his way to protest Jim Crow laws. In 1956, Louisiana banned the mixing of races at social events, including basketball games. New Orleans tried in vain to get the Sugar Bowl sports events exempt from the law. That year's basketball tournament entries were Kentucky, Dayton, Notre Dame, and St. Louis. When the three Catholic schools pulled out to protest the state law, Rupp urged Houston, Alabama, and Virginia Tech to accept bids. The Sugar Bowl honored Rupp in 1973.

Still, Rupp could rationalize keeping the Wildcats all-white. He used the example of the abuse he and his team suffered at Mississippi State, where he once found a stuffed skunk under his seat on the bench, and where fans loved to pull Cotton Nash's blond leg hairs out by the roots when he tumbled out of bounds.

"If they treat me and my boys like that now, what do you think they would do if I brought a Negro to town?" Rupp asked. "I've had many fine black prospects tell me they did not want to be the first to go to Mississippi and play, and I don't blame them."

In 1961 Rupp announced that he would sign and play black players. Southeastern Conference schools that refused to play Kentucky would have to forfeit the games. He said two of the state's finest players, both blacks, would enroll at Kentucky. Later, though, he said, "I was talking about a hypothetical case. I'd like to know what those schools will do if I bring an integrated team into their cities?"

Nor were Rupp and the Wildcats above profiting from the racist attitudes in Dixie. The 1959 Bulldogs won the SEC crown but was forced to decline the NCAA bid that went with it because the team might have to play against blacks. Kentucky gladly filled in. Four years later Mississippi State coach James "Babe" McCarthy pulled a fast one on the lawmakers. Determined that the Bulldogs would keep their NCAA date, he sent a squad to the airport, where the authorities accosted them—only to discover that these were the MSU benchwarmers. Then he sneaked his regulars out of town and into the tourney.

"That took some nerve on his part," Rupp said. "Maybe that will wise those people up down there."

The people "down there" may have been backward, but Lexington wasn't exactly famous for its enlightened attitudes. Three racial incidents during the late 1950s and early 1960s defined the city's reputation. Two involved a hotel dining room's refusal to serve black athletes. In the fall of 1961, the Boston Celtics and St. Louis Hawks were in town for a benefit game. Each team had a former Wildcat star on the roster—Cliff Hagan for the Hawks, Frank Ramsey for the Celts—but some members of the community were more concerned about the black players on each team. Bill Russell led a Celtics contingent that included Al Butler, Sam Jones, K.C. Jones, and Tom Sanders. Woody Sauldsberry and Cleo Hill were with the Hawks.

The teams stayed at the Phoenix Hotel, which had promised to treat the black guests fairly. When the hotel dining room refused to serve three of the blacks, the entire group caught the first plane out of town. Without those players, the game was a dud.

Temple and Kentucky played eighteen games from 1944 to 1962, but after a Lexington hotel refused to serve black members of the Temple team, the Owls canceled the series the following year. Three years earlier, the Owls had come to Lexington with black stars Guy Rodgers and Bill "Pickles" Kennedy. By some quirk, two black educators, Paul L. Guthrie and S. T. Roach, were able to purchase prize seats for the game. "I guess it was the rush of selling tickets," Roach said, "but we got two seats midway in the lower section." Lower seating was considered a birthright—the presence of any stranger in the section was cause for alarm. When the strangers were black—never mind that Guthrie was the principal and Roach the basketball coach at Dunbar High School—it was cause for panic.

When a Boy Scout told Roach and Guthrie they would have to leave the lower section, they produced their tickets. The boy summoned his Scoutmaster, who repeated the request. Then Bernie Shively told the pair that they had to move. Since the men were employees of the Board of Education, they feared that creating a disturbance might cost them their jobs.

"The only move we were going to make was out of there," Roach said. "We were not going to move just because the people behind us complained that two niggers were sitting in front of them." Rupp had no part in that incident, but some people thought that he was part of the problem. Knowing Rupp coached a black player at Freeport High School, Roach just don't understand his attitude," Roach said. Roach had mixed feeling toward the UK coach; the two met only once, when Rupp congratulated Roach for winning his five hundredth game. Later Rupp would open the UK gym for Dunbar to practice.

"He did it out of the goodness of his heart," Roach admitted. "That allowed us to work out for the various tournament games that we played there." Dunbar had a number of good players, but Rupp did not recruit any of them. "I'm sorry he didn't see fit to open the door to blacks," Roach said. "He apparently didn't want to be the first to set a trend of recruiting a black in the conference." He said blacks throughout Kentucky still have negative feelings toward the university because of the Rupp era. "With his stature, he could have made all the difference in the world."

When Dr. John W. Oswald became Kentucky's sixth president in 1963, he was a man with a mission: to integrate the school's athletic teams. Not only was it the right thing to do, it would also help the school get federal funds. But first he had to neutralize Rupp. Oswald's strategy was simple: create a new department and put his own representative in charge of athletics. Thus was born the Department of Student Affairs, with Vice President Robert L. Johnson as its first director.

Florida, Tennessee, and Vanderbilt indicated that they were ready to integrate their teams, but the schools felt that Kentucky should be the first to integrate. Finally, in 1965, Kentucky signed black track star Jim Green and black football players Nat Northington and Greg Page. Vanderbilt quickly signed Perry Wallace to a basketball scholarship.

Oswald told Rupp it would mean a lot to everyone if there were blacks on the UK basketball team. He told him to recruit one, even if the player just sat on the bench. Rupp said he didn't recruit players to sit on the bench. Harry Lancaster wrote that Rupp would return from a meeting with Oswald and say the president was ordering him to get some black players, whether or not they could play.

Wesley Unseld was the target of Rupp's first real effort to recruit a black player. Not only was Unseld the best high school player in the nation, but he was also more brown than black—Rupp couldn't have asked for a better package. But when Rupp made an official visit to the Unseld home, the player walked in with Louisville coach John Dromo.

"We shook hands, and the boy said he was going to hear Dromo speak somewhere," Rupp said. "I knew then we had no chance at him." In fact, Unseld welcomed a chance to integrate the UK team, but he said there was always some excuse, including a lack of grades and skills, for the school not to recruit a black player.

"There was much pressure brought to bear from the black community to do it," Unseld said. "There was also pressure brought from many other people that I better not do it."

Butch Beard signed a UK grant but had already signed with Louisville. The UL pact took precedence. Then in 1968 Rupp was stymied at every turn in his attempt to integrate the team. Hazard star Jim Rose promised that he would not sign with any school until he talked to UK; Rupp later learned that Rose had already signed with both Houston and Western Kentucky. Jim McDaniels of Allen County turned down Kentucky's offer of a scholarship and signed with Western. Jerome Perry of Louisville was Rupp's last hope, but he joined Rose and McDaniels at WKU.

The following year, Rupp finally got on board when he signed Tom Payne to a grant-in-aid. Payne, only the second 7-footer to play for Rupp, thought the Baron could bring out his potential more than any other coach. But he didn't stick around long enough to find out, turning pro after his sophomore year. Black football players Darryl Bishop and Elmore Stephens played briefly for Rupp in his final season at UK. He dismissed both after they missed a team plane.

Bob Johnson never thought that Rupp was feigning interest in recruiting blacks, but Rupp had little use for recruiting of any sort. Rupp had been on top of the heap so long that players came to him and asked to play.

"I never got the impression that Adolph was hostile to blacks," Johnson said. "He just wasn't making overtures to them." Wes Unseld said, "You're talking about a different time and different people. There's no sense dwelling on any of that."

Chapter
Seventeen

Mountain to Mohammads

R upp believed that if he offered a boy a scholarship to play basketball at Kentucky, that boy would be a fool not to accept. He thought that when a Kentucky baby was born, the mother had two wishes for him: to grow up to be like another native son, Abraham Lincoln, and to play basketball for Adolph Rupp.

That was the Baron's attitude, at least, when he was on top of the collegiate basketball world and fine high school players were beating a path to his door. The talent began to ebb in the late 1950s, when competition for players became more intense. Rupp had gotten where he was by recruiting, but he was too proud to beg a boy to play for him. He hated visitations, feeling that the mountain should not go to the little Mohammads. As recruiting began to escalate, one prize prospect after another escaped Rupp.

"King" Kelly Coleman, 6-foot-2, averaged more than thirty-one points a game during his four years at Wayland High School in Kentucky. He scored 185 points in four state tournament games, including a record sixty-eight in one game. Rupp offered Coleman a grant-in-aid although he had doubts about the boy's ability to fit into his system. Some UK boosters offered Coleman more than a scholarship, but they did not dare tell Rupp, who hated that type of dealing. West Virginia boosters got into the hunt, offering him a Dodge automobile, a gasoline credit card, and clothes. They also enrolled him in Greenbrier Military Academy, but he chose to spend his senior year at Wayland.

The NCAA placed the Mountaineers on probation, stipulating that Coleman could not play for them, and he enrolled at Eastern Kentucky. As Rupp had predicted, Paul McBrayer's discipline was too tough, and Coleman transferred to Kentucky Wesleyan, where he set a school mark of 2,077 points that would stand for twenty-nine years. A weight problem kept Coleman from starring in the pros. Rupp called his failure a case of a very talented basketball player spoiled by too much attention.

While Coleman was dominating the news, Harry Lancaster signed Jackie Moreland to a UK grant. Moreland, a 6-foot-7 center-forward, scored a national record of 5,030 points in four seasons at Minden High in Louisiana. Lancaster was unaware that Moreland had also committed to Texas A&M and Centenary, and that North Carolina State was in the hunt as well. Moreland shipped his trunk to Lexington, but North Carolina State took both him and the trunk to Raleigh, where he enrolled in school. Railroad officials put a tracer on the trunk and located the missing person. In addition to probation, the NCAA ordered State to pay a $5,000 fine if Moreland did not complete his four years there. Moreland transferred to Louisiana Tech, where he was a two-time All-American and a first-round draft choice of the Detroit Pistons.

After UK won the 1958 NCAA championship, Rupp ran out of "big" players. "We could find plenty 6-footers," he said, "but the schedule we played required us to have bigger boys than were available either on our varsity or freshman squads." (Actually, several big Kentuckians were available—but they were all black.)

Gary Bradds, a 6-foot-8 all-state forward-center, signed an SEC grant with Kentucky after graduating from Greenview (Ohio) High in the spring of 1960. Two days after enrolling at Lexington, he left for Ohio State. Harry Lancaster claimed someone in Columbus gave Bradds' father a job after Kentucky had refused to do so. Rupp reported the matter to the NCAA, which later said it had considered the case. That was the last UK heard about it. Bradds averaged 28.0 and 30.6 points a game in his last two years at Ohio State. He was twice All-American and a Big Ten Player of the Year, and he had a successful career in the pros.

Jerry Lucas, 6-foot-9 forward-center, led Middletown High in Ohio to seventy-six straight victories and two state titles. He told the *Saturday Evening Post* that forty recruiters—out of the more than 150 who came to call—offered his parents a new home. Lucas added that one school also offered him a car, a job for his father, and all the spending money Jerry needed, plus a house for him after he married. The article reported that Lucas gave Rupp ten seconds of his time.

"It was more like twenty seconds," Rupp corrected. "I met him in the cafeteria in the presence of his football coach, and when I offered him an application for a scholarship, he laughed at me and walked away."

Rupp had parents ask him for clothing for their boys and extra spending money. Some wanted a package deal—a scholarship for the athlete's brother or sister; one boy wanted a grant for his girlfriend.

"Basketball used be a coaching proposition," Rupp complained in 1969. "Now it is a recruiting proposition. There are some coaches who feel you must cheat to win." He did not subscribe to that philosophy, but as he neared retirement age, he could see that he was dealing with an entirely different type of athlete, boys who had their hands out when he first came to call. Offered a scholarship, many asked, "How much on top of that?" He did not understand how boys from low-income families could attend school, have a five-room apartment and own a car without arousing the NCAA's suspicion. "When I see one of those boys driving a car better than mine," he said, "I suspect something is taking place."

Not only was Rupp dead set against recruits receiving any illegal inducements, he was skimpy with the legal perks as well. He protected the university's money as if it were his own, and he took good care of his own. Dave Kindred, in *Basketball, the Dream Game in Kentucky*, said there were more sightings of the abominable snowman than of Rupp picking up a tab. Larry Boeck, a reporter for the *Courier-Journal*, recalled when Rupp called Ralph Beard and Wah Jones to the hotel desk during a tournament in New York. They were checking out after winning the event.

"Did you boys have radios in your room?" Rupp asked. When they acknowledged that they had, he said, "Well, boys, you each owe the university one dollar a day for the three days you had the radio."

In the aftermath of another failed recruiting bid—for Bill Hosket, a 6-foot-7 forward from Belmont High in Dayton— Rupp's stewardship of UK funds was put in a rather embarrassing spotlight. The coach once said that he had learned to handle the invitations himself on recruiting trips.

"Do not invite anybody you do not want," he said, "because there are many deadheads who will not help a bit, but will eat and run up the check."

Hosket, the Player of the Year in Ohio after leading his team to the state championship, was the son of the late Wilmer Hosket, captain of the Ohio State team that had beaten Kentucky in Alumni Gym in 1932. Rupp said that Armand Angelucci, a UK booster, contacted him during practice and said the boy was ready to sign. They had arranged a party for the announcement. Rupp left practice with a scholarship application in his pocket and accompanied Angelucci to the Hosket home. They went to a restaurant, where Rupp said Hosket ordered a $7.50 steak, supreme shrimp cocktail, and an extra order of mushrooms. After dinner, Hosket informed Rupp that he was going to Ohio State.

The coach's version of the story appeared in the October 1987 issue of *Big Blue Basketball*. Three months later, Hosket wrote Oscar Combs, the publisher, with his side of the story. He said he had never called anyone from Kentucky and said he was ready to sign; Rupp's visit to his home was unexpected. Angelucci had called and said Rupp and a few other men were on their way to Dayton and wanted to take the family to dinner. Mrs. Hosket explained that she had guests—her mother, her daughter, and Bill's girlfriend—but she invited them to stop by. Five UK boosters, all dressed in business suits, accompanied the coach. Rupp told Hosket how much he admired the play of his father back in 1932, and the group insisted on taking the family out to dinner.

Bill Hosket never forgot that meal. The men ordered steaks for everyone except his grandmother, who ordered fish, and Rupp, who got liver. The grandmother, who called Rupp "Sonny," asked if he had an iron deficiency. Hosket did not recall Rupp picking up the check, nor did he tell Rupp after dinner that he was going to Ohio State.

Hosket said he enjoyed the time he spent with Rupp. He visited the UK campus in the fall of his senior year and met Wildcat star Cotton Nash. A telegram in March congratulated him on the state championship and the Player of the Year honors; it was signed, "Respectfully Yours, Cotton Nash." Hosket didn't prize the telegram quite as much, however, when he talked to Nash later "and he asked me how my season had gone.

"Perhaps the phony telegram was sent by some of the 'deadheads' that Rupp referred to in your article." Hosket never regretted his decision to stay in his home state and play for Fred Taylor, and he said he received nothing other than what the NCAA allowed during his four years there. He did not know of any OSU players who received illegal aid.

Not only was Rupp having trouble recruiting in Ohio, more and more Kentucky boys were getting away. Jeff Mullins was the state's best player in 1958, and he was right there in Lexington. Mullins led Lafayette High School to the state championship. His coach, former Wildcat Ralph Carlisle, was not close to Rupp. Mullins' parents had come to Lexington from New York with IBM, so Big Blue basketball tradition didn't mean much to them. Mullins enrolled at Duke, where he became an All-American.

During that period, Charles "Cotton" Nash was the only good big man that Rupp recruited. Nash was 6-foot-5, weighed 220 pounds, and could make a basketball do tricks. He was an all-star in baseball and basketball, twice all-state in football, and holder of the discus record at Lake Charles High School in Louisiana. Nash played his first two years of basketball at Jeffersonville High School in Indiana, where his coach was former Wildcat Cliff Barker.

Rupp could not have recruited Nash at a more opportune time. His Wildcats were 24-3 in 1958-59, but there was no replacement in sight for Johnny Cox. One of Kentucky's wins was against Maryland 58-56 in overtime. Kentucky trailed the Terrapins by three points with sixteen seconds to play when Rupp called time out. He told his players to drive for the basket, try to make the shot, and draw a foul. Coach Bud Milliken cautioned his players against fouling, but Bennie Coffman took the inbounds pass, drove, scored, and was fouled by Al Bunge. Coffman's free throw sent the game into over-time.

Kentucky lost to Mississippi State, which repeated as conference champion but again refused an NCAA bid. The conference chose Kentucky as its representative to the Mid-east Regional. The Wildcats were leading Louisville by fifteen points in the first half when Cardinal coach Peck Hickman called time out and told his guards to smother the UK guards. In the second half Louisville pressed the Wildcats all over the floor, and the Cardinals won 75-61.

"You know what Louisville is eating tonight?" Rupp demanded, as he handed each Wildcat a dollar for hamburg-ers. "T-bone steaks, because they are winners." After beating Marquette for third place, the Wildcats sat behind the UL bench and rooted for the Cardinals in the championship. Louisville defeated Michigan State 88-81 and advanced to the Final Four, where it lost to West Virginia. Wildcats Cox and Billy Ray Lickert made the All-SEC team, and Cox was All-America.

The following year, Rupp had no player of Cox's stature, and the Wildcats went 18-7. Before practice started, Rupp lost four players. He dismissed Bobby Slusher and Howard Deenen for disciplinary reasons, the NCAA declared Roger Newman ineligible for playing in a summer basketball league, and Carroll Burchett had hepatitis. Bennie Coffman missed some early games with academic problems, and Ned Jennings and Dick Parsons were injured at crucial stages of the campaign. Rupp opened the season with Lickert and 6-foot-5 Allen Feldhaus at forward, 6-foot-9 Ned Jennings at center, and 5-foot-10 Dick Parsons and 6-foot-1 Sid Cohen at guard. Senior Don Mills started at center at times, and Burchett played forward.

Kentucky opened with a 106-73 win over Colorado State. Walk-on Herky Rupp tipped in the shot that put UK over the century mark, and the crowd gave him the only ovation he would receive in his career. The Wildcats then took their first trip to the West Coast, with return stops at St. Louis and Kansas. They defeated John Wooden's UCLA team 68-66 but lost to Southern Cal 87-73. En route to the hotel after the USC game, the team bus hit a car. The UK party escaped injury, but a woman in the car was killed and some others received serious injuries.

St. Louis beat the Wildcats 73-61, and Rupp was a nervous wreck when they arrived in Kansas. It was the first time he had brought one of his teams back to play his alma mater. On the eve of the game, he took the UK media to the Jayhawk Cafe, where he shared some memories. His sister Elizabeth Lawson was at the game with his old coach Phog Allen, who had been forced to retire and was bitter over it.

After the team went over game plans, Lancaster asked Rupp to leave so he could talk to the team. He told the Wildcats that Rupp had won every honor in the world, but nothing would make him happier than a win there that night. They gave him that win, 77-72 in overtime.

But they didn't give him as many wins as he was used to. Third place in the SEC was Kentucky's lowest finish since 1942, and for the first time since 1955, they did not participate in the NCAA tournament.

Kentucky Wildcats continued to struggle in 1960-61, going 19-9 and losing four SEC games for the second year in a row. After twenty-seven years, Louisiana State finally beat a UK team. The Wildcats did win the final nine games of the season, including a 68-62 victory over eventual conference champion Mississippi State at Starkville.

Mississippi State again declined an NCAA bid, and with Kentucky and Vanderbilt tied for second place, the conference scheduled a playoff game at Knoxville. On the afternoon of the game, the team doctor called Dick Parsons to Rupp's room. Rupp was in bed and looking weak. The doctor didn't know whether he could make it to the pregame meal. Parsons said that was all right, he would explain it to the squad. Rupp said he wasn't sure he could even make it to the game. Parsons told the coach not to worry—the team was ready to play. Rupp sat up and said, "Heck, I feel better already." The Baron sat weakly on the bench until the Wildcats started pulling ahead, then he got fired up. After UK beat the Commodores 88-67, the Wildcats carried their coach off the floor. It was a rare occasion. Rupp gave the game ball to Parsons.

There was talk of Rupp having another Fiddlin' Five on his hands. "I won't say my club now is as good unless it can do what the '58 bunch did," he said, "and that is win the NCAA." A record crowd of 18,883 was in attendance at the regional finals in Louisville's Freedom Hall as Lickert's twenty-eight points and sixteen rebounds led Kentucky to a 71-64 win over Morehead. In the other game, top-ranked Ohio State edged Louisville 56-55. Kentucky had defeated the Buckeyes, 96-93, earlier that season in Lexington.

Ned Jennings was the only Wildcat big enough to control Jerry Lucas, and he fouled out early in the championship game. Lucas hit fourteen of eighteen shots and scored thirty-three points in OSU's 87-74 win. It was Kentucky's ninth loss, the most for Rupp in a season. Lickert made All-Regional and was All-SEC for the third straight year. He, Jennings, Newman, and Parsons would not return the following year. Cotton Nash would have a big load to carry.

Chapter
Eighteen

Picking Cotton

C otton Nash's timing on the basketball court was impeccable, and he couldn't have picked a better time to step onto the basketball floor for the University of Kentucky. The Wildcats needed him more than he needed them. Rupp had lost Jeff Mullins and several other prime recruits. Nash was his crutch. The Louisiana boy was big, and he could play. He was white, too, from his blond head to the hairs on his feet. Before he was through, he would earn All-America honors three times and score 1,770 points, twenty-six more than Alex Groza's career total.

As a freshman, Nash lived up to his advance billing, averaging 26.4 points a game and twice hitting forty for the 13-5 Kittens. This was not one of Harry Lancaster's stronger freshman teams—Ted Deeken was the only other player who would start with the varsity.

Rupp hoped for an inside-outside punch, with Nash in the middle and 5-foot-11 Larry Pursiful at shooting guard. Starting every game in 1960-61, Pursiful averaged 13.4 points per game and led the team with a shooting percentage of 41.1.

The other starters were 5-foot-11 Scotty Baesler at guard and 6-foot-4 Roy Roberts and 6-foot-5 Allen Feldhaus at forward. Carroll Burchett eventually would start in place of Feldhaus.

Kentucky opened with eight straight home games—a schedule made in heaven. Nash had twenty-five points and seventeen rebounds in a 93-61 opener against Miami of Ohio. But after he made three straight bad passes with twelve minutes left against Southern California, Rupp pulled him and kept him out. Kentucky lost to the third-ranked Trojans 79-77.

In an 86-77 win over St. Louis, Baesler scored twenty points, and Roberts and McDonald held the Billikens' Tom Kieffer to thirteen. That was the beginning of a sixteen-game UK win streak. Temple came in with four black starters who tried to rattle Nash by calling him "poor white trash." He lost his cool but thought he still played a good game. He didn't realize how good until he checked the totals for Kentucky's 78-55 win. "I looked at the stats sheet and saw I had thirty rebounds," Nash said.

Tennessee was struggling to survive its own point-shaving scandal, so Rupp invited the Vols to the Invitational in recognition of the school's earlier refusal to jump on the anti-UK bandwagon. Pursiful scored thirty-four points and Kentucky coasted, 96-69. In the title game, the unranked Wildcats played Tex Winter's Kansas State, a top five choice in both major polls. Pursiful scored twenty-six in an 80-67 win.

The streak grew. Nash scored thirty-one points in a 100-53 thumping of Notre Dame in Louisville. Against Tennessee at Knoxville, Nash and Pursiful scored thirty apiece. After the Wildcats beat Georgia Tech 71-62 in Atlanta, Furman Bisher wrote, "You will seldom, if ever, see a boy so big with so much grace, so much agility, so much maneuverability and with so soft and velvety touch as Nash. There were times when Rupp was using this versatile young man to bring the ball down court when Georgia Tech pressed its defense. With his size and his massive hands, Nash gave the impression of a circus giant dribbling an orange."

On February 12, Kentucky had a 17-1 record and was 8-0 in the SEC. The Wildcats were ranked No. 2 in the nation behind Ohio State. Mississippi State was 18-1 and 7-1 and ranked ninth. Babe McCarthy told his Bulldogs to "dribble for fifteen minutes and play defense for five." State hit eleven of eighteen shots in the first half and was ahead 28-22. The Bulldogs made seven of eight in the second half and won 49-44.

"I was hoping one of you fellows would ask me how we handled Nash," McCarthy said to reporters at Memorial Coliseum. "I was going to tell you my daddy used to have a cotton gin, and I was always good at handling cotton." Someone reminded him that Nash had scored twenty-three points. "But that wasn't enough," McCarthy said.

Kentucky did not lose another game and finished 17-1 in the conference. Mississippi State had an identical record, and the victory over the Wildcats gave the Bulldogs the SEC's automatic bid to the NCAA playoffs. For the third time, State officials turned down the bid because of its stand on integrated athletics. Babe McCarthy was getting tired of that. He would do something about it, and perhaps lose his job in the process.

Kentucky was leading Butler by one point at halftime of the Mideast Regional at Iowa City when Rupp switched from a single-post attack to the double-post offense he had used against Ohio State two years earlier. Pursiful scored twenty-six points, Nash twenty- three, and Kentucky won 81-60. In the regional final against Ohio State, Rupp and Lancaster designed a defense they hoped would stop Jerry Lucas. To keep Nash from fouling out, they stationed Carroll Burchett in front of Lucas. Nash was to help anytime the ball came inside to Lucas. Instead, Lancaster said, Nash "didn't do a damn thing all night."

Some observers said Nash was not quick enough. John Havlicek held him to fourteen points, Lucas scored thirty-four, and the Buckeyes won 74-64. Nash was first-team All-America, SEC Player of the Year, and All-NCAA tournament. With 608 points, he was the highest-scoring sophomore in UK history. His 23.8 average made him the first SEC sophomore scoring champ in ten years, since Bob Pettit in 1952.

Lancaster said he and Rupp did a foolish thing after the Ohio State game. They chewed Nash out, called him every name in the book. "We ruined Cotton as a great basketball player for us," Lancaster said. During an interview in March 1994, Nash did not remember it that way. He said "just the normal yelling and screaming" went on after the game. He did not remember being told to help Burchett with Lucas. If they told him that, it was like many other things they said—he let it all go over his head. Nash just did not pay any attention to their ranting and raving.

Nash gave Rupp notice that he was leaving. Rupp said that was just fine with him. But Nash finished the semester and played baseball for Lancaster. Before the final deadline, Rupp called Nash into his office and they made their peace, after a fashion. Rupp said he would put Nash's picture on the cover of the media guide; his picture was right there alongside Nash. They were kneeling behind a basketball and Kentucky's four NCAA trophies; their smiles seemed forced.

From then on, Rupp and Nash were at odds; they were tolerating each other. It afforded Lancaster an opportunity to ingratiate himself with Nash, as did similar situations with other players.

If Nash had not returned as a junior, the Wildcats would have been in serious trouble. As it was, they managed only a 16-9 record. Nash drew a crowd everywhere he went on the court. Every opponent would double-team him, and there was no other Wildcat to take up the slack. Nash and Roy Roberts were the forwards. Ohioan Don Rolfes, 6-foot-6, was in the pivot. Sam Harper and Scotty Baesler were the guards.

Nash scored thirty-four points in the home opener against Virginia Tech, but the Wildcats lost 80-77—the first opening loss in Rupp's career and the program's first since a 48-10 loss to Cincinnati in 1926. Leland Melear, a product of Louisville Manual High, led all scorers with thirty-seven points. Bill Matthews was in his first year as Tech coach, and Guy Strong, who lettered for Rupp in the early 1950s, was his assistant. Strong scouted the Wildcats, and Rupp called him a traitor. The Baron never forgave him.

C. M. Newton had a similar experience when he was working on his doctorate at Alabama and coaching the freshman basketball team. Hayden Riley asked him to scout Kentucky. Newton, who knew he was going back to Transyvlania University and would have to live in the same town as Rupp, refused Riley's request. But he later rode to a Kentucky game at Auburn with Tide assistant Wimp Sanderson. Rupp was cool to Newton after that Saturday game, and C. M. could not understand why. Newton was on the Alabama bench when Kentucky played at Tuscaloosa the following Monday before a full house.

Rupp started the game with the old guard-around play, as everybody who'd been paying attention over the decades knew he would. A Tide player jumped out and took the charge. Rupp turned to Lancaster and said, "Newton's a Benedict Arnold; they know everything we're doing." Relations were still strained when Newton returned to Transylvania. Rupp made it known that he didn't want Newton around. Finally Newton made an appointment to see Rupp.

"I never thought you'd turn on me," Rupp began.

"Coach, I did not turn on you," Newton said. "Let me tell you how it was." Then he explained what had happened.

Rupp was not one to admit he was wrong or to say he was sorry. "We'll go on from here," he said.

Nash had a stone bruise on his heel during his entire junior season. Dr. Maurice Royalty shot it with novocaine before each game and put impact-cushioning "donuts" in the heel of his shoe. It was an injury that needed time to heal, but Nash played every game—and the coaches rode him constantly.

After the loss to Virginia Tech, Rupp called his team selfish. That was mild compared to what he would call them later in the season. They lost twice each to Georgia Tech and Tennessee and once to Mississippi and Vanderbilt. One of the losses to Georgia Tech was in double-overtime at Lexington. Rupp pulled Nash and Rolfes out of the game after twelve minutes of the first half with Kentucky down by ten. Only eight minutes remained when they returned to the game. Mike Tomasovich hit two free throws with seven seconds left and Tech won 86-85. Nash got three shots the entire game, hitting two of them.

Rupp was not too fond of Nash, and he didn't care for Rolfes, either, who would quit after the 1963 season. The Baron was dealing with a different breed of 'Cat. Nash passed the one thousand-point mark in career scoring with fourteen points against Florida, the nineteenth game of his second varsity season. He reached the milestone faster than any other player in UK history. His mark was still standing in 1994.

Tennessee rallied from a sixteen-point deficit to pull a stunning overtime upset in Memorial Coliseum. After back-to-back losses to Mississippi State and Vanderbilt, Rupp said his boys lacked "intestinal fortitude." They defeated Auburn and Alabama in Lexington and closed the season with a loss to Tennessee at Knoxville. Rupp missed that game with the flu. The 16-9 record was his worst yet at Kentucky. Some fans even booed him near the end of the season, and many were saying that he was too old.

But for all the team's problems, Nash was third in conference scoring with a 20.6 average. The U.S. Basketball Writers again named him to their All-America team. Near the end of that year, the UK ticket office announced that four of the five remaining home games were sold out. When season tickets went on sale the following season, a long line was waiting for the doors to open. After that season, there would be no more season basketball tickets for sale to the general public. The House that Rupp Built had become the House that Cotton Filled, but it was a happy home for neither man.

The best newcomers in 1963-64 were Larry Conley, a 6-4 forward from Ashland; Tom Kron, a 6-5 guard from Tell City, Indiana, and Lloyd "Mickey" Gibson, a 6-3 forward from Hazard. Rupp called them the "Katzenjammer Kids" because they were "always popping off like the kids in the comic strip." Gibson missed the first five games because of disciplinary problems, and would quit the team before the NCAA tournament. Nash and Deeken were co-captains and the starters at forward. John Adams, a 6-6 sophomore from Rising Sun, Indiana, was the center. Terry Mobley and Randy Embry were junior guards who had started the last few games in 1962-63. Rupp seemed to have enough players to complement his embittered star Nash.

Nash and Deeken scored twenty-eight points each in an opening win over Virginia. Nash had thirty-three and Deeken twenty in a 107-91 win over Texas Tech. Larry Conley added seventeen points off the bench and thrilled the fans with his clever passes to Nash. He started the next game, against Northwestern, and Nash moved to the pivot. Billy Cunningham outscored Nash 32-23, but four other Wildcats scored in double figures, and Kentucky beat North Carolina 100-80. A win over Baylor boosted Kentucky to No. 2 in the nation entering the UKIT.

Bill Bradley scored thirty-three points in the opening game of the tournament, but Princeton lost to Wake Forest. Bradley scored a tournament-record forty-seven the next night against Wisconsin. Rupp had tried to recruit Bradley, but an offer of a scholarship meant nothing to the Missourian. His father was a banker.

The Wildcats easily won the UKIT and whipped Notre Dame 101-81 in Louisville. They were ranked No. 1 in both polls for the first time in five years.

Kentucky disposed of Loyola of New Orleans in the opening round of the Sugar Bowl, then met Duke in the championship game. Mobley's basket sent the game into overtime, and the score was tied at 79 when Rupp called a timeout to set up a play for Nash. Mobley dribbled around the keyhole and he saw nobody open, so he threw up a last-second shot to win the game.

Some members of Nash's family had traveled to New Orleans for the bowl games, and Cotton was having trouble getting tickets for them. Nash knew there was no use asking Rupp—he'd tried that route the year before in Atlanta. He was on Peachtree Street buying tickets for his future wife and her parents while Rupp was giving tickets to servicemen back at the hotel. In New Orleans, Nash told Lancaster his problem. A student manager later knocked on Nash's door and gave him four tickets.

The Wildcats were 10-0 and rated No. 1 when they returned to Lexington on a cold, icy night. They rested only two days before heading south again for a disastrous trip to Atlanta and Nashville. R. D. Craddock, a Kentuckian from Hart County High, scored twenty-four points and Georgia Tech upset Kentucky 76-67. Two nights later, John Ed Miller hit a last-second jump shot from the top of the key with one second remaining to lift Vanderbilt over the Wildcats 85-83. Nash was scoreless in the first half and hit only four of twenty shots in the game.

Late in the Tech game, Rupp experimented with a 1-3-1 zone trap defense that Lancaster had taught the freshmen. Not long after, Rupp surprised Ray Mears with the defense and Kentucky beat Tennessee 66-57 at Knoxville. The key to the defense was moving Tom Kron to the point.

"We never have played a zone," Rupp explained. "That was a stratified transitional, hyperbolic paraboloid defense." His description sounded a lot like one Phog Allen had used many years earlier.

Rupp said he and Lancaster had invented the defense on a trip to Japan. Lancaster said he got it from Virginia Tech's Chuck Noe at a coaching clinic. C. M. Newton provides another source. When he was coaching at Transylvania in the early 1950s, the Pioneers participated in an invitational tournament at Williamson, West Virginia. They played West Virginia Tech, which was averaging more than one hundred points a game.

"What they were doing was zone-pressing," Newton said. "They were carrying to the college level what John Bill Trivette was doing at Pikeville (KY) High School." When Newton returned to Lexington, he told Lancaster what he had seen. He explained the full-court press with trapping and Lancaster got excited. When they took the idea to Rupp, he listened for a while, then brushed them off: "That would be a great defense if you had six men."

Kentucky won the SEC that year and played Ohio University in the Mideast Regional. Jim Snyder's black stars Mike Haley, Jerry Jackson, and Don Hilt dominated the boards and the game, 85-69. Nash hit only four of fourteen shots and scored ten points. Kentucky also lost the third-place game to Loyola, 100-91, as black players Les Hunter and Vic Rouse led the Rambler attack. It was Kentucky's worst showing in an NCAA tournament, and it moved Kentuckians to a radical notion: it was time Rupp started recruiting some blacks.

Rupp started Louie Dampier and Pat Riley in the opening game of the 1964-65 season. Other starters were Randy Embry at guard, John Adams at center, and Larry Conley at forward. Terry Mobley missed two weeks of preseason practice because of an eye injury. Dampier hit nine of eighteen shots as Kentucky beat Iowa in the opener. Tom Kron replaced Dampier to provide more height against North Carolina, but Billy Cunningham scored twenty-two points and the Tar Heels won 82-67 at Charlotte.

Dampier was back in the lineup for the Iowa State game. He scored nineteen points in the first half. "If you get the shots, take them," Rupp told him at halftime, "but don't be a hog." He scored eighteen more as the Wildcats won 100-74. Thirty-seven points was an all-time high for a UK guard. Kron replaced Embry and scored thirty-one points in that game.

Notre Dame outrebounded the Wildcats 81-44 and beat them 111-97. Kentucky continued to struggle; a 4-4 start was the worst of Rupp's career. Fans were saying he didn't work hard enough to get players.

"People who say that are just fools," he said. "The only reason we don't have big men on our team now is because boys who said they were coming didn't keep their word." He was talking about Gary Bradds and Bill Hosket, as well as Ron Kozlicki of Northwestern. He had also visited Dick and Tom Van Arsdale, but the twins from Greenwood, Indiana, stayed home to star for the Hoosiers.

Midway through the season, Rupp said it was his worst team. The final record bore out that assessment: 15-10. Dampier was the lone bright spot, averaging seventeen points a game and connecting on a school-record 51.2 percent of his field goal attempts.

The summer before, Rupp had hired Joe B. Hall as his No. 2 assistant. Hall was one of Adolph's boys. He had played some during the Fabulous Five era before transferring to Sewanee. "Joe B." was a successful coach at Regis College and at Central Missouri. His first recruit at Regis was Louis Stout, a 6-7 black from Hall's hometown of Cynthiana. At Regis, Hall was a Protestant coaching black players at a Catholic school. Rupp wanted Hall as a recruiter, and he promised to share the coaching chores.

Kentucky's recruiting system needed a complete overhaul, and Hall took charge, spending far more time landing players than coaching them. He would bring those Mohammads to the Mountain.

Chapter
Nineteen

Rupp's Runts

After suffering through his worst season, Rupp came back in the fall of 1965 with a group of "Runts" who would set the basketball world on fire. The team was so improbable that, on paper, it looked as if it might not win a game. On hardwood, it won twenty-seven. The tallest starter, Tom Kron, approached 6-foot-6 and played guard. Pat Riley was a forward who jumped center. Those who kept track claim that the 6-foot-3 Riley lost only twelve of fifty-eight taps. Playmaker Larry Conley was also a forward. He turned beet-red in the heat of battle. The center, Thad Jaracz, was 6-foot-5. Guard Louie Dampier was known for his quiet demeanor, his shooting, and his defense.

There were a couple of 6-foot-8 reserves on the team, but when someone named the squad "Rupp's Runts," the nickname caught everybody's fancy. The smaller Wildcats could hold their own with anybody on the boards, and all of them loved to shoot. It may not have been Rupp's best team, but it warmed his heart to close his eyes and listen to the pit-pat of the ball being passed to perfection. Basketball is a game of rhythm, and the Runts had it. They won twenty-three straight games before losing to Tennessee at Knoxville. They shook off that loss and went all the way to the championship game of the NCAA tournament. For a while, they made people stop saying Rupp was old and feeble. It was a sad day in the Bluegrass state when the Runts lost to Texas Western.

Conley and Kron took it on themselves to be passers and playmakers, and they were the heart and soul of the team, the ones whose unselfishness helped make Dampier and Riley All-Americans. Kron was a strong, tough point guard and a fine rebounder. Rupp had never seen a boy who could play the point on defense the way Kron did. He was fast, aggressive, and he never quit. Conley—the son of former Marshall College player and well-known referee George Conley—had been a starting junior forward on Ashland's 1961 state championship team. He was a pinpoint passer and a great rebounder, and, a bonus, he was one of the few players who knew how to talk to Rupp. It was hard not to like him.

Louie Dampier scored a school-record 1,011 points in two years at Southport High School in Indianapolis. He wanted to play for Indiana University, so his Uncle Louie, who was president of the IU alumni association, talked Branch McCracken into offering his godson a scholarship. But when Dampier got the feeling that the Hoosier coach was only mildly interested, he decided to visit Lexington, where the people actually seemed to want him. Rupp had seen Dampier hit nine of ten shots in the first half of a high school tournament game. The UK coach left at intermission, and Louie had a shaky second half.

"The first thing I noticed about meeting Coach Rupp was his handshake," Dampier said. "It was real soft." He had expected a real tough grip from the gruff Baron, and that soft handshake changed his opinion of Rupp. Dampier's specialty was a jump shot over a center screen at the top of the key. Once at Kentucky, he led the UK freshmen with 427 points—forty-nine fewer than Cotton Nash's record, and Nash had played two more games.

Pat Riley was the best athlete on the team and one of the strongest players Rupp ever coached. He grew up in Schenectady, New York, where he earned all-star honors in basketball and football at Linton High School. His father was a former minor league baseball manager. The family lived in Knott Terrace, a rough area in the middle of town. As a teenager, Riley wore rebel-without-a-cause attire—peg pants and a T-shirt with a pack of cigarettes in a rolled-up sleeve. At the Catholic high school, the nuns did what they could to keep him in line.

Rupp was planning on Conley, Kron, Dampier, and Riley in the starting lineup, but he still needed a man in the middle. Thad Jaracz was a pleasant surprise. The 6-foot-5, 230-pound center-forward was light on his feet. Jaracz had played for Lexington Lafayette High School. Rupp saw him in a losing effort in the 1963 regional tournament, but something about the big, left-handed kid caught his eye. Recruiting Thad was easy. Jaracz's father had played football and ran track for Kentucky in the early 1940s, and Lancaster had once dated a girl who was close to the family.

At first, Rupp and Lancaster disagreed on the boy. Lancaster thought he only knew how to hit layups. "Get out there and sign him," Rupp said. "The kid showed me some moves, and I think we can teach him how to play basketball." Speed and quickness helped Jaracz overcome a lack of height. He was deceptively quick on the fast break. One coach said he looked like a big freight train barreling down the floor. Jaracz was a good driver, and he had a deadly looping hook shot from the corner. He beat out fellow sophomore Cliff Berger, who was 6-foot-8.

Seeing that Riley had strong legs, Harry Lancaster decided to teach him how to get the tip. Most pivot men spread their legs and jump with one leg. Lancaster told Riley to jump off both legs, to get up first and into the other guy. Riley dug an elbow into the opponent's shoulder for leverage. That was how he got the tip over 7-foot Bill Uhl of Dayton. He "rode" his shoulder.

Kentucky won the opening game with Hardin-Simmons 83-55, though Jaracz was the only Wildcat to score in double figures. Hardin-Simmons coach Lou Henson called Kentucky "a good little team" but predicted that the Runts would have trouble when they ran into a big man. Jaracz scored twenty-two points and pulled down thirteen rebounds as Kentucky beat Virginia, and he scored thirty-two at Illinois.

Pollsters suddenly began to take notice of little Kentucky. The Wildcats were 6-0 after defeating Indiana 91-56 for the UKIT title. With Dampier hurt, Kentucky trailed Texas Tech at Lubbock. Rupp sent Bob Tallent into the game, and the reserve scored thirteen points and sparked a rally that gave the Wildcats an 89-73 win. Then Kentucky pounded the Irish 103-69 before 17,952 fans in Freedom Hall, as Riley scored thirty-six points and held Notre Dame's scoring ace, Jim Monohan, to seven. Jaracz scored 26 points in a 78-64 win at Florida. Against Georgia, Cliff Berger hit four free throws in double-overtime and Kentucky won 69-65.

Tennessee and Kentucky played back-to-back games that year. Ray Mears wore a brown suit to the game in Lexington. Rupp was not amused. Kentucky won 78-64 as the Vols played without muscular Howard Bayne. The Wildcats were 23-0. Two days later in Knoxville, Bayne was back to help Tennessee to a 43-31 rebounding edge. Ron Widby scored twenty-two points, Red Robbins eighteen, and Bayne twelve as Tennessee won 69-62.

The Wildcats returned home and beat Tulane 103-74, and four nights later, they were in Iowa City to play Dayton in the NCAA regional tournament. Henry Finkel scored thirty-six points and Don May sixteen for the Flyers, but Kentucky's balanced attack prevailed 86-79. Rupp went to the 1-3-1 defense in the second half to slow Finkel. Kentucky also used a 1-3-1 offense, with Jaracz setting screens at the top of the circle for Dampier. The little guard scored thirty-four points, five more than Pat Riley.

Riley repeated his twenty-nine-point performance as Kentucky defeated Michigan 84-77 in the regional final. Cazzie Russell had twenty-nine for the Wolverines, but it was not enough. Conley took the worst beating of his career in that game, complaining of chest pains afterward. Jaracz had a cold. Rupp was taking a group of sick boys to the Final Four at College Park, Maryland.

In the semifinals Kentucky met Duke, its rival for the No. 1 position. The Blue Devils had three future pro players—Jack Marin and Mike Lewis, both 6-foot-7, and 6-foot-1 Bob Verga. Both Conley and Verga were sick and saw limited action. The Wildcats got twenty-three points from Dampier and nineteen from Riley to win 83-79. Conley was still ailing and Riley had an infected toe.

Texas Western was ranked No. 3, but the Miners did not get much respect. Don Haskins' team was 23-1—the loss was to Seattle in the final game of the regular season—but it had not beaten a single Top Ten team. The Miners were a collection of street fighters from the city sidewalks. Haskins had played under Hank Iba at Oklahoma City, and he carried his mentor's values to El Paso: tough practice sessions and hard work on defense. In the Midwest Regional, the Miners won two games by a total of three points in a total of three overtime periods. They beat Cincinnati 78-76 in overtime and edged Kansas 81-80 in double-overtime.

Texas Western beat Utah 85-78 in the semifinals, despite thirty-eight points by the Utes' Jerry Chambers. Haskins surprised Rupp by starting 5-foot-6 Willie Worsley in place of 6-foot-8 Neville Shed in the final. The regular guards were 5-foot-10 Bobby Joe Hill and 6-foot-1 Orsten Artis. Haskins believed that 6-foot-7 David "Big Daddy" Lattin and 6-foot-5 Harry Flournoy could take care of the rebounding, and they did. The three-guard lineup would allow the Miners to control the pace of the game.

A turning point came midway through the first half. Texas Western was leading 10-9 when Hill stole the ball from Kron, dribbled half the length of the court, and made a layup. Moments later, he stole the ball from Dampier and made another layup. The Wildcats kept it close, but they never recovered from that volley. The Miners led by one point with 12:26 left to play, and Kentucky missed three consecutive chances to tie or take the lead. Late in the game the desperate Wildcats began to foul. Texas Western made twenty-eight of thirty-four attempts from the line. Kentucky, which had five more field goals than the Miners, made only eleven of thirteen free throws. Texas Western won the title 72-65. Hill finished with twenty points, while Dampier and Riley scored nineteen each.

Pat Riley returned to the UK athletic complex after coaching the 1982 Los Angeles Lakers to an NBA championship. He said the Texas Western game was the most miserable experience of his life. He could still see "Big Daddy" dunking over him and Willie Cager taking the ball down the lane and slamming over UK's 1-3-1 zone. Neville Shed scored one field goal, but it was a thunder dunk that would haunt Riley's dreams for decades.

"There's a safe-deposit box in my mind with the memories of that game—the Ultimate Game—stored in it," Riley said. "When you get that far, whether it's the seventh game of the NBA championship or the NCAA finals, nothing else suffices but winning." Rupp carried the memory of that game to his grave. On his deathbed, he still woke up in the middle of the night wondering what he could have done to turn the tide.

Haskins had used seven players against Kentucky, all of them black. Texas Western's five white players rode the bench. "I never thought a thing about it, but after we won the title with five black guys, everybody made a big deal out of it," Don Haskins said. "You play your five best guys." Haskins received thousands of pieces of hate mail—both from racist whites and from blacks who accused him of exploitation. A quarter-century's hindsight recognizes the game as a turning point for college basketball, but the players involved at the time did not realize its impact. Soon it dawned on Kentuckians and people throughout the nation that an all-black team had whipped a lily-white team. The time had come for Rupp and other coaches in the South to start bringing in the black basketball talent that was right under their noses.

The following season, Dampier and Riley were back, but the Runts were history. The team missed Conley and Kron. "Nobody will ever realize what they meant to the team," Riley said. "They made all the sacrifices." All Pat and Louie had to do was run up and down the floor and shoot the ball when the playmakers got it to them. Bob Tallent and Gary Gamble replaced Conley and Kron in the lineup.

Riley was slowed by a back injury he had suffered in a summer water skiing accident. He spent days in pain and nights in traction; surgery was imminent. Rupp needed Pat too much to hold him out of competition. Riley scored twenty-three points and grabbed eleven rebounds in a 104-84 win at Virginia. Three quick fouls reduced Riley's playing time against Illinois, and the Wildcats lost 98-97 at home. Four Wildcats scored twenty or more points—Riley with thirty-three, Dampier thirty-two, Jaracz twenty-three, and Tallent twenty—as Kentucky beat Northwestern 118-116 at Evanston. Riley hit the two winning free throws.

But Florida and North Carolina beat Kentucky in Memorial Coliseum—the first time a Rupp team had lost three consecutive home games. Later, lightly regarded Cornell won 92-77 at the Coliseum. Twice the Wildcats lost three consecutive games to conference foes.

Tallent was playing with a sore ankle, and Rupp blamed him for the breakdown. At Knoxville, Rupp moved Phil Argento into Tallent's spot. Tallent came off the bench and lost the ball, and out he came again. The same sequence of events happened a few minutes later. As Tallent walked to the bench this time, he and Rupp had words. They got into it again in the locker room. At Monday's practice, an empty locker greeted Tallent, and equipment manager George Hukle refused to issue him any gear. The student newspaper demanded a public apology from the coach. John W. Oswald, the UK president, called Rupp to his office and made it clear that public censure of a student had no place among staff members at the university. The coach who had once told his players to report to practice or find their clothing in the middle of Euclid Avenue was caught in a new age.

The Wildcats were 12-13 entering the final home game against Alabama. Rupp was in danger of experiencing his first losing season. Pat Riley came to the rescue. The lame knight scored twenty-eight points, and Kentucky won 110-78. Not long after, doctors removed two disks from his back. Rupp looked forward to the next season and the surgical removal of his worst record ever. He could hardly wait to get his hands on the fine group of sophomores that Joe Hall had recruited.

Chapter
Twenty

Issel-Pratt-Casey

Whenever Rupp seemed to have come to a dead end, a new group of boys with a catchy nickname came to the rescue. The teams following the 13-13 nightmare were missing just one thing—the nickname. Wildcat fans called them "Issel-Pratt-Casey."

Dan Issel was the leader. He may have been the best ever to play at Kentucky, and his name tops most of the scoring lists, but he almost missed out on a Wildcat career. Rupp was still looking for that good big man. Issel was 6-foot-8 but unknown, an all-sports star at Batavia High, a small school in Illinois. Dan was only third or fourth on the UK most-wanted list, and in the spring of his junior year, he got a letter from the University of Wisconsin. It was good to know somebody wanted him.

During Issel's junior and senior years, Batavia put together a 53-5 record, which got Issel a little more attention from college recruiters. Joe Hall made a visit, but Issel showed no interest in Kentucky—Wisconsin was his choice, while his parents preferred Northwestern. Visiting Kentucky was a compromise of sorts.

Hall and Phil Argento met Issel at the Louisville airport and drove him to Lexington. It was a good trip until Issel picked up the school newspaper and read a story on recruiting. He couldn't find his name. Dan went home and signed with Wisconsin.

His father, Bob, still wasn't convinced Dan was making the right move. "Let's take another trip to Kentucky," Bob said, offering to pay for the second visit. Bluegrass Airport manager Logan Gray rolled out a plush red carpet. The stewardesses were running around looking for the Big Shot. It impressed Dan: Kentucky was serious. He didn't know that Hall had just lost recruiting battles for two big men. Hall got Dan's name on the dotted line.

"I remember the first time I saw Coach Rupp," Issel said. "Everybody treated him like a king on the throne." Phil Argento gave Dan some advice before his first meeting with the coach.

"Coach Rupp will say things that will crack you up," Argento said, "but if he's not laughing, you don't laugh. Then he'll say something that's not funny at all, but he'll laugh, and that's when you laugh."

Mike Casey was a free spirit, 6-foot-4 and slightly bow-legged. He was Mr. Basketball in Kentucky after leading Shelby County to the 1966 state tournament championship. Recruiting Mike was easy. His father was sheriff of Shelby County, where Harry Lancaster had taught, coached, and served as principal. Mike was listening to the radio when Kentucky won the 1958 NCAA championship. He told his father he wanted to be a Wildcat.

Mike Pratt was only 6-foot-4, but he was big where it counted—hands, feet, shoulders, butt, heart. Rupp had seen some strong players, like Leroy Edwards and Pat Riley, but Pratt was as tough as any of them. He played his first basketball on outdoor courts, where a player learns to take care of himself under the basket. At Meadowdale High School, Pratt scored 1,396 points in seventy-six games, a Dayton-area record, but Rupp's Runts were the Ohioan's favorite team. Hall had little trouble persuading him to become a Wildcat.

Pratt was ill and missed the first five games of his sophomore season. Issel had a benign tumor removed from the roof of his mouth after his freshman season, but Rupp started him as a sophomore. "It would have been easy to explain if they had let me sit on the bench," Issel said. But Rupp had big plans for the big soph. Starting with Issel and Casey were seniors Thad Jaracz at forward and Steve Clevenger and Jim LeMaster at guard.

Casey scored twenty-eight points and got fourteen re-bounds— one fewer than Issel—in a 96-79 win over Michigan. Rudy Tomjanovich had twenty-seven rebounds and seventeen points for the Wolverines. After an easy victory over Florida, Phil Argento started in place of Clevenger and scored twenty-three points in a win over Xavier. Two games later, Clevenger was back in the lineup. The Wildcats lost to North Carolina 84-77 at Greensboro, as Casey got only seven shots and Dick Grubar and Charlie Scott outplayed Kentucky's guards.

Pratt made his first start against Dayton in the UKIT, with Casey moving from forward to guard and Clevenger sitting again. Pratt had fifteen points and fifteen rebounds. Casey scored twenty-seven points, and Kentucky won 88-85. After some early-season shuffling, Rupp had his starting lineup: Issel, Casey, Pratt, Jaracz, and Argento.

In an 81-73 win over Notre Dame in Freedom Hall, Casey stole the ball six times and scored twenty-six points and was rewarded with the first Bernie A. Shively award as the most valuable player in that annual game. That was victory No. 767 for Rupp, who insisted that the total should be 772—he wanted to count five wins in the 1966 International Universi-ties Tournament in Tel Aviv. The NCAA said no—Rupp would have to earn a few more victories to move ahead of Phog Allen as the winningest coach.

Kentucky lost only to Florida, Auburn, and Tennessee on the road that season. Neal Walk, Florida's 6-foot-11 center, outscored Issel 28-12 and outrebounded him 23-7. Issel scored twenty against Auburn, but the Wildcats lost 74-73. Bobby Croft, Bill Justus, and Tom Boerwinkle combined for fifty-four points in Tennessee's 87-59 victory at Knoxville. Argento suffered an ankle injury against the Vols and was out for the season.

Pete Maravich was the talk of the SEC, and the Wildcats' game at Baton Rouge against LSU was televised. The "Pistol" hit nineteen field goals and scored fifty-three points, both records against Kentucky. But it took him fifty-one shots to get the job done, and the Wildcats won 121-95 behind Casey's thirty-one points. The two-team total of 216 points broke the SEC mark of 209 set in 1956, when Kentucky buried Georgia 143-66. The teams also combined for ninety field goals, five more than in that earlier UK-UG game.

Next the Wildcats went to Oxford to play Mississippi. Rupp now had 771 wins—officially—and was tied with Allen. No one in the UK party dared mention the record. When Kentucky pulled out a hard-fought 85-76 victory, Rupp had his 772nd triumph in thirty- eight seasons. He pointed out that it had taken Dr. Allen forty-six seasons at Kansas to set his mark.

In a UK-LSU rematch at Lexington, Maravich scored forty-four points, but Kentucky won 109-96. Mike Casey had twenty-nine for Kentucky. "Let Pete have his points," Rupp said. "We'll stop the other guys." After Kentucky beat Mississippi and Mississippi State, Tennessee came to town for a conference showdown. Jaracz scored six points in the last six minutes, then hit Issel with a pass under the basket with twenty-five seconds to play. The big guy scored the winning basket in a one-point game.

The Wildcats won their last eleven games and the SEC title. They took a 21-4 record into the Mideast Regional, which was on their home court. In the opening round, Kentucky played Marquette, and Ohio State met East Tennessee State. The Buckeyes had won their bid by beating Iowa State in a playoff game.

Al McGuire, Marquette's brash young coach, baited Rupp at a press party, then refused to go on the Baron's television show unless he received some pay. McGuire objected to Kentucky's being designated the home team, so Rupp told him to go ahead and dress the Warriors in their home uniforms. McGuire said he did not want Rupp to give him anything—he had worked for everything he'd gotten in life. McGuire later admitted that he'd gone out of his way to create waves—he got Rupp mad, and he got Marquette fans excited. Issel remained calm, though. He scored thirty-six points, and Kentucky won 107-89. Ohio State, meanwhile, defeated East

Tennessee by five points. Some Wildcat fans began packing for a trip to Los Angeles, site of the Final Four.

Kentucky was leading Ohio State by one point with six seconds left when the Buckeyes missed a shot from the corner. Casey got a hand on the rebound but fumbled it out of bounds when he was jostled from behind by Bill Hosket. During a timeout, Buckeye coach Fred Taylor told Dave Sorenson and Steve Howell to cross and look for a close-in shot. In the UK huddle, someone suggested fouling immediately. Under the rules of the time, a player fouled while not in the act of shooting got one shot; even if the Buckeye made the pressure free throw, the Wildcats would get one more crack at the basket and, at worst, overtime. Rupp rejected the strategy. The teams took the court, and Sorenson got the ball on the inbounds play. He squared up in front of the basket and made a medium-range jump shot, and Ohio State won 82-81.

"The whole world fell in when Sorenson hit that shot," Dan Issel remembered. "I think half of us already had our bags packed for California."

The 1968-69 season was a year-long Kentucky basketball highlight film. The Wildcats became the first college team to win one thousand games. Rupp recorded his eight hundredth victory. Pete Maravich hit twenty of forty-eight shots and scored fifty-two points, but Kentucky beat LSU 108-96 at Baton Rouge. "Pistol" scored forty-five in Memorial Coliseum against Rupp's zone defense, but the Wildcats won again, 103-89. Kentucky helped dedicate Miami's new Millett Assembly in Oxford, Ohio, Mike Casey spoiling the ceremony with three late baskets in a 86-77 UK victory. At season's end, Issel made All-America.

Two weeks before the opening game that year, Pratt broke a finger on his left hand. Rupp moved Casey to forward with Larry Steele, a 6-foot-6 sophomore from Bainbridge, Indiana. Terry Mills and Phil Argento, both 6-foot-2, were the guards. The Wildcats hit their first eleven field goal attempts and first nine free throws in a 102-78 win over Pennsylvania in the Palestra. Kentucky beat Michigan and Army in the UKIT, as Issel was the most outstanding player. Argento scored twenty-seven points in a 110-90 win over Notre Dame in Louisville and received the Shively Trophy.

On New Year's Eve, it was sixteen degrees below zero in Chicago when Kentucky played Wisconsin. In his first appearance before the home folks, Issel bombed. "That happens sometimes when you try too hard," Harry Lancaster told him at halftime. Issel relaxed and played better the second half, but the Wildcats hit only 38 percent of their shots and lost by four points. In January, Kentucky beat Mississippi State, and Rupp claimed that was the school's one thousandth victory— he was still counting those five wins in Tel Aviv. Again the NCAA denied the claim.

"Why the hell not?" Rupp demanded. "You sent us over there to play those games." A check of old files revealed four previously unreported games—two wins and two losses. NCAA verified the claim; Kentucky and Kansas each had 997 victories. Oregon State trailed by five. As Kansas faltered, Kentucky won three straight games. The one thousandth win came on January 13, 88-68 over Georgia in Lexington. With former Wildcat All-Americans in the background, Rupp cut the victory cake. Fans came out of the stands to help eat it.

Rupp got his own victory No. 800 two weeks later at Tuscaloosa, and it wasn't easy. Alabama missed a shot in the closing seconds of regulation, and Kentucky won 83-70 in overtime.

The Wildcats were 22-4 entering a rematch with Marquette in the Mideast Regional at Madison, Wisconsin. The game took on racial overtones as the Marquette supporters took Kentucky to task for its all-white roster. "Hey, Hitler," some Warrior fans yelled at Rupp. Marquette's players were no gentler, bumping Wildcat players even when they didn't have the ball. Rupp feared a riot might ensue if his boys retaliated. Marquette won, 81-74.

"You could almost feel the [racial] tension in the crowd," Dan Issel said. "I'm sure that played a big part in the outcome."

I was attending an NCAA meeting in New York the following summer when Rupp called and told me about Mike Casey's accident. The All-SEC guard-forward had been en route to play a softball game when his car wrecked on I-64. He sustained several broken bones in his leg.

"Fate has dealt us a cruel blow," Rupp said. "There goes our chance to win the NCAA tournament." Jim Dinwiddie moved into the starting lineup with Issel, Pratt, Mills and Steele.

Joe Hall put together a tough running program that fall. After the players met and aired their gripes, Issel and Pratt asked Hall to let up. When the assistant coach held firm, the team captains decided to take their complaint to Rupp. The Baron sent for Issel.

"Dan," he said, "do you realize that you have an opportunity to be the all-time leading scorer for the University of Kentucky? You go out there and run today and I will do everything in my power to see that you achieve that." Issel and the five freshmen ran that day. The remaining players reported a day later.

Rupp continued to have health problems. He was diabetic, and when a shoe rubbed his foot and caused an ulceration, it was slow to heal. Doctors told him to stay away from the office and keep the foot elevated, but he refused to miss practices and the games. There was too much at stake. A stool and cushion propped his foot on the sideline.

Issel picked up where he had left off as a junior, scoring thirty-four points against West Virginia. Pratt added twenty-eight as Kentucky beat the Mountaineers 106-87. Bob McCowan was most valuable player in the UKIT after scoring forty-one points in two games. After a victory at Mississippi State, Joe Hall and trainer Claude Vaughan caught McCowan, Randy Pool, and some other reserves in a bar on Sunday afternoon. Rupp had no choice but to suspend them from the team, but he said Vaughan's vigilance had cost him a national championship.

Another trip to Mississippi had a happier ending. Seventy-five hundred fans were in the Coliseum at Oxford as Issel scored twenty-nine points in the first half. Though Ole Miss was behind by twenty-eight points, the fans stayed around to see the big guy run up and down the floor. Issel started the second half with a barrage of hooks and layups. He was nearing Cliff Hagan's UK mark of fifty-one points when Rupp took him out of the game. I got up from the scorer's table, hustled to the bench, and told Rupp that Issel was near the record. He sent Dan back into the game. Issel tied Hagan's mark with a drive to the basket. His turnaround jump shot gave him fifty-three and the record. Rupp took Issel out of the game again with five minutes left. The Ole Miss crowd gave him a standing ovation, and Rupp shook his hand. Baron Rupp had kept his promise. Twenty-five years later, Issel's record was still on the books.

Rupp surprised LSU with a man-to-man defense against Maravich. Terry Mills started out guarding the Pistol. McCowan took a turn, then gave way to Larry Steele. Pistol responded with fifty-five points, a Coliseum record, but Kentucky won 109-96. In the return game at Baton Rouge, Maravich outscored Issel 64-51, but the Wildcats won again, 121-105.

Issel had a sore foot when Kentucky suffered its only loss of the season, losing by eight at Vanderbilt. The Wildcats were 25-1 entering the Mideast Regional at Columbus, Ohio. Austin Carr scored fifty-two points, eight more than Issel, but Kentucky beat Notre Dame 109-99. Jacksonville beat Iowa in the other bracket. Jacksonville had the biggest team Rupp had ever seen, featuring seven-footers Artis Gilmore and Pembrook Burrows.

Issel had twenty-eight with ten minutes to play when Vaughn Wedeking ran in front of him at midcourt on a break. The two collided, and Kentuckians cheered what they thought was a clear foul on Wedeking. Instead, Issel was whistled for his fifth foul. Pratt, Steele, and Mills also fouled out. The teams combined to shoot fifty-four free throws in the foul-plagued game, which Jacksonville won 106-100. Rupp complained about the officiating, and Issel was angry at having fouled out. But he had gone out as he had always played, playing the game hard, playing aggressively. He was the most prolific scorer in UK history. His 948 points that season brought his career total to 2,138 in eighty-three games, still a UK record in 1994.

Harry Lancaster thought that Rupp had started slipping as a coach right after the Runts. As with many assistants, Lancaster thought he ran the team, and he did, to a certain extent, but there were times when he overstepped his bounds. Players from earlier days liked Harry because he was the "good cop," but more than once he ran off a player he didn't like. Rupp let him get away with it because he needed him—and Joe Hall was in the same category.

An aging Rupp was struggling to preserve his barony, but the price was high. It meant learning how to swallow his pride and make concessions sometimes. A young Rupp would never exchange favors with a player, as the Baron did with Dan Issel. Rupp's biggest concession came when he agreed to give a 7-foot black player a scholarship. That person would have to step into Dan Issel's shoes, but there was no way he— or anyone else—could fill them.

Chapter
Twenty-One

Milestones

The date was June 9, 1969. Memorial Coliseum's clock struck nine. Joe B. Hall and I were jittery as we waited for the Baron. It was a momentous day, and we wondered how he felt about it. It wasn't every day—it hadn't been any day until then—that our university signed a black basketball player.

Tom Payne was 7-foot-1, and he could play the game. His grades were a question mark, but the powers that be had told us to forget about his report card. Just get him—that was our mission.

We were glad Joe Hall was there. He had resigned two months earlier to take the head coaching job at St. Louis University. Rupp grumped that Joe had left him holding the bag. Some prominent people—UK board chairman Albert Clay, attorney Harry B. Miller Jr. and businessman Jim Host—pulled some strings, and Hall returned to Lexington. It was understood, though not written in stone, that he would be Rupp's successor.

The Baron arrived at his office at 9:40 a.m.—rank has its privilege. He spent a few minutes there—I'm sure he counted them— then walked out, saying, "Let's go." We went. On the way, Rupp talked business, not basketball. We passed various fried chicken establishments along the route, and he went into detail about a new food chain. We knew he was an investor. He also discussed Hereford cattle, tobacco, and the stock market.

We passed a black business district in Louisville's west end. "This is where they had the riot," Joe said. Rupp jerked his ahead around, then smiled: surely, Joe was kidding. Joe wasn't kidding. We arrived early at the home of retired Army Sergeant and Mrs. Thomas R. Payne Sr. Rupp told Hall to drive around the block—he didn't want to seem overeager. Ten seconds before the appointed time, we knocked on the door. Members of the media were waiting, along with Mr. and Mrs. Payne, who were gracious hosts. Their son was shy, and Rupp glowed. Linville Puckett once said you could lead Rupp around with a microphone or a camera.

Young Tom was an "Army brat" who had lived in Europe and throughout the United States. More than 150 schools sought his services. He planned to study sociology so he could go into people's homes and help them with their problems. Mr. Payne wanted the best for his son, and he was convinced that it didn't get any better than Rupp. While everybody else beamed, Tom showed no emotion. Over a pot of his mother's coffee, we sealed the bargain.

"Yes sir, Tom is farther along than Bill Spivey was," Rupp said. "He will fit into our plans perfectly." Rupp knew he was taking a risk. Payne had not participated in an organized sport until his sophomore year at Shawnee High School. He was rough, unpolished, and inexperienced. There was also the matter of a low entrance test score. Payne did not qualify for a scholarship. He could neither practice nor play with the freshmen. He would play on a local AAU team. After Payne made the grades, Rupp would give him a scholarship.

Mike Casey and Larry Steele were co-captains of the 1970-71 team. Casey was a step slower, with a noticeable limp, and an ankle sprain didn't help his speed. Mark Soderberg broke a bone in his hand. He didn't like competing with a 7-footer. Neither did 6-foot-11 sophomore Jim Andrews, but he stuck it out. Randy Noll transferred to Marshall. Steele and Tom Parker were the forwards. They combined for forty-three points in an opening 115-100 victory over Northwestern at Evanston. Payne scored fourteen points, but only got one rebound in that game. In Lexington, Henry Wilmore hit seventeen of twenty-one field goals and scored forty points for Michigan, but Kentucky beat the Wolverines 104-93 as Payne had seventeen points and ten rebounds. Casey scored twenty-five points. Kent Hollenbeck, Jim Dinwiddie, Terry Mills, and Stan Key fought for the other guard spot.

Kentucky helped West Virginia dedicate its new arena, which was designed by Carl Staker, the UK team captain in 1941-42. Payne scored nineteen points and had nineteen rebounds in a 106-100 win over the Mountaineers. Rupp said the big center was coming along nicely. Before a game with Indiana, Steele had broken a bone in his hand, so Larry Stamper took his place. Kentucky beat the Hoosiers 95-93. Payne scored thirteen points, but he had only four rebounds. In the UKIT, the Wildcats defeated DePaul 106-85, then lost to Purdue 89-83 in the championship game. Payne totaled thirty-five points and thirty-two rebounds in those games.

Soderberg started at forward against Notre Dame in Louisville. Austin Carr scored fifty points, and Notre Dame won 99-92. After a trip to the two Mississippi schools, Soderberg went home to California. Playing basketball at Kentucky demanded too much of a player and gave too little in return, he said. The problem, as he saw it, was a lack of communication between the coaches and the players. Soderberg said Rupp had very little rapport with the team; he was cold to his players, made no effort to get to know them, and regularly forgot their names. Rupp wanted 100 percent effort, but Soderberg felt he was "using my body to get another trophy."

In the next sixteen games, Kentucky lost only at Tennessee and Florida. Rupp was in the hospital with a foot ailment and didn't make the trip to Gainesville. Joe Hall coached that game. Hall had been the No. 1 assistant since Harry Lancaster became UK athletic director in 1968. He took the Wildcats from Gainesville at Athens, where Payne scored thirty-four points in a 107-95 win over Georgia. Rupp was back on the bench in Lexington as Payne scored thirty-nine points and got nineteen rebounds in a televised 110-73 win over LSU. Rupp returned to the Medical Center after the game, but two nights later, he was back on the bench again to watch Payne score sixteen points and pull down nine boards in a 101-74 win over Alabama. At Auburn, Rupp was absent when Kentucky beat the Tigers 119-90. Payne led the scoring with thirty points. Rupp returned for the closing game against Tennessee, sitting courtside in a wheelchair.

The game was a rematch between Payne and Tennessee's Jim Woodall. At Knoxville, Payne had flipped Woodall head over heels in a battle for a rebound. Payne said it was unintentional, but he drew a flagrant technical foul—and boos and namecalling from the UT fans. In the rematch, officials again ejected Payne for flagrantly fouling Woodall. Payne left the game with twenty points and eight rebounds.

Payne had also been tossed from a game against Alabama in Lexington when he objected to an official's decision. Payne's temper and gestures were drawing criticism from some UK fans. He irritated them with his victory salute: he would clinch his fists and pump them up and down over his head after a particularly good play. Some fans thought he was giving the "Black Power" sign. There were scuffles with teammates, especially Larry Stamper, but they were kept quiet. On the road, Payne was a lone warrior, hiding behind sunglasses and keeping his distance from the other players. His classwork was below par; summer school awaited.

The Wildcats beat Tennessee 84-78 and were 20-4 entering the Mideast Regional at Athens. They had scored more than one hundred points in fifteen of twenty-four games. Rupp was SEC Coach of the Year, and Payne, Parker, and Steele made the All-SEC team. In a preliminary game at South Bend, Indiana, Western Kentucky beat Jacksonville by two points to set up the first basketball meeting between Kentucky and Western.

"We've been waiting thirty-two years to play them," Jim McDaniels said, "and we're gonna get them Thursday night." McDaniels thought so little of Rupp that he had refused to play for him in a charity game between Kentucky and Tennessee in late March. Then he changed his mind, deciding to play for the handicapped and retarded children who would benefit from the game.

Joining Kentucky and Western in the regional finals were Ohio State and Marquette. Al McGuire praised Rupp during a press conference. "He's probably the finest coach who ever lived," McGuire said. "Coach Rupp has contributed more to basketball by accident than most of us have on purpose."

All of Western's starters were black. For Wildcat fans, it was Texas Western all over again. Coach John Oldham's team wiped out Kentucky 107-83. After picking up three fouls, McDaniels missed seven minutes of the first half, but he still scored thirty-five points. Midway through the second half, with Western leading by twenty-three points, McDaniels walked to the bench with arms outstretched in victory.

It was the most humiliating loss of Rupp's career. "I was thinking about turning this thing over to Joe Hall and taking it easy, but I can't leave him with a mess like this," Rupp said. "They'll think I'm dying on the vine." The Wildcats had some fine freshmen, and he was going to wait until he could leave Hall in good shape. "I can't go out on a sour note like this," he said, "not after a game in which not one of our boys would do what I wanted them to do." In the third-place game, Marquette defeated Kentucky 91-74. Western beat Ohio State and advanced to the Final Four in Houston, losing to Villanova in the semifinals. Payne got fifteen points and ten rebounds against Western, but he only had a single point and two rebounds in the Marquette game. Rupp said the boy's mind must have been somewhere else. Payne finished the season as UK's top rebounder (10.1 per game) and third-leading scorer (16.9 ppg).

In April, Rupp had surgery on his ailing foot. He returned to work the following month. It was clear that he intended to be around for the next season—maybe longer if the university decided to waive its mandatory age-70 retirement.

In August, a state policeman cited Tom Payne for speeding in his new Cadillac. There were other tickets on file, some more than a year old—citations for failing to dim lights, illegal parking, and operating a vehicle with a defective muffler. In September, Payne quit the university and joined thirteen other underclassmen in the National Basketball Association's first supplemental draft, signing with the Atlanta Hawks. Rupp had been fair with him, Payne said—the coach, a counselor, and a lawyer were the only persons he could believe. No one else offered a helping hand without expecting something in return. At Tennessee, he had endured racial slurs on the blackboard and such vicious booing that Mike Casey and Larry Steele had told officials the Wildcats would walk off the court if it didn't stop. But while the co-captains had stood up for him at Knoxville, Payne claimed Kent Hollenbeck was his only friend on the team. The other players wouldn't throw him the ball.

Payne's departure left Kentucky as the only SEC school without a black player. Alabama and Florida each had four blacks on scholarship. Team captain Henry Harris was one of three blacks at Auburn. Even Mississippi and Mississippi State had two black players each.

Rupp celebrated his seventieth birthday in September. University President Otis Singletary told Rupp that there would be no exceptions to the school's mandatory retirement age. Rupp rallied his forces, and several of his former players petitioned the athletic board to waive the rule. John Y. Brown Sr. and Jr., both active in senior citizens' causes, joined the campaign, appearing before the board with Colonel Harlan Sanders at their side. The Kentucky Fried Chicken king was still active in his eighties. The board stood firm. In an attempt to appease Rupp, the board offered him free use of his office after he retired and an annual consulting fee of $10,000. His pension guaranteed him 62 percent of his salary, so he would lose no income upon retirement.

Not that money was a problem for Adolph at this stage. He had learned early on that he had as good a head for business as for basketball. While he was still in Freeport, he and Elmer Hoffman made some money on stock tips from friends, but they lost it in the crash of 1929. In the early 1940s, though, he made a profit on some stock he had bought in a distillery, and then he began buying stock in the Central District Warehousing Corporation. Twenty years later, he was one of the firm's three largest shareholders and a member of the board. In another business venture, Rupp, Herky, and former UK player Roger Layne started the Rupp Oil Company, incorporating with the intent to drill for oil in Kentucky and elsewhere. The value of his farms, meanwhile, reached an estimated quarter of a million dollars.

"The thing about Adolph is that he did all those things well," Esther said. "He wasn't one to handle things once over lightly." Rupp credited his good business fortune to "sound investments, good friends who helped me with them, and to just good, old-fashioned free enterprise." He often said, "Free enterprise is the greatest thing we've got. It means that a man has the right to go as far as his ability will take him." To him it was the same in sports as in business.

The board was making every effort to ease Rupp out gracefully—even having Harry Lancaster install a special $10,000-bronze plaque in Memorial Coliseum listing Rupp's accomplishments—but the Baron would have no part of it. As heir apparent to the throne, Joe Hall was in Rupp's direct line of fire. Hall had recruited the best freshman group in the country, and Rupp wanted to coach those boys. He asked why Hall had not recruited that caliber of players for him.

That year, Gale Catlett joined the UK coaching staff after serving four years as an assistant varsity coach and freshman coach at the University of Kansas. Rupp began to praise Catlett and slight Hall. The loss of Payne had dealt a severe blow to Rupp's hopes for another national championship, and before the season started Kent Hollenbeck broke a bone in his foot three times. Bob McCowan tore a shoulder muscle, and Jim Andrews sprained an ankle.

Rupp opened with Andrews at center, Tom Parker and Larry Stamper at forward, and Stan Key and Ronnie Lyons at guard. Andrews scored thirty-seven points in an opening victory over Northwestern. On a western swing, Kentucky defeated Kansas and Kansas State. It was at Kansas that the Wildcats realized it might be Rupp's last year. Before the pregame talk, Catlett got Rupp out of the room and told the players how important the game was to Rupp. The Wildcats won by ten points. Parker injured an ankle against Indiana, and the Wildcats lost by one point in double-overtime, as Steve Downing scored forty points and had twenty-five rebounds for IU. Rupp said Payne would have prevented that. After Michigan State upset Kentucky 91-85, Rupp said his players lacked talent.

"If we had Tom Payne, we'd be undefeated," he said. "The pros don't care whether they destroy a good college team or not." They had ruined him by drafting his center, Rupp complained. He was making noises like a coach on his way out.

"His retirement wasn't mentioned until the last game of the season," Tom Parker said in his diary, but he added, "there were certain games— Georgia, Ole Miss, Mississippi State, Tennessee—that we thought had to be Coach's last at those places." Parker said Rupp's reception everywhere he went was uncharacteristically warm. "The Mississippi State crowd that hates everything about Kentucky gave him a standing ovation," Parker said. "They honored him for what he had done for basketball."

The Wildcats won their next five games and were 8-2 when they lost back-to-back games at Florida and Georgia. Then they won ten conference games before losing at LSU and Alabama. They finished with a 102-67 victory over Auburn at home and a 67-66 win over Tennessee at Knoxville.

Before the Auburn game, the university staged its farewell celebration for Rupp. Many of his All-Americans were on the floor before the tip-off to unveil the bronze plaque commemorating his record. After the national anthem, the Coliseum was dark except for a single spotlight circle in front of the UK bench. Harry Lancaster was at the microphone.

"Coach Rupp," the Baron's old friend said, "we want to thank you for what you have done the past forty years for college basketball. We want you in the spotlight." Lancaster said nothing about that being Rupp's last home game as UK coach, and Tom Parker regretted that the crowd—uncertain whether it was indeed his last game—didn't give Rupp the applause that was his due. "If they had known," Parker said, "they would have blown the roof off the place."

Kentucky defeated Marquette and lost to Florida State in the Mideast Regional. The NCAA credited Rupp with 875 wins and 190 losses. (In 1992, the NCAA increased the win total to 876, accepting a previously unreported UK win over an Alumni team in 1932) He told the media he would like to hang around and improve on that record, but a few days later the athletic board made his retirement official. Harry Lancaster chose to remain as athletic director and let a younger man coach the team. Joe B. Hall got the job. The university made the announcement at a press conference, which Rupp did not attend. Hall understood—he had talked to Rupp before the session.

Rupp often described positive reactions to his speeches. "They were all adults, and they gave me a standing ovation," he would say. "There wasn't a dry eye in the house." That was the case at the last UK basketball banquet he attended. After hearing praise from Dr. Singletary, the Baron walked slowly to the dais. He choked back the tears, looked lovingly at the faithful, and said, "For those of you who have gone down the glory road with me, my eternal thanks."

Epilogue

The University of Kentucky wanted to make peace with Rupp, but he would have no part of it. He had given them so much during the past forty-two years, and they had rejected him. It did not matter that they had also retired the noted historian Dr. Thomas D. Clark. Baron Rupp had given much more than he had received. Still, the board thought that no one, including Rupp, should be exempt from the mandatory retirement rule. To do otherwise would be in violation of a state law.

When Kansas retired Phog Allen, the story goes, he had a firm grip on the door knob as they dragged him out of his office. That was equally true of Rupp. But the Baron got more than his old coach: he got to keep his office, and he also received a $10,000 annual salary as a consultant, in addition to his pension. But there was a problem: "I am a consultant, but nobody wants to consult with me," he told me. Joe B. Hall respected his old coach, but he maintained a distance between them.

When Hall gave Rupp a box of popcorn at the opening game of the 1972-73 season, flashbulbs popped. Rupp continued his Sunday television show on Channel 18. Hall's show was on Channel 27. Viewers were uncomfortable with the competition. Something had to give—it was another battle Rupp couldn't win.

Just before the 1972-73 season started, Bucky Waters resigned as Duke coach with one year remaining on a five-year contract. Duke's president was Terry Sanford, a former North Carolina governor who later became a U.S. Senator. Herky Rupp said Sanford and other school officials asked Rupp if he would like to coach the Blue Devils. Adolph said that would be fine. He planned to take Herky along as his chief assistant.

Herky was working at a bank in Lexington, but he had seven years of coaching experience on the high school level, two at Louisville Atherton, three at Lexington Lafayette, and two at Shelby County. He compiled a 55-9 record at Shelby County, taking two teams to the state tournament. Sandy Rice and Cathy Smith, who were students at Lafayette when Herky was coaching there, remember arriving at the gym one night at the same time as Adolph and Esther. When Rupp couldn't get the door open—he was pushing it the wrong way—he went into a rage, calling it some of the same names he'd used on his players. Esther was still one of the few people who could handle Adolph on those not-so-rare occasions when he got rambunctious. A soft "now, Adolph," did the trick, and the two entered the gym.

Two days before the start of basketball practice, Rupp's farm manager died. The farm was a substantial investment, and there was no one to run it. Duke gave Rupp one week to straighten out his business affairs. Unable to find anyone that quickly to tend the farm, he told them to go ahead and hire someone else.

The farm had always been Rupp's third love anyway, after his family and basketball. He savored the nickname "Baron"—German for *landowner*. Hereford cattle were an obsession for him. Rupp had gotten hooked on purebred cattle while studying at Kansas. He skipped classes one day to attend a livestock show in Kansas City. There were no cattle other than Herefords in Kansas, so naturally he chose that breed. He was eighteen years old before he knew cattle had anything but white faces. In 1944, he started stocking his farm with cattle, putting all of them in Herky's name.

By 1951, he had more than 150 head of stock on the farm. He later bought 198 acres in Scott County and 240 acres in Harrison County, each farm only a short distance from Lexington. When he died, Rupp owned a five hundred-acre spread at Centerville in Bourbon County. Although the value of Rupp's land investments reached an estimated $250,000, he denied being a wealthy man. "I am comfortable, but not wealthy," he said. "I'm selling one farm, maybe two, to help pay for my new purchase."

Carl Yazell managed Rupp's farm for a time and owned a half-interest in the operation—but not the land. When Rupp was around, there was no doubt who was boss. For years he visited the farm almost every afternoon, but as time passed and basketball and business pressures mounted, he had to limit his visits. Even so, he always found time to take members of the press out to the farm. Furman Bisher, the sports editor of the *Atlanta Journal*, got the grand tour when he was in town to do a story on Rupp for *Sport* magazine.

"We had gone out to look at his farm and were driving around the pasture with Chester Jones, his foreman," Bisher wrote. "Adolph was admiring the bovine lines of the herd as if it were a basketball squad when we came upon a heifer lying on the ground. Adolph asked Chester, 'What's wrong with her?' Chester replied, 'She just lays down and coughs all the time. I can't find a thing wrong with her.' Adolph said abruptly, 'Get rid of her. She is not a credit to the place. She's like a sub sitting on the bench rooting for the other team. Get rid of her.'"

Rupp impressed Tom Lord during a tour of the farm. Lord, who worked for a New York men's clothing firm, had met Rupp through his friend and clothier Paul Nickell. During a cookout at Nickell's home, Rupp said, "Let's get together tomorrow, Tom, and go to my farm; you damn Yankees don't know what farming means."

During the tour, Rupp would come upon a Hereford and say, "Now, Tom, this one is by Domino II." Since all the Herefords looked alike to Lord, he could not fathom how Rupp could identify each one of those cattle. Lord went back to New York and told his friends of the prodigy he had met in Kentucky, who had a hundred head of cattle and knew them all by name and could even tell you who their parents were. He discovered later that he had been the victim of a con: each cow had its vital statistics imprinted on one of its horns.

Having given up the Duke job, the Baron also turned down a coaching offer from Charles O. Finley, owner of the Memphis Tams in the ABA. Finley told Rupp he could be president, coach, general manager, or any combination of the three. Rupp became president and general manager of the Tams. He later was an executive with Kentucky Colonels of the ABA, but neither job was satisfying to the aged and ailing Baron.

When Rupp went to UK basketball games, he sat in the front row behind the scorer's table. As the university's guest at the 1975 NCAA Final Four in San Diego, he saw the Wildcats lose to UCLA in the championship game. On March 8, 1976, the Wildcats played their last game in Memorial Coliseum, beating Mississippi State 94-93 in overtime. Hall presented the game ball to Rupp, who accompanied the team to the 1976 NIT in New York.

On November 30, 1976, the university moved into Rupp Arena. Rupp left the UK Medical Center to attend an opening victory over Wisconsin. There were 23,266 fans in attendance. After being introduced, Rupp said, "This is the best place in the world." At the dedication ceremonies on December 11, Rupp received a blue easy chair to replace his regular sideline seat— he sat in the chair once before returning to the hard-back seat. Athletic director Cliff Hagan also offered him the game ball, but with Kentucky leading Kansas 41-27, Rupp suggested that the Wildcats keep the ball in play. They rolled to a 90-63 victory.

On December 10 of the following year, the Wildcats played Kansas in Lawrence on Adolph Rupp Night. Jayhawk fans bowed their heads in a moment of silence for the famous alumnus, who was back in Lexington fighting a losing battle with cancer. Kentucky defeated Kansas 73-66, but Rupp did not live long enough to hear the score.

At a farewell tribute to Rupp two nights later in Lexington, Cliff Hagan suggested that we do more than observe the usual moment of silence. I remembered that one of Rupp's favorite poems was Kipling's "L'Envoi"—he had recited it two years earlier at a dinner in his honor. We dimmed the arena lights at halftime of the game against South Carolina and played a recording of that recital. There wasn't a dry eye in the house.

When we buried Rupp, I remembered the fears he had voiced in his last years as UK coach.

"If they retire me," he had said, "they might as well take me on out to the Lexington Cemetery." He lived five years beyond retirement. On his death bed, I had asked for a summation of his life.

"Just say he did the best he could," Adolph said. "That's good enough for me."

Appendix One

RUPP ASSISTANTS

Name	Colleges	Years at UK
Atkinson, Mike (Volunteer)	(Southwest Texas '60)	1962-63
Catlett, Gale	(West Virginia '67)	1971-72
Combs, Cecil	(Kentucky '30)	1930-31
Davalos, Rudy	(Southwest Texas '60)	1962-63
Gilb, Elmer	(Kentucky '29)	1944-45–1945-46
Hall, Joe B.	(Kentucky '63)	1965-66–1971-72
Hines Doug	(Eastern Kentucky '55)	1960-61
Lancaster, Harry	(Georgetown '32)	1945-46–1968-69
Lenhardt, Ted	(Western Mich. '58)	1960-61–1961-62
Lykins, John (G.A.)	(Georgetown '64)	1964-65
McBrayer, Paul	(Kentucky '30)	1934-35–1942-43
Miller, Len	(Kentucky '28)	1931-32–1933-34
Moore, Ballard (G.A.)	(Western Kentucky '59)	1962-63
Plain, T. L.	(Western Kentucky '50)	1969-70–1970-71
Reed, Neil (G.A.)	(Illinois '59)	1962-63–1964-65

RUPP'S COMPOSITE UK BASKETBALL PLAYER

Shooting: Larry Pursiful, Louie Dampier
Drive: Frank Ramsey
Speed: Ralph Beard
Grace: Cliff Hagan
Defense: Billy Evans, Kenny Rollins
Temperament: Aggie Sale
Rebounding: Bob Burrow
Passing: Cliff Barker
Competitiveness: Wallace Jones
Scholastics: Jim McDonald
Hands: Cotton Nash
Strength: Leroy Edwards, Pat Riley, Mike Pratt
Unselfishness: Larry Conley, Tom Kron
Togetherness: 1965-66 team

RUPP'S ALL-OPPONENT TEAM

George Mikan, DePaul, 1945
Bob Kurland, Oklahoma A&M, 1946
Sparky Wade, LSU, 1935
Pinky Lipscomb, Vanderbilt, 1941
Bob Cousy, Holy Cross, 1950
Vince Boryla, Notre Dame, 1946
Clyde Lovellette, Kansas, 1952
Bob Pettit, LSU, 1954
Jerry West, West Virginia, 1960
Tom Gola, La Salle, 1955
Elgin Baylor, Seattle, 1958
Cazzie Russell, Michigan, 1966
Austin Carr, Notre Dame, 1971
John Mengelt, Auburn, 1972
Charlie Scott, North Carolina, 1970
Bailey Howell, Mississippi State, 1959
Guy Rodgers, Temple, 1958

GENERAL RULES OF CONDUCT — BASKETBALL 1969–70

Varsity and Freshmen

1. From Sunday through Friday, players are expected to be in their rooms by 11 p.m. Lights will be out at 12 midnight unless actively studying.

2. On Saturday night, players are to be in their rooms by 1:15 a.m. Lights will be out by 1:30 a.m.

3. All rules are in effect immediately and will continue through the basketball season.

4. All rules apply to guests as well as resident players.

5. Players are expected to conform to the rules of no alcohol or tobacco. This pertains to the use or possession of the above.

6. Card playing is also prohibited.

7. Players who are below a 2.0 standing at mid-term will be confined to their room at 7:30 p.m. until further notice.

8. Players guilty of excessive class cutting will be required to report to the Coliseum at 7:30 a.m.

9. Players are expected to conform to the dress and grooming code that was explained and stressed at the initial squad meeting.

10. Permission must be obtained to leave the metropolitan area of Lexington.

11. Players must obtain permission from Coach Rupp before making statements to the press or radio.

ADOLPH F. RUPP

Head Basketball Coach

October 20, 1969

RUPP's RECORD AT FREEPORT

YEAR	W	L	CONF.	DIST.	SECT.	STATE
1924-25	10	6		2nd		
1925-26	11	5	3rd	2nd		
1926-27	18	6	2nd	1st	1st	3rd
1929-30	20	4	1st	1st	Semi.	
TOTAL	59	21				

HONORS, ETC.

Certification by the NCAA Service Bureau as the nation's most successful collegiate basketball coach: 876 wins, 190 losses (.822).

Elected to the Helms Hall of Fame in 1944.

Selected as the unanimous national "Coach of the Year" in 1966 for the fourth time. He was a two-time runner-up.

Columbus Touchdown Club's "Coach of the Century" in 1967.

Four NCAA championships. A record twenty appearances in the tournament.

Coach of the International Universities Tournament champions in 1966 at Tel Aviv.

Associate coach of the successful U.S. entry in the 1948 Olympic Games in London.

Producer of more Olympic Gold Medal winners (seven) than any other college coach.

A record of twenty-seven Southeastern Conference championships.

Elected to Naismith Basketball Hall of Fame in 1959.

Trustee and member of the selections and honors committee of the Basketball Hall of Fame. Chairman of the NABC Hall of Fame Committee.

Recipient of the Governor's Medal in 1959 for meritorious service to the Commonwealth of Kentucky.

SEC coach of the year in 1964, '66, '68, '69, '70, and '71.

Chosen "Deltasig of the Year" for 1966 by the International Fraternity of Sigma Delta Phi, professional fraternity in commerce and business administration.

Development of more All-America players (twenty-two players honored thirty-three times) and more material for the pro ranks (30) than any other coach.

Five Sugar Bowl Tournament champions, an NIT title and thirteen championships in nineteen UKITs.

Member of the Basketball Rules Committee.

More overseas clinic trips (seven to Europe, three to the Far East, and one to the Near East) than any other coach. He also held a clinic in Alaska in 1968.

Selected as an official goodwill ambassador to the 1968 Olympics in Mexico City, representing the NCAA.

Member of Kansas and Kentucky halls of fame.

President of the National Association of Basketball Coaches in 1971.

Recipient of University of Kansas' Distinguished Service Award in 1970.

Appendix Two
Letters from Rupp

April 2, 1965
Mr. Bill Myers
Paulsboro, New Jersey

1. Some of my interests are education, sports, and farming.
2. The only way to become a basketball coach is to actively play and make a study of the game.
3. Yes, I enjoy my work.
4. The requirements are, of course, the same as in any other profession: application.
5. The working conditions are excellent.
6. The pay is satisfactory.
7. Very little advancement in this field.

In order to be successful, a coach must create within his boys a competitive spirit that will bring success. In our free enterprise system, we should encourage competition.

When Grantland Rice wrote, "When the Great Scorer comes to mark against your name, he writes not that you won or lost, but how you played the game," I do not believe that he meant that to apply to sports. If he did, why do they keep score at all these games?

May 11, 1965
Mr. J. S. Grigsby, Jr.
Nashville, Tennessee

If nothing else, sports at least teach a man to be on his own. Something we need today.

February 5, 1964
George S. Thayer
Sanford, Maine

If you can't rebound, you don't have a ball to pass, shoot or dribble. Shooting is to basketball what putting is to golf.

I would rate dribbling the least important of all, but I hesitate to evaluate the others.

January 7, 1958
Mr. Bob Husten
Cincinnati Enquirer
Cincinnati, Ohio

It has always been my idea that there is a reason for a golf course having par. I have always thought that my greatest team was the Hagan, Ramsey, Evans and Tsioropoulos team that won 25 games and was named National Champions. They finished with the highest rating of any team up to that date. I call that par for the course. Whenever we cease to strive for excellence we cease to be useful and every coach should establish a par course and try to play up to it. It is a simple philosophy, but it has helped me a lot.

January 2, 1959
Mr. William P. J. Drakeley, Jr.
Wilmington, Delaware

Whenever you eliminate the personal desire to be successful in any walk of life, then you have destroyed the very foundation that our pioneer fathers brought with them to this country.

March 12, 1959
Mr. Joe Warren
Lexington, Kentucky

I feel very strongly that it should be the duty of every professor to take a personal interest in the boys, the way we do here in the Athletic Department. If they would do that, they would get a lot more accomplished. I have been needling some of our professors in my talks and maybe we will get the idea across to them one of these days.

January 4, 1961
Mr. Ed Sword
Wellington, Ohio

You request information regarding the effects of athletic sports on the body. That is something you have to get from the medical profession. I could only vent an opinion, which is that all sports help in body development, coordination and thinking; therefore, we should encourage participation in sports.

January 18, 1962
Mr. Larry Glaser
Fair Lawn, New Jersey

Some people are just born more graceful than others and with more ability, and regardless of how long you work with a boy who does not have it you seldom are able to develop him into a great athlete.

You ask whether or not a boy could be good at any sport he tries. I would say no. There are thousands of boys who try to play baseball who are never able to do so well.

November 6, 1963
Sacred Heart Tigers
Oelwein, Iowa

I understand that you are starting your third year of basket-ball without a gymnasium. It is difficult for some people to understand how a group of youngsters can maintain an interest in a sport when they do not have a gymnasium. It is so commend-able that you boys are doing this.

A boy sincerely interested in a sport can overcome any handi-cap.

February 7, 1961
Mr. Jim Ausenbaugh
Louisville, Kentucky

You mentioned coaching good material and material not so good. The test of a coach is if he can win with good material. There are many coaches in the U.S. who have excellent material but just simply don't seem to be able to put over the clincher games.

A good coach is a coach who can win when he has the mate-rial. It is very seldom that you can take indifferent material and develop it into a championship team. It has occurred several times. The 1958 Kentucky team was an example.

There wasn't a single outstanding boy on that team. In comparison with the teams that played in the last four games of the NCAA Tournament, they were out-manned every night. However, there are many coaches in the U.S. who do not have great material that other coaches manage to find. These coaches develop strong teams every year. Maybe not winning champion-ships, but still being contenders.

April 5, 1967
Mr. Curt Gordon, Sports Editor
Fernandia News-Leader
Fernandia Beach, Florida

The thing we look for in a boy first is his grades. Here at Kentucky, that is an important thing. Then we look at his reflexes. If he is slow, we virtually discard him. Then we want size and coordination.

I don't believe I ever made a statement that I wanted our boys to shoot 500 times at a basket each day. I gave this assignment to Ralph Beard in 1948 after he made All-America in order to correct a bad habit and I am sure it helped him.

January 17, 1967
Mr. Phillip Carr
Nashville, Tennessee

One of the first things that we look for in an athlete is his quickness. Then we want this quickness accompanied by size and determination. In order to be a great athlete you must be able to do everything well. The shots you practice should be of every variety.

Loyalty is a prerequisite to becoming successful in anything. In basketball, a young man must first be loyal to himself, his teammates, his coach, and his school. To be loyal, he must play up to his capabilities. Building character is teaching boys to be successful in all their undertakings.

January 9, 1964
Mr. Kenneth Gee
Pleasantville, New Jersey

There are three requirements that we ask of our boys: 1, is that they be genuine boys to begin with; 2, that they are excellent students; and 3, that they are excellent basketball players. It is in these three categories that we evaluate our players.

Mr. James Proffitt
Louisville, KY

Some stupid jackass sent me this letter and I am sure you will want to run him down, and reprimand him for his stupidity.

I have talked with people who know you and they all say you

have more sense than to write such a letter, so I am sure you will
want to take the proper steps.

Mr. C. D. Loewer
Prichard, Alabama

I resent your letter saying that we were trying to alibi out of
the Mississippi State defeat. I am sure you know very little about
basketball and the shock was that you would attempt to tell me
something about it. A team that gets an early lead can play to
that advantage. I don't think you understand that.

Whenever you folks down that way have a record in basketball such as we have here at the University of Kentucky, drop up
here sometime and try to tell us something about the game, but
until you have at least won the SEC once, I would just sit back
and listen.

March 29, 1962
Mr. Watt Bishop
Cleveland, Mississippi

I think the only way for you to improve your basketball is to
continually stay at it with determination. You will never learn to
play and be a great athlete unless you have the determination to
do so. Constant practice on fundamentals is the key to good
basketball.

February 9, 1966
Mr. Jerry Watt
Aurora, Illinois

The best way for a youngster to develop in the awkward ages
that your sons are in is only one of constant practice.

The only way to learn to play basketball is to play it. If your
boys can get under the supervision of a good junior high coach, I
am sure they will learn the necessary fundamentals. Fundamentals are polish and a polished team wins.

Jan. 14, 1963
Mr. Bob Prather
Decatur, Georgia

We permit our boys to lay it (shoot) up any way they can just so that it goes in. The ball possibly leaves the hand easier with the underhand method. Our boys do it about 50/50 and I see little difference.

The initial move in assembling a basketball team or any other undertaking is to understand the problems involved.Then it is necessary to get the right kind of material for the purpose and to instill a winning complex. Never talk about defeat. This simply breeds defeat.

January 11, 1961
Mr. John Burt
Director of Personnel NIBCO, Inc.
Elkhart, Indiana

Today, life does not present enough of a challenge to our youngsters. Too much is being done for them in such an easy fashion that they expect the same treatment in all other phases of life. If you eliminate competition from our everyday life, you do not present a challenge to our youngsters.

I would not care to live in a society unless it be competitive. I think our sports teach that better than most other phases of education.

March 3, 1962
Mr. Robert Bailine
Margate, New Jersey

Ability has a lot to do in basketball, as it does in all sports. However, the difference between the ability in one person and possibility in another is a genuine desire to succeed. A boy without ability isn't much of an athlete any way you look at him, but the desire to succeed is certainly important.

May 9, 1966
Mr. George Samuel Majic
Toronto, Ontario, Canada

You must have complete confidence in what you teach. The second important thing is to have enthusiasm every day. The third is that you are able to communicate with your boys. Those are the three ingredients of a successful coach. Don't get too close to your boys. In other words, you must have their respect at all times.

July 13, 1946
Pvt. Ernest Sparkman
Sqd. E - Army Air Corps, Box 98
Keesler Field, Mississippi

I was glad to get your letter for I was wondering what had happened to you.

I see that you beat Tulane University and I am wondering what kind of teams Tulane and LSU have. I wish you would sit down and write me a letter, giving me your honest opinion as to their ability. I presume Tulane uses the three out and two in. Is that correct, or do they use the pivot type of offense?

Our team is going along nicely and I believe that, if we can get over Saturday night, we should do pretty well from here on out.

Please write whenever you have time for I always enjoy hearing from you.